Philosophy for Children Across the Primary Curriculum

This is an easy-to-use, theme-based resource book for Philosophy for Children (P4C) practitioners in primary school settings. It covers ten popular themes, which include many current affair issues and enduring curriculum themes such as artificial intelligence, biodiversity, resilience, and waste.

Each theme provides planning for every subject and links to the relevant English national curriculum expectations. Offering ideas for a year's worth of work, it can be dipped into for inspiration or used for step-by-step sessions. There are links to video clips, websites, and stories that teachers and practitioners can use to base their concept exploration and enquiries on.

Presenting a range of philosophical ideas, activities, and resources, this book is essential for all primary P4C facilitators excited by embedding and exploring philosophy across the curriculum.

Alison Shorer is a P4C facilitator (SAPERE trained) and Thinking Moves Trainer for DialogueWorks. She specialises in oracy teaching and is a co-founder of Articulacy and TalkTastic. During her career in education, she has been a primary school teacher, given oracy intervention programmes to secondary school students, been a lecturer in language and literacy, and served as a teacher trainer and mentor. Her first degree was in reading philosophy, and she has a master's in education.

Katie Quinn is the Philosophy for Children (P4C) Lead and SAPERE Trainer at a large city-centre primary school in Exeter. She has worked with senior leadership to link philosophy to the learning and behaviour values already in place, and to develop ways of systematically incorporating it into topic planning, across all year groups and all curriculum areas, from science to maths to religious education. Her first degree was also in reading philosophy.

"Absolutely packed with great ideas and resources, this book shows that Philosophy for Children truly can be cross curricular, and used within a holistic approach to education, throughout primary education and beyond. For educators new to P4C up to those who have been doing it for years, this book will prove to be an essential tool. An absolute treasure trove of lessons to take you through a full year and beyond."

Dulcinea Norton-Morris, author of *Beautiful Thinking: Metacognition from Birth to Five*

"I really like that the cross-curricular links were shown and linked to the questions. This makes it easy for teachers to embed P4C into the curriculum."

Natalie Padley, Deputy Head Teacher, St. Martin's Primary

Philosophy for Children Across the Primary Curriculum

Inspirational Themed Planning

Alison Shorer and Katie Quinn

LONDON AND NEW YORK

Cover image: © Getty Images

First published 2023
by Routledge
4 Park Square, Milton Park, Abingdon, Oxon OX14 4RN

and by Routledge
605 Third Avenue, New York, NY 10158

Routledge is an imprint of the Taylor & Francis Group, an informa business

© 2023 Alison Shorer and Katie Quinn

The right of Alison Shorer and Katie Quinn to be identified as authors of this work has been asserted in accordance with sections 77 and 78 of the Copyright, Designs and Patents Act 1988.

All rights reserved. No part of this book may be reprinted or reproduced or utilised in any form or by any electronic, mechanical, or other means, now known or hereafter invented, including photocopying and recording, or in any information storage or retrieval system, without permission in writing from the publishers.

The content of this publication has not been approved by the United Nations and does not reflect the views of the United Nations or its officials or Member States.

Trademark notice: Product or corporate names may be trademarks or registered trademarks, and are used only for identification and explanation without intent to infringe.

British Library Cataloguing-in-Publication Data
A catalogue record for this book is available from the British Library

Library of Congress Cataloging-in-Publication Data
Names: Shorer, Alison, author. | Quinn, Katie (Primary school teacher), author.
Title: Philosophy for children across the primary curriculum : inspirational themed planning / Alison Shorer and Katie Quinn.
Description: Abingdon, Oxon ; New York, NY : Routledge, 2023. | Includes bibliographical references and index.
Identifiers: LCCN 2022004009 | ISBN 9780367207113 (hardback) | ISBN 9780367207137 (paperback) | ISBN 9780429263033 (ebook)
Subjects: LCSH: Children and philosophy. | Philosophy—Study and teaching (Primary)—Great Britain. | Education, Primary—Curricula—Great Britain.
Classification: LCC B105.C45 S56 2023 | DDC 107.0941—dc23/eng/20220505
LC record available at https://lccn.loc.gov/2022004009

ISBN: 978-0-367-20711-3 (hbk)
ISBN: 978-0-367-20713-7 (pbk)
ISBN: 978-0-429-26303-3 (ebk)

DOI: 10.4324/9780429263033

Typeset in Helvetica
by Apex CoVantage, LLC

Access the Support Material: www.routledge.com/9780367207137

For my co-author, Katie Quinn, who has endured long COVID since March 2020.

Alison

Contents

Foreword
Nick Chandley ix

Preface xi

1 About the authors 1

2 How to use this book 2

3 Philosophy at the heart by Alison Shorer 4

4 The philosophical teacher by Lizzie Lewis 6

5 Making metacognition simple: philosophising and thinking moves by Roger Sutcliffe, Bob House, and Nick Chandley 11

6 Artificial intelligence 16

7 Biodiversity 40

8 Heart and lungs 64

9 Journeys 88

10 Money 114

11 Resilience 138

12 Time 166

13 War and peace 190

14 Waste 218

15 Water 246

Appendix A: P4C generic worksheets 270

    1 SAPERE – Developing 4C thinking 270

    2 SAPERE – Identifying philosophical concepts 271

    3 A new thought – evidence of thinking 272

    5 SPEC Grids 273

    6 Group, divide activity 274

Appendix B: Commemoration dates 275

Index 279

Foreword

Nick Chandley

Philosophy for Children, or as it is commonly known, P4C, has been the slow-burn initiative within the education world. Since its development 50 years ago, by Professor Matthew Lipman and Ann Margaret Sharp, it's never gone away, nor gone out of fashion, nor suffered the fate of many other newcomers of disappearing and returning years later under another name. Now practised in over 60 countries, Lipman's aim for P4C was to help children become 'more thoughtful, more reflective, more considerate and more reasonable individuals' (Philosophy in the Classroom, p. 15). It does this through presenting children with something interesting – a story, poem, or picture, for example – and encouraging them to come up with their own questions about it, rather than answering the teacher's. The teacher then manages, or 'facilitates', the subsequent discussion, encouraging children to build on – and respect – each other's ideas.

Lipman's own description of P4C as a thinking skills programme certainly helped its spread, as most curricula aspire in some way to promote critical and creative thinking, core elements of P4C. However, 'thoughtful', 'reflective', 'considerate', and 'reasonable' are rather less likely to appear as outcomes within subjects, which may be a reason why P4C has been so enduring. The addition of the caring thinking dimension (to critical and creative), encourages students to care about being involved, to care enough to want to 'entertain' the thoughts of others (a mark of an educated person, according to Aristotle), to care about the feelings of others and those of their own, and to care enough about the progress of the enquiry at hand that they share their personal feelings and experiences and reflect on the lives they lead.

This all-too-brief explanation of caring thinking does little to convey its richness, but it goes some way to show why P4C is the tortoise in the hare-and-tortoise education race. Children and young people are entering a world that is moving at a relentless pace, with whole new fields of employment springing up between the time children start school and the time they enter the workplace. The development of critical, creative, caring, and (particularly in the UK) collaborative thinking skills that are inherent in P4C, through participation in classroom (and beyond) communities of enquiry, may be viewed on one level as essential for the workplace. At another level, though, these '4Cs' are powerful companions on the journey to living a good life.

One of the challenges that P4C faces is the giving over of curriculum time to discrete sessions, despite the value that these bring. Students, in the main, love this time for them to talk about things that matter to them, so for many schools, this is something precious and worth timetabling. As one 10-year-old girl said to me, 'It's important that we do P4C because when we get older, we won't have time to think'.[1]

For others though, incorporating P4C into curriculum subjects and topics may be the only way to access it, which is why a book like this is important. There is a philosophical dimension to every subject, which shouldn't be viewed as icing on the cake if there is time at the end of a lesson. Any topic on World War One should surely include some exploration of the concept of conflict, just as any study of a particular artist should explore elements of the field of aesthetics, lest we demote education to simply learning facts.

P4C may not be the only way to do this, but for me, it is the most complete, with a rich past and an assured future. This book will help those both experienced and inexperienced in P4C take a step towards truly philosophical teaching and learning.

Note

1 'Older', by the way, meant '15 years-old and above', which may explain certain exasperations of secondary school colleagues.

Preface

"Philosophy is not a theory but an activity" – Ludwig Wittgenstein.

This book is a practical guide for experienced P4C practitioners who want to place philosophical thinking at the heart of the curriculum. We have selected modern themes, such as biodiversity and artificial intelligence, that will refresh topic planning.

It was inspired after Katie and I attended a P4C SAPERE course led by Nick Chandley in which we explored how to embed across the curriculum and we noticed that some teachers struggled to find philosophical questions for all subjects.

We felt compelled to write an inspirational resource book that was easy for practitioners to use. We know as teachers ourselves how much preparation goes into planning, resource management, and referencing the curriculum, so each activity is a photocopiable page with the English national curriculum references included.

As experienced practitioners you have the option to use as much of the suggested activity as you choose and to tailor it for the needs of the class. For the introduction of the theme there are concept stretchers so the learners can explore the words and semantics for deeper understanding before philosophical enquiries. Each theme has an activity for each subject and a philosophical question, but these are merely suggestions.

We have selected modern themes, as we feel that young children want to discuss current global issues and that exploring them is important so children understand the world around them. Even as I write, we are experiencing a two-year pandemic in which children have been exposed to an existential threat. They deserve a space for thinking and talking about these real and complex issues. The next generation will have to think deeply and make decisions about important global issues.

We hope this book inspires you to place philosophy at the heart of your practice.

Alison Shorer
January 2022

1 About the authors

Alison Shorer

Alison graduated with a BA (Hons) Philosophy in 1997 from Hertfordshire University and continued to study a PGCE in primary teaching with Qualified Teacher Status at Plymouth University. She became a primary teacher in 1998 and during her teaching career taught across the whole age range. In 2009 Alison received a master's in education at Exeter University and became a lecturer in language and literacy at the Plymouth Institute of Education, teaching from 2009–2020 on the BEd, PGCE, School Direct, and BA Education Studies.

During her time lecturing, Alison developed an interest in Philosophy for Children (P4C), which blended her love for philosophy and education. She practised it in local primary schools and taught it within the BA Education modules: Philosophy in Practice; Learning through Children's Literature; and Childhood, Philosophy, and Education. She believes critical thinking should be central in pedagogy and education programmes.

Alison is a Thinking Moves A-Z and P4C Plus Trainer for Dialogue Works and has trained with Society for Advancing Philosophical Enquiry and Reflection in Education (SAPERE) in Levels 1, 2B, and 2A. She also has two education organisations that she co-founded called TalkTastic CIC and Articulacy, which specialise in teaching oracy. Her fields of specialism are critical thinking skills, literacy, children's literature, and oracy practice. Alison lives in Devon, England, with her husband, two children, and spaniel. She loves sailing, walking and enjoying the outdoors with her family.

Katie Quinn

Now with over 15 years' experience, Katie loves facilitating enquiry-led, project-based, thematic learning in her classroom teaching, with an ideal of preparing children for their 21st-century future. P4C practice closely echoes her pedagogical values by enabling children to model language connections and meaning making for each other in real contexts, as co-enquirers. Having studied philosophy as an undergraduate at the University of Bristol, Katie's interest in P4C first arose from a workshop with Barry Hymer in 2013, before going on to train with Steve Bramall, Nick Chandley, Roger Sutcliffe, and Sara Liptai at SAPERE up to Level 3. Since then, she has taught P4C across KS1 and KS2, for some years facilitating several P4C sessions a day in all classes from Year 1 to 6 in a three-form entry state primary school. As well as modelling lessons and P4C activities for teacher CPD sessions, Katie has been the subject of a doctoral international P4C comparison study and worked with Plymouth University as a guest P4C practitioner/lecturer on their PGCE programme. She currently works as Curriculum Lead and continues to advocate for P4C. Outside work, she loves the joy of sharing the outdoors with her family in Devon, be that walking on the Moors or jumping in the sea.

DOI: 10.4324/9780429263033-1

2 How to use this book

Who is this book for?

Our book is aimed at P4C practitioners who are looking for inspirational topics and themes to teach all the curriculum subjects via a philosophical pedagogy. It is based on the national curriculum in England, but we hope that other facilitators teaching different curricula can use it in their educational setting as well.

Why did we write this book?

We wanted to help fellow P4C practitioners place philosophy at the heart of children's learning and demonstrate that philosophical thinking can be linked to all curriculum subjects and their learning objectives. P4C is often taught as a discrete subject, but we have placed P4C at the centre of the pedagogy.

How to use this book

First, select the theme from the contents page and scan the opening two-page spread to see the overview of activities for each subject along with their suggested philosophical questions. These are purely suggestions and are for you to use as a starting point if you are looking for philosophical inspiration.

Next, read the following activity pages. They are written in the form of a worksheet for you to photocopy directly from the page for ease of use.

On the top left is a philosophical question, on the top right the subject, and at the bottom a link to the national curriculum objective. We have designed the pages so that you have flexibility in how you want to use them – for example we say, "discuss with a partner", but this can be done within a circle discussion or in a group. We may suggest that questions be put to P4C enquiry, but of course you can decide when the children are ready for this. We want you to be able to use your professional judgement and our activities, with the aim to make this book a helpful guide and resource for you.

Many activities are intended to be used as a springboard for more P4C enquiries and activities than we suggest. As experienced teachers, you can find your own path with your learners. It is not intended to be restrictive in any way.

Also, at the end of each theme chapter there is a national curriculum grid that captures all the objectives for each topic, which is useful for your teaching plans.

Furthermore, in Appendix A there are P4C generic worksheets, which are blank for photocopying. These are blank SPEC grids, Venn diagrams, helpful SAPERE P4C posters, and assessment sheets that you may find useful. Also, in Appendix B there is a usual list of commemoration dates that relate to the book's themes.

P4C and spoken language

In the national curriculum for England, the spoken language (formally called speaking and listening) objectives are only two pages, and the expectation is for teachers to integrate them into all the other subjects. These are only referenced for the concept-stretching activities but are equally relevant for the other activities.

3 Philosophy at the heart

Alison Shorer

The national curriculum in England is a knowledge-based curriculum, as it stipulates what the children should know, but many schools are moving towards a value-based or concept-based curriculum. Many modern constructionist educators promote a paradigm shift for teachers to become "teachers of thinking". The Philosophy for Children (P4C) practice promotes thinking skills, and as Matthew Lipman, the founder of P4C, explains, that thinking is about process and not content. We want children to be thoughtful and curious in all subjects and be creative thinkers.

Today's young learners can easily find information online, often instantly, and many agree that the knowledge-based curriculum that we have in England is not fit for purpose. Learners need the skills to find reliable and credible information, but also the thinking skills, such as critical evaluation, problem-solving, deduction, inference, and creative thinking. We also need originality of thought to find solutions. Originality comes from creativity, and creativity comes from playful thought exercises, where children ask questions such as "what if".

P4C and its inquiry method (SAPERE)

The P4C enquiry approach allows these skills to develop by using a community, usually peer groups, to explore together any philosophical questions that they have raised from a stimulus, such as a book, image, story, or object. This practice allows open discussion for children. Both authors believe that the children should create their own philosophical question and use concept-stretching activities around the enquiry to gain the depth of understanding needed for semantics and rich discussion.

The philosophical teacher

In Chapter 4 Lizzy Lewis explores the notion of the philosophical teacher and how she, after many years of teaching P4C, has navigated and blended teaching philosophy into all of her practice. As an experienced P4C practitioner, she recommends that it is more about being a "philosophical teacher" with a critical and reflective stance, and to see the philosophical questions in topics and themes that require one to have a thoughtful disposition (Lewis and Sutcliffe). Also, the philosophical teacher explores deeply the semantics of words to attend to what their learners understand them to mean. Lewis argue that the exploration of concepts leads to the learners' deeper understanding. With this approach in mind, we have selected concepts and themes relevant to the curriculum that have rich concepts to discuss.

Metacognition

In Chapter 5 Bob House introduces the 26 Thinking Moves created by Sutcliffe, Bigglestone, and Buckley, which identify a common language for teachers and learners to use. This complements the P4C enquiry perfectly. Educators ask children to think, but there is not explicit language to name the thinking we do and how we describe it. The Thinking Moves can be blended into concept-stretching activities and all your P4C enquiry wor with the children, and all the moves are available in the appendix.

Teaching cognition

Educationalists, such as Fisher, Sutcliffe, and Lipman, along with many education organisations, such as SAPERE, DialogueWorks, and Thinking Matters, promote the teaching of thinking in particularly, philosophical teaching and learning. Innovative thinking skills equip young people with the mental skills needed for modern life, not just for educational success or financial success. Learning should help people be happy and fulfilled in their lives. We need to teach the mental skills needed to navigate the many cognitive conflicts that we meet throughout our lives.

Cognitive conflict is where we can have two universal principles, or beliefs, that we concurrently believe, such as "We should look after animals" and "I think that I should eat meat". Philosophers, such as James Nottingham, have looked at this phenomenon in more depth with children and created "The Learning Pit", which is a fascinating process of thinking to make sure that learners test their thoughts thoroughly (see www.challenginglearning.com/learning-pit/). The P4C community of enquiry allows that space for children to think about how to apply principles that we teach and encourage how principles vary once applied to contexts. The new Thinking Moves programme gives P4C practitioners the language with which to teach cognition explicitly.

Modern themes

Chapters 6 to 15 are themed plans for topics that we believe are more relevant, or current. We feel that many of the topics covered in the curriculum are outdated in a time when children are becoming more aware of the pressing current issues that affect all of us. There are other organisations promoting the discussion of current affairs and ways for children to find a voice to articulate their opinions, such as *VotesforSchools, Citizenship One, TalkTastic CIC, Noisy Classroom, Articulacy, RECLAIM project, Thinking Matters,* and *Dialogue Works*. The *Week Junior* also has a weekly debate which is well worth looking at with your class. Children, such as Greta Thunberg, are finding their voice and speaking up for issues that they want to address.

Exploring difficult topics

There is often a fear among educators that they should avoid discussions about difficult or contentious subjects, but many modern philosophers agree that taboo subjects need to be discussed with children, in an appropriate way, for several reasons. One of them is very serious. Joanna Haynes argues that the gap between what they know and what they don't know, among other things, leaves them vulnerable to abuse. Many adults assume that children are not able to discuss nor cognitively ready to think about difficult subjects, and this is what we call "adultism". This is an interesting debate, and one that we feel educators should consider.

4 The philosophical teacher

Lizzie Lewis

When I started practising Philosophy for Children (P4C) in the mid 1990s in a key stage one classroom, I felt quite isolated; none of my colleagues had heard of P4C, and the headteacher commented that my class talked too much. However, doing P4C was the highlight of my week, and I was thrilled by the creativity and engagement of the children. I knew that P4C was benefitting their confidence, language skills, and ability to think and reflect. However, I began to feel uneasy, moving back and forward between two emerging teacher personas. Wearing one teacher hat I felt the security of the step-by-step script of a lesson plan. It felt safe, like having my hand held, but it wasn't always very enjoyable or stimulating for me or the children. Wearing the other teacher hat, that of a P4C facilitator, I felt excited by having to think on my feet by being responsive to the children's interests and questions. I began to realise that I preferred facilitative philosophical teaching because it seemed to make the most impact on the children's learning, and personal and social development.

Two teacher personas

Then I became aware that these different modes of teaching might become problematic for the children. How were they to make sense of these two modes, not just with me, but when they encountered other teachers? Some colleagues were not so impressed by the curiosity, confidence, and questioning that I fostered. I rejoiced when a 5-year-old in my class said 'I disagree with you, Ms. Lewis', but I was all too aware that other teachers would feel quite differently about this. I then met other P4C facilitators who also described feeling as though they were two different kinds of teacher. Since then, we have been on a journey in P4C, to find ways to overcome this unease by becoming more philosophical in all our teaching.

I learned this lesson more profoundly from the children, who gradually transferred the language, confidence, and skills from our P4C enquiries to their play and other aspects of learning and life. They became better able to listen and talk together, more questioning, curious, articulate, and interested, giving reasons, asking for help and clarification, giving examples, etc. And so, we slowly transformed how we worked together for the better, and increasingly I felt my teacher personas merging into one: that of a philosophical teacher wearing one pedagogical hat!

One teaching persona

I have since been able to understand my experience in the context of the bigger picture of the development of P4C in the UK. Placing P4C in the curriculum – in subjects – has been a challenge for teachers and schools since it was introduced in the UK in the early 1990s. Schools are notoriously time-poor, and many cannot give P4C a dedicated weekly session. However, what has emerged over years of practice is that a sustainable, whole-school approach to P4C has helped teachers and schools have a holistic and long-term vision.

Becoming a philosophical teacher does involve a long journey, commitment, and hard work. Many UK teachers have no prior experience or understanding of philosophy, which is a further challenge. But this can be overcome over time, and it is a very worthwhile personal and professional journey.

Becoming a philosophical teacher

So, we are now going to explore what it means to be a philosophical teacher with some insights into overcoming some of the likely obstacles.

First and foremost, a philosophical teacher has done their own philosophising about education, informed by experience, inner reflection, and enquiry. Teachers need to think philosophically about the pedagogical and ethical judgements we make that inform our actions and behaviour. There is no such thing as a values-free teacher, and we model our values, even unconsciously, to children all the time. P4C challenges our expectations of what children are capable of, and so urges us to rethink our approach to teaching. Being a philosophical teacher involves constant reflecting and rethinking about what we are doing in the classroom and why.

The philosophical teacher also makes judgements about how to approach the curriculum, looking for areas of philosophical potential. Teachers who make use of the philosophical dimensions of the curriculum are able to enrich and deepen teaching and learning. The use of P4C in curriculum subjects can reveal questions and concepts that may otherwise go unnoticed and unexplored. For example, in a topic on the environment my infant class asked the question 'Who owns the air?', eliciting an exploration of the concept of 'ownership' that we related to other natural resources. This is central and crucial to environmental issues.

One critique of P4C is that children need prior knowledge to have a meaningful dialogue. Anyone with experience of practising P4C with very young children knows that they are more than capable of discussing philosophical ideas and concepts, such as ownership. Children have experience of owning toys, for example, and often have a strong sense of what is 'mine', what it means to share something, and how difficult this can be. We know that making learning meaningful to young people is crucial to their engagement and enjoyment of learning. Joanna Haynes reminds us that:

> From an early age, and provided they are not ignored, children ask questions with philosopher cool potential such as, Am I real? How do thoughts get into your mind? Where did the first chickens come from? How do you know when you're dreaming? Why do people have secrets? Why do husbands split up from their wives? The horizons of such questions are not boundless but the mystification they express is profound. Part of the appeal of such questions is that they are not drawn from within the confines of what, through schooling, we come to know as the 'subjects' within the framework of knowledge. They take us away from these narrow paths and beyond to bigger and deeper spaces of knowing and being where the edges are blurred or beyond our reckoning.
>
> (Haynes, 2002: p. 41)

A philosophical perspective

Most teachers in the UK have little or no experience of formal philosophy, or even informal philosophical inquiry, in their own education. It was in this context that SAPERE, the charity that promotes P4C, always aspired to promote Lipman's aim for P4C:

> The approach that I have created in Philosophy for Children is . . . not about prescribing any one philosophy to children, but about encouraging them to develop their own philosophy, their own way of thinking about the world. It is about giving the youngest of minds the opportunity to express ideas with confidence and in an environment where they feel safe to do so.
>
> (Lipman, 2008: p. 166)

Having a philosophical perspective can also be motivating for teachers; it can open their eyes to new possibilities and transform how they teach. As a philosophical teacher, we usually begin by planning for philosophical inquiry, but as we grow in experience and confidence, we can also respond spontaneously to opportunities for philosophy as they arise. Naturally, as children become more philosophically aware and confident, they bring philosophical concepts and questions to light and initiate inquiry for themselves.

Furthermore, philosophical teaching has the potential to not only be integrated in school curricula but also within the school's ethos and pedagogy. This was the vision of Matthew Lipman and Ann Margaret Sharp who founded P4C,

> The philosophy for children program has the clear potential to become the central paradigmatic discourse model underlying all levels of school life, both children and adult. It can shape pedagogy, planning, evaluation, conflict resolution, and management and organisation in general. It can shape the approach to the disciplines: by approaching each content area from the point of view of the 'philosophy of' a more synergistic, integrated curriculum will emerge.
>
> (Kennedy, 1993: p. 355)

Perhaps one reason that P4C has been successful in the UK is that schools have been able to make it their own and explore ways to make P4C work in their context. As a result, different models of P4C have emerged. It is helpful to offer teachers different models, especially bearing in mind that it is possible to begin with discrete, stand-alone P4C sessions and move towards an integrated model, or ideally to maintain both.

Discreet/stand-alone P4C sessions

This is the most common model in UK primary schools, where time is dedicated for *open* philosophical inquiry that is not situated within a curriculum subject. This allows for the development, in Lipman's words, of children's 'own' philosophy, their own way of thinking about the world. This is often how P4C teachers start but then, over time, the children's philosophical thinking starts to 'spill out' across the curriculum, the dining table, the playground, and into their homes and lives. Quite often the impact of one teacher doing P4C gradually impacts the whole school through a kind of philosophical 'ripple effect'. Both teachers and children enjoy time and space that is liberated from curricula matters, and they want to feel free to pursue philosophical questions that are meaningful to them. In this way, the model promotes philosophy as valuable in itself and as the best way of enabling young people to recognise and resolve for themselves the many ethical and personal challenges they face. Many schools find it helpful to begin their P4C journey in this way to give children time to internalise the process, the skills, and the language of philosophical inquiry.

Philosophy in subjects

Many schools have introduced P4C in curriculum subjects, more so in secondary schools and particularly in the humanities and sciences, in which contestable philosophical concepts are readily found. Knight and Collins give examples of the philosophical concepts that can be explored philosophically:

> Philosophical issues are embedded in many, if not all, curriculum areas. Here are some familiar examples: in Maths, deduction and induction; the concepts of number, space and infinity; the big questions of aesthetics in the Arts; in Health, a plethora of ethical questions, as well as metaphysical questions about change, and about the nature of human beings; in English, questions of truth and meaning, deductive reasoning, and the logical structure of language; in Science, questions about scientific method, the roles of theory and observation in scientific proof and the nature of scientific laws; and in SOSE [Studies of Society and Environment], the question of justification in ethics and numerous substantive moral issues – our responsibility to future generations, animal rights and so on.

(2000: p. 8)

With a revitalisation of topic-based, value-based, or concept-based curriculum planning, the ground for including philosophical inquiry in the curriculum is becoming more fertile. Teachers are increasingly ready to see that P4C is the best way of deepening students' understanding and appreciation of 'big' ideas, not to mention those that Splitter and Sharp (1995) characterized as 'common and central' to human thinking.

Concept and semantics exploration

Every subject within the curriculum has its philosophical dimensions – particular questions or concepts that lend themselves to philosophical interest and inquiry. Pupils' *understanding* of even the most 'ordinary' of concepts benefits from philosophical inquiry – which is, after all, inquiry into *meaning*. Every teacher needs to be sensitive to students' *lack* of understanding of everyday vocabulary, such as *believe, story, situation, real, made up, fact, possible, problem, freedom, rules, family, act, right* (all concepts explored in Lipman's *Pixie* [1981] for 6 to 8-year-olds) – not to mention the basic 'thinking' vocabulary, such as: *equal, alike, different, opposite, contrast, association, relationship, names, parts, characteristics, belong, kind, example, ways, ideas, definition, ambiguity, consequences, dimensions, models, metaphors, arguments, principles, reasons,* etc.

Moreover, when a teacher introduces new technical vocabulary – say, *environment* in geography, or *revolution* in history, or *force* in science – it has to be *connected* with every pupil's prior knowledge *and understanding*, and the semantics explored in depth.

Metacognition in the classroom

Schools worldwide are under increasing pressure to include the explicit teaching of general, cognitive, and particular academic skills, as well as content, in their curriculum. Regular experience of P4C can go a long way to equipping young people with desirable, if not necessary, skills and dispositions for learning and life. Some teachers use aspects of P4C to develop thinking and learning skills, sometimes framed as 'life' skills. The skills might involve games and activities or questioning the meaning of something and evaluating the reasoning behind it. However, if there is no development of a community of inquiry, then this is not P4C. There is a danger of introducing P4C as a skills-based programme, as it could play into a merely instrumental and instructional agenda (at its worst, geared to passing exams), without respect to deeper, philosophical understanding and dispositions. This is a vital concern – precisely the one that Lipman railed against in *Philosophy Goes to School* (1988) when he talked of the 'information-acquisition' model that dominated education then, and arguably is even more dominant now. Philosophical teaching and learning has a holistic vision of doing good, both for the individual and for society.

References

Dewey, J. (1916). *Democracy and Education: An Introduction to the Philosophy of Education*. New York: The Free Press (cited in Makaiau and Miller, 2010: 328).

Haynes, J. (2002). *Children as Philosophers: Learning Through Enquiry and Dialogue in the Primary School*. New York: Routledge.

Kennedy, D. (1993). The community of inquiry and educational structure. In: M. Lipman ed. *Thinking Children and Education*. Dubuque IO: Kendall/Hunt Publishing Company, 357.

Knight, S. and Collins, C. (2000). The curriculum transformed: Philosophy embedded in the learning areas. *Critical and Creative Thinking*, 8(1), 8–14.

Lipman, M. (1980). *Philosophy in the Classroom*. Philadelphia: Temple University Press.

Lipman, M. (1981). *Pixie*. Montclair, NJ: Institute for the Advancement of Philosophy for Children.

Lipman, M. (1988). *Philosophy Goes to School*. Philadelphia: Temple University Press.

Lipman, M. (2008). *A Life Teaching Thinking*. Montclair: Institute for the Advancement of Philosophy for Children.

Makaiau, A. S. and Miller, C. (2010). The philosopher's pedagogy. *Educational Perspectives*, 44(1, 2), 8–19.

Splitter, L. (2006). Philosophy in a crowded curriculum. *Critical and Creative Thinking*, 14(2), 4–14.

Splitter, L. and Sharp, A.M. (1995). *Teaching for Better Thinking*. Melbourne: Australian Council for Educational Research.

5 Making metacognition simple

Philosophising and thinking moves

Roger Sutcliffe, Bob House, and Nick Chandley

Introduction

Our thinking ability is what makes us distinctively human. Yet we have no generally accepted approach to teaching thinking – and no common vocabulary to describe different ways of thinking. This, when you think about it, is extraordinary. Imagine trying to teach or learn maths if we did not have commonly accepted terms such as *add*, *subtract*, *multiply*, or *divide*. However, all teachers teach thinking.

Roger Sutcliffe (founder of SAPERE) realised this need and that, although there are many lists of thinking skills and such as the Frameworks for Thinking (Moseley et al., 2005), none were what teachers needed them to be: easy to explain to students and easy for students to memorise. In fact, there were no fewer than 42 schemes reviewed. It was when Sutcliffe attended a workshop on the Habits of Mind, led by Art Costa nearly 10 years ago, that he conceived of the possibility of constructing a memorable list of distinct acts of thinking. He called them Thinking Moves.

What Sutcliffe decided was needed was not so much the theoretical construct of human thinking but a matter-of-fact, methodical, and memorable way of thinking about one's thinking without resorting to technical terms. That is how the A – Z was conceived. It was constructed through regular reflection on thinking in practice. From the start, it uses the language of moves rather than skills so that it can analyse thinking more precisely – as a progression of simple steps rather than as a set of complex strategies.

Sutcliffe's Thinking Moves A – Z simply encourages teaching thinking explicitly, drawing attention to the thinking already used in schools and in everyday life so that students become able to choose the right tools for the job in hand. In short, Thinking Moves A – Z is a framework for developing metacognition via a common vocabulary.

The new Thinking Moves A – Z identifies 26 "thinking moves", and each has an icon to match.

DOI: 10.4324/9780429263033-5

12   *Making metacognition simple*

The A – Z provides a common vocabulary for metacognition because of its completeness, simplicity, and memorability. If students can master the moves, to the point where they can not only recognise them but also apply them independently and effectively, they will truly become metacognitive learners.

Thinking Moves A – Z

Thinking Moves A – Z provides a vocabulary for thinking. The moves themselves are not new – we all use them in our learning and our lives every day. But we need a way of talking about how we think and a means to work on improving the effectiveness of our thinking. The moves are designed to satisfy these needs by being:

- **Comprehensive**: collectively, the moves cover every type of thinking that teachers and students are likely to come across in their education and their daily lives;
- **Understandable**: the moves are expressed in everyday language and are backed up by different devices to aid understanding across all age ranges;
- **Memorable**: by linking the moves to the alphabet, students have the most fundamental of all mnemonics to help them remember the moves.

The full A – Z, with icons to help understanding

| DIALOGUE WORKS |

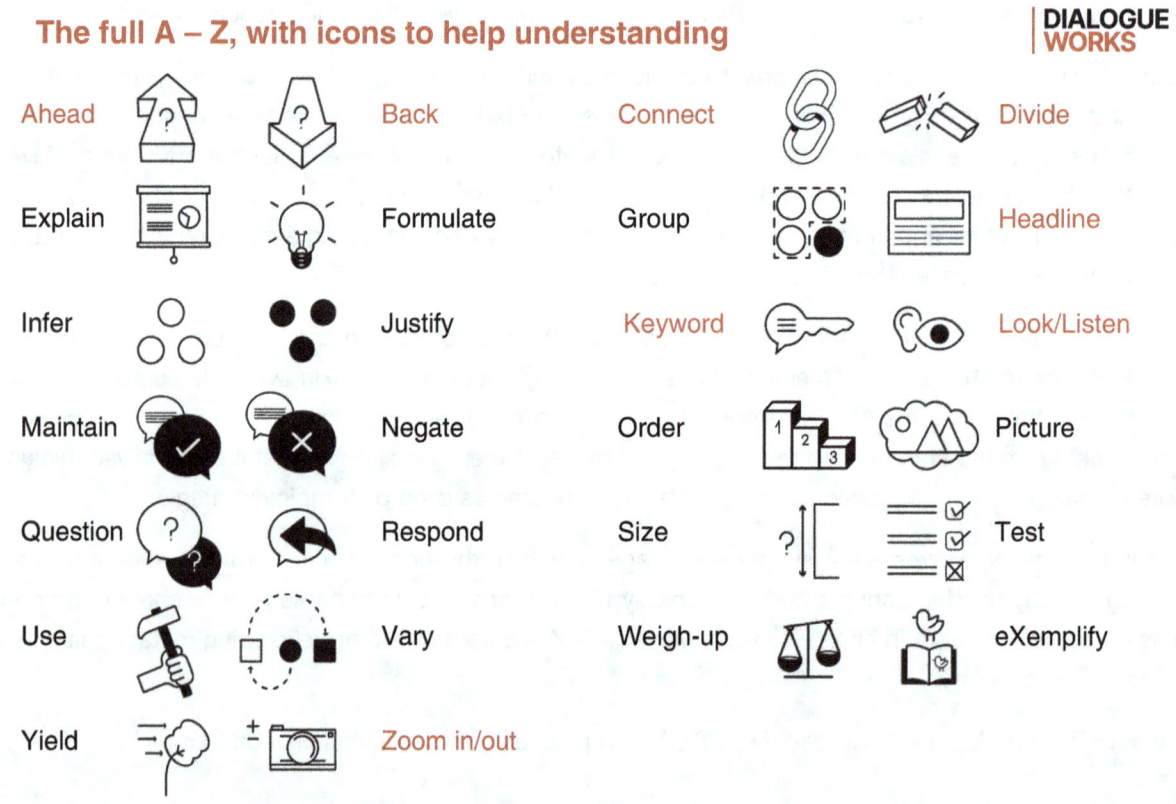

Thinking Grooves

As this book is a resource for P4C practitioners to find the philosophical within each topic, it is exciting to contemplate that Thinking Moves can be put into combinations or sequences for thinkers called "Thinking Grooves". These can be subject-specific or general. Thinking Grooves are a great tool, as you can select moves and apply them to suit the subject. Here are some examples.

Maths

- LOOK at the problem;
- FORMULATE a mathematical expression or equation;
- USE the expression to solve the problem;
- TEST the solution for accuracy.

Geography

- HEADLINE the main message;
- ORDER the supporting information;
- PICTURE an interesting way to design the slides;
- ZOOM out to make sure that the overall storyline is coherent.

In modelling such "Thinking Grooves", the teacher's aim is for the students to start developing their own Grooves, initially with guidance and encouragement but eventually becoming spontaneous and internalised as a way of managing thinking in a purposeful and effective manner. Once that stage is achieved, the school can justly claim to have made major progress in building metacognition and self-directed learning among its students.

Thinking Moves and philosophising

Thinking Moves and Thinking Grooves can be blended into teaching between P4C enquiries to help deepen the children's understanding of their own thinking skills. As more practitioners are discovering them, individual schools and school groups around the world are starting to use Thinking Moves A – Z across a wide range of student ages.

The moves have been working well with Early Years, using simplified vocabulary and a limited range of moves. Students as young as 7 years old have found it easy to access the full range of 26 moves, and to remember them remarkably quickly. Older students have found the moves engaging and helpful in a broad range of subject areas. Trainee teachers have found the moves to be an effective and accessible tool to help them plan and deliver lessons during their school placements.

Experienced teachers and school leaders have reported that the moves are easy to build into lesson plans, that students find them fun to work with, and that they can see evidence of impact on the quality of student thinking within a few weeks of introducing the moves. There will, of course, need to be formal research to assess the full impact of Thinking Moves, but the early indications are that the moves will be a powerful tool for better thinking in education and everyday life.

To find out more about Dialogue Works and Thinking Moves, see the appendices.

English

> What makes a techie tick?

STEM Ambassador
Invite a STEM ambassador to your school. Prepare questions to ask them.

> Would a universal language make the world a better place?

Definition of A.I.
Explore what A.I. means. The definitions can vary. Create your own definition.

Maths

> Is A.I. magic or just mathematics?

Maths in A.I.
Use software to demonstrate the mathematics in the computer programming.
Learn how to use numbers to control a robot.

R.E.

> Is programming the new universal language?

Tower of Babel
The biblical story of The Tower of Babel tells how humans decided to build a tower up to the sky to find the heavens. Think about how this was one language and how computing language is universal.

Music

> Can artificial music created by a computer be any good?

Computers making music
It is interesting to play with artificial sounds on computer software and relatively easy.
Make some music with software.

History

> Who controls the future of robots?

The recent history of computers
Explore the history of computers, as well as the new software applications that we can use on smartphones.

Computing

> Is code the same as speaking?

Codes and how to use them
Create your own codes and learn to use the flag semaphore system.

Artificial Intelligence

Science

> Should robots do human's work?

Ten robots that will change the world
Explore what robots are capable of. Analyse what they can do.

> Do computers make your life better?

Famous computer scientists
Research famous computer scientists and select one for your school's Achievement Medal.

Geography

> Can we use artificial intelligence to find anything?

> Question?

Geo-caching
Learn how to use computers, such as SATNAVs to find your way around. Try geo-caching to practise finding places with geo-locators.

Art

> Is binary beautiful?

The art of binary
The binary numeral system is a way to write numbers using only two digits: 0 and 1. Learn how to make a binary image or a binary bead string.

Design and Technology

> Should robots move like humans?

The future of design
Create a 3D robot model using pivots, levers, and pulleys that has limbs that you can move. Try using a computer to design it.

Citizenship

> Should robots be citizens?

Robots that can think
As robots get better at performing cognitive skills it raises the question of whether they become human. Sophia, an A.I. robot, was the first robot to be given citizenship in the world. Discuss this together.

PSHE

> Are we safe in a virtual world?

Using our devices safely
Explore the word "safe". Share all the associations using words, phrases or pictures that you have with this word. Use your schools' rules about online safety.

P.E.

> Can a machine help you get better at sport?

Sport and artificial intelligence
Over the last decade artificial intelligence has started to creep into the world of sport.
Think about the new devices and what makes us better at sport.

6 Artificial intelligence

Concept stretchers   **SPEC grid**

As part of a P4C enquiry, children brainstorm synonyms, phrases, connections, and examples (SPEC) in a SPEC grid, as in this example.

Synonyms	Phrases
• Bot	• That doesn't compute.
• Digital	• I am not programmed that way.
• Function	• I switched off.
• Alien	• I just blew a fuse.
• Ether	• Light-bulb moment.
• Tablet	• I malfunctioned.
• Cyber	• Are your calculations right?
• Cloud	• My computer has died.
• Technology – Tech	
Connections	**Examples**
• ICT learning	• Mobile phone
• Home	• PC computer
• School computers	• Home appliances
• Tablets	• E-menu in fast food restaurant
	• Cloud storage

Curriculum connections

Spoken language – Pupils should use spoken language to develop understanding through speculating, hypothesising, imagining, and exploring ideas.

SPEC grids are the work of Roger Sutcliffe, Director and Programme Designer of P4C Plus and Thinking Moves A – Z at Dialogue Works, Philosophical Teaching and Learning. www.dialogueworks.co.uk

DOI: 10.4324/9780429263033-6

Quotes to explore   **P4C**

"If a robot can do it, then it should."

Anon.

"Man is a robot with defects."

Emil Cioran

"I just want the future to happen faster. I can't imagine the future without robots."

Nolan Bushnell

"I believe that robots should only have faces if they truly need them."

Donald A. Norman

Concept line activity   **P4C**

Give a card to each child and ask them to consider where these objects would sit along a continuum of a robot.

Place cards along a line from yes (a robot) and no (not a robot) page and discuss.

A robot <-----------------------------------> Not a robot

Clock

Mobile phone

Kettle

Microwave

Car

Bus

Computer

Machine in factory

Till

Checkout operator

Teacher

TV

Curriculum connections

Years 1–6 Spoken language – Pupils should be able to articulate and justify answers, arguments, and opinions.

Years 1–6 Spoken language – Pupils should be taught to gain and maintain attention and participate actively in collaborative conversations, staying on topic and initiating and imitating and responding to comments.

18 Artificial intelligence

Concept stretcher P4C

Decision corner

Read the children "Would you rather?" by John Burningham. Ask the children to:

1. Decide which corner to go to.
2. Share how they made their decision.

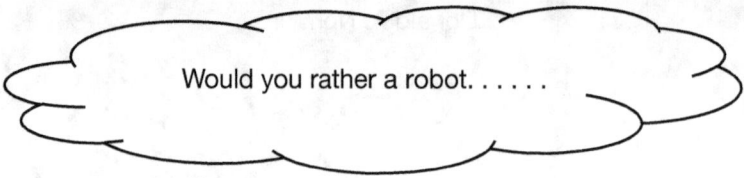

Would you rather a robot......

KS1

... made your bed OR did the washing up?

... read you a bedtime story OR taught you to read?

... played with you in the garden OR took you to the seaside?

... brushed your teeth OR brushed your hair?

KS2

... wash your clothes OR do your homework?

... calculate your maths work OR record your money in a bank?

... tell you the time OR tell you when you have made a mistake?

... measure your skills and talent OR be your cheerleader?

Further activities:

- Ask the children to think of their own pairs of choices.
- Ask the children to ask the questions of family and friends.

Curriculum connections

Spoken language – Pupils should be able to participate in discussions, presentations, performances, role play/improvisations, and debates.

Spoken language – Pupils should use spoken language to develop understanding through speculating, hypothesising, imagining, and exploring ideas.

What makes a techie tick?   **English**

STEM Ambassador

Invite a technology ambassador into the classroom. There are over 2,000 IET members acting as STEM Ambassadors.

www.theiet.org/involved/volunteering-for-the-iet/volunteer-roles/education-roles/stem-ambassador/

Write down all information you know about this person from your research.

Now write down some probing questions to ask them.

1.

2.

3.

4.

5.

Notes from interview:

Curriculum connections

Spoken language – Pupils should be able to ask relevant questions to extend their understanding and knowledge.

Would a universal language make the world a better place? English

Definition of artificial intelligence

The definition of what artificial intelligence is varies. Here are two definitions.

Read, compare, and discuss in pairs, groups, or in a P4C enquiry.

> The theory and development of computer systems able to perform tasks normally requiring human intelligence, such as visual perception, speech recognition, decision-making, and translation between languages (Oxford Language, 21/09/2020)

> Artificial intelligence (AI), sometimes called machine intelligence, is intelligence demonstrated by machines, unlike the natural intelligence displayed by humans and animals. Leading AI textbooks define the field as the study of "intelligent agents": any device that perceives its environment and takes actions that maximize its chance of successfully achieving its goals.[3] Colloquially, the term "artificial intelligence" is often used to describe machines (or computers) that mimic "cognitive" functions that humans associate with the human mind, such as "learning" and "problem solving".[4]
>
> https://en.wikipedia.org/wiki/Artificial_intelligence (accessed 21/09/2020)

Create your own definition of AI.

Curriculum connections

Spoken language – Pupils should consider and evaluate different viewpoints, attending to and building on the contributions of others.

Spoken language – Pupils should be taught to articulate and justify answers, arguments, and opinions.

Is AI magic or just mathematics?   **Maths**

Maths in AI

Many computer scientists agree that artificial intelligence is just mathematics. Let's see an example of this.

> **How do you programme a robot?**
>
> BBC has a game that you can play which teaches you how to use mathematical language to make the robot do your errands.
>
> https://toybox-assets.files.bbci.co.uk/activities/legacy-bitesize-games/robot/navigation/index.html (accessed 21/07/2021)

Challenge

Create a programme that tells a robot how to get from one place to another in your school.

1. Think about how to get from your classroom to a particular place in your school.
2. Then walk the path to see how many steps you would need to go forward, then to the right/left, then how many forward again.
3. Next include turns. (You can use 90°.)

Create a programme for a maze

www.coderkids.com/blog/scratch-projects-for-kids (accessed 21/07/2021)

> Write some of the thoughts that you have discussed with your partner or circle about the philosophical question at the top.

Curriculum connections

The purpose of the curriculum is to deliver a high-quality computing education which equips pupils to use computational thinking and creativity to understand and change the world. Computing has deep links with mathematics, science, and design and technology, and it provides insights into both natural and artificial systems.

Do computers make your life better? Science

Famous computer scientists

Research these famous people and write four facts about each of them here.		
Charles Babbage	**Margaret Hamilton**	**Grace Hopper**
1	1	1
2	2	2
3	3	3
4	4	4

Imagine you have to pick someone for your school's achievement medal. Who would you choose from these three famous computer scientists, and how would you say they have made your life better?

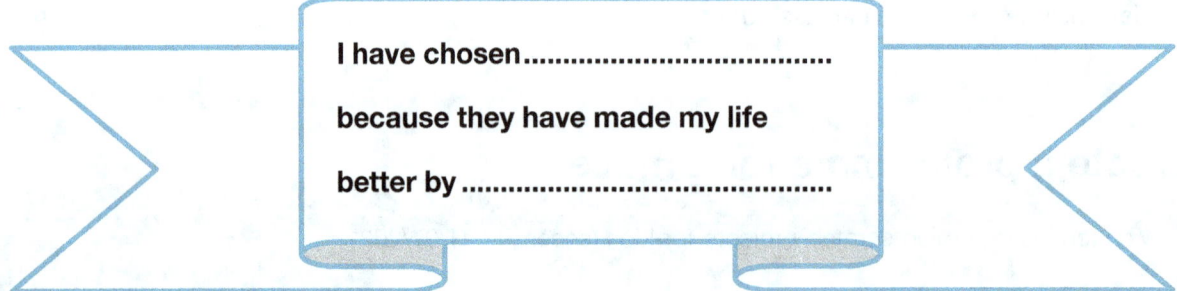

I have chosen………………………………

because they have made my life

better by ………………………………

Curriculum connections

Computing – Pupils should use search technologies effectively.

Spoken language – Pupils should participate in presentations.

Should robots do humans' work? Science

10 Amazing Robots that Will Change the World

Let children see what the robots can do.

Watch the video called "10 Amazing Robots that Will Change the World". What would your dream robot do? www.youtube.com/watch?v=6feEE716UEk

Watch again! Note what you see the robots doing.

Running	Walking		

Curriculum connections

Computing – Pupils should be able to recognise common uses of IT beyond school.

Is programming the new universal language? RE

Tower of Babel

The biblical story of the Tower of Babel tells how humans decided to build a tower up to the sky to find the heavens. God was not pleased and said that humans had become too clever. To prevent this happening again he gave people different languages so that they would not be able to collaborate again.

Read the story or watch it. www.youtube.com/watch?v=-X0i22IM1sQ (accessed 28/06/2021)

Think about what the world would be like if we all spoke one language. What do you think would be a benefit of this?

Curriculum connections

Computing – Pupils should understand computer networks including the internet – how they provide multiple services, such as the WWW, and the opportunities they offer for communication and collaboration.

Who controls the future of robots?   History

The recent history of computers

Computers started to be invented from 1822. The first computer, called the Babbage Difference Engine, was one of the first mechanical computers. Computers as we know them today are very different and have become much smaller, lighter, and faster. In particularly, the last 25 years have seen many software applications change the way we live our lives. Here are some of those and when they were created.

The recent past

2004	Facebook launched
2006	VDSL used in BT's Infinity approved
2006	Twitter launched
2007	Windows Vista launched
2007	iPhone launched
2008	First Android smartphones
2009	Windows 7 launched
2010	iPad launched; other Android ones followed

Activity – Create a poster that is a visual timeline of the recent past of computers.

Interview

Interview people born in the 1970s, 1980s, and 1990s. See what they remember about computers and technology.

Notes from your interview

Curriculum connections

History – Pupils should be learning links to change since 1948 in Year 6.

Is binary beautiful?   **Art and Design**

The art of binary

The binary numeral system is a way to write numbers using only two digits: 0 and 1. See Innovationkidslab.com for a good description of how to make a binary bead string.

Create a pen and ink binary image.

1. Draw a shape (e.g. a bird).

2. Fill the shape with big 0s and big 1s.

3. Fill in the spaces in between so there are no gaps with smaller 0s and 1s.

> Is binary beautiful?

In pairs, groups, or in a philosophy circle discuss whether binary beautiful.

Curriculum connections

Art – Pupils should develop a wide range of art and design techniques in using colour, pattern, texture, line, shape, form, and space. The pupils produce creative work, exploring their ideas.

KS1 – Pupils should learn about a range of artists.

KS2 – Pupils learn to use charcoal or pen and ink to explore their mastery of art and design techniques.

Is code the same as speaking?   **Computing**

Computing codes and how to use them

How have codes been used in the past?

Try the Flag Semaphore technique that passes messages silently via code and was used in war time. People used two flags in different positions. Have a go yourself.

https://en.wikipedia.org/wiki/Flag_semaphore (accessed 13/10/2021)

Pick one of these to investigate.

Road signs	Emojis	Flags of the world	Flags for sailing
Clothes labels	Smoke SOS	Sign language	Morse code

Further activities:

Write your own secret code using numbers instead of letters. Finish the alphabet. You could make up your own symbol to denote a letter when you run out of digits. Give your friend a message in code and ask then to decode it using your method.

A	B	C	D	E	F	G	H	I	J	K	L	M	N	O	P	Q	R	S	T	U	V	W	X	Y	Z
3	6	5																							

Famous codebreakers

Bletchley Park is famous for the role it had during a war. Learn about the mastermind codebreakers of the time. Write some of the names and your notes below.

https://bletchleypark.org.uk/our-story/bletchley-park-people/who-were-the-codebreakers

Coding explained

Explore what software (coding) is. The following link shows a really good video that you can watch to explain the basics.

www.youtube.com/watch?v=RmbFJq2jADY (accessed 25/05/2020)

Curriculum connections

Computing KS1 and 2 – Pupils can understand and apply the fundamental principles and concepts of computer science including data representation.

Computing – Pupils should understand computer networks including the internet – how they provide multiple services, such as the WWW, and the opportunities they offer for communication and collaboration.

Can we use artificial intelligence to find anything?   **Geography**

Geocaching

Equipment needed – GPS or smartphone with 4G

We can use computers to help us find our way around. Your parents may have a SATNAV that uses a postcode to get to places without getting lost. You may have used other tools with maps to help know where you are or where you are going.

A global positioning system (GPS) or smartphone uses the position of your coordinates to find your way. Use one to find out where you are sitting right now.

- What are your global coordinates?
- What is your latitude?
- What is your longitude?

Now find out about geocaching. You can find out where your local caches are.

www.geocaching.com/play

As research from home, see if you can go on a geocache walk with your family near your home. How about setting up a new cache somewhere?

www.maps.ie/coordinates.html

Curriculum connections

KS1 – Pupils should learn to use aerial photographs and plan perspectives to recognise landmarks and basic human and physical features; devise a simple map; and use and construct basic symbols in a key.

KS2 – Pupils should learn to use maps, atlases, globes, and digital/computer mapping to locate countries and describe features studied.

Will artificial intelligence take over human design?   **Design and Technology**

The future of design

Use pivots, levers, and pulleys to create a 3D robot model that has limbs you can move. Think about how you make it stand, walk, twist, and bend. Work with a partner or group on your robot.

Think about how you can improve it.

Try using a computer design to help you, such as Tinkercad. www.tinkercad.com/

Curriculum connections

Pupils should learn to generate, develop, model, and communicate their ideas through discussion, annotated sketches, cross-sectional and exploded diagrams, prototypes, pattern pieces, and computer-aided design.

Artificial intelligence

Are we safe in a virtual world?   PSHE

Using our devices safely

Marketplace activity

Explore the word *safe*. Share all the associations using words, phrases, or pictures that you have with this word.

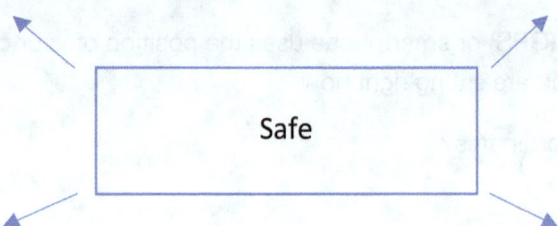

Next share them with a partner. Give one that your partner doesn't have, and note one that you haven't got. Now go find another partner until your teacher says stop.

What is a virtual world?

What does it mean when we say that we are using a virtual world? Write some of your thoughts here.

Online rules for children

With a trusted adult, explore the rules of internet safety using a rules list like the one here: www.safekids.com/kids-rules-for-online-safety/ (accessed 21/07/2021)

Curriculum connections

KS1 Keeping Safe H34 – Pupils should learn about the basic rules to keep safe online, including what is meant by personal information and what should be kept private; the importance of telling a trusted adult if they come across something that scares them.

KS2 Keeping Safe H42 – Pupils should learn about the importance of keeping personal information private; strategies for keeping safe online, including how to manage requests for personal information or images of themselves and others; what to do if frightened or worried by something seen or read online, and how to report concerns or inappropriate content and contact.

Can a machine help you get better at sport? PE

Sport and artificial intelligence

Over the last decade artificial intelligence has started to creep into the world of sport, whether it is measuring a penalty kick in football or recording your running time with the help of wearable sensors and high-speed cameras.

What makes you get better at sport? Write some ideas here.

What is needed for improvement in sport?

Attitude	Dedication	Fun	Ability	Diet
Space	Weather	Competition	Time	Water
Coach	Teacher	Friends	Carers	Love

Discuss with a partner or group what you think is more important, not so important, and least important. Write your ideas along a decision line.

Capture what you have discussed here.

More important	Not so important	Least important

Write some reflections about what you are thinking.

Curriculum connections

The purpose of study is to deliver a high-quality physical education curriculum which inspires all pupils to succeed and excel in competitive sport and other physically demanding activities.

Can artificial music created by a computer be any good? Music

Computers making music

So, we already have begun to hear computer-generated sounds in songs instead of musicians using the real instrument, such as an artificial violin instead of a real violin.

It is interesting and relatively easy to play with artificial sounds on computer software. Why not try making some music with some of the free software listed here?

Ocean – create a jam on this. It is very easy to get started. Select all the noises and just put them in the places/blocks of when you want them to make their sound.

www.oceanwaves.io/currents/jHsAC3s2KSZA8pemy (accessed 23/07/2021)

Scribble – using shapes, selecting notes and how many times you would like to repeat the sound, you can create a piece of music.

http://scribble.audio/ (accessed 23/07/2021)

> Now that you have used some software to create computer-generated sounds, do you like it?

> Some computer programmers have come up with codes that allow the computer to design the music. Is this the same as a human creating a piece?

Curriculum connections

Pupils should learn to sing and to use their voices, to create and compose music on their own and with others, have the opportunity to learn a musical instrument, use technology appropriately, and have the opportunity to progress to the next level of musical excellence.

Should robots be citizens? Citizenship

Robots that can think

Sophia, an AI robot built by Hanson Laboratories, was the first robot in the world to be given citizenship, and this was done by the Saudi Arabian government.

Here she is being interviewed. https://youtu.be/78-1Mlkxyql

> Write your thoughts here.

> Write your questions here.

She was also awarded by the UN Development Programme in Asia and the Pacific as the first non-human Innovative Champion.

www.asia-pacific.undp.org/content/rbap/en/home/presscenter/pressreleases/2017/11/22/rbfsingapore.html

https://youtu.be/AGFIzM4Wva0?list=TLGGZmzuVcOXtxQyNDA5MjAyMQ

Think about the following concepts. Select two and say how they are linked.

Clever	Smart	Obedient
Intelligent	False	Natural
Research	Data	Controlled

Curriculum connections

A high-quality computing education equips pupils to use computational thinking and creativity to understand and change the world. Computing has deep links with mathematics, science, and design and technology, and it provides insights into both natural and artificial systems.

Inspirational people

Grace Hopper

Grace was a professor in mathematics and a pioneer in computer science, as she invented one of the first linkers. Hopper was the first to devise the theory of machine-independent programming languages and the FLOW-MATIC programming language.

Charles Babbage

Considered as the Father of Computers, he is believed to be the first person to think of the concept of a digital programmable computer. He invented the first mechanical computer called the Difference Machine.

Ada Lovelace

Often considered the first computer programmer, she wrote and published the first algorithm for Babbage's proposed machine called the Analytical Machine. She wrote notes on both the Analytical Machine and the Difference Machine, as many people couldn't understand what they did.

Elon Musk

A modern-day scientist and game-changer, he likes to explore and do things differently. He has created companies, such as PayPal, but more relevant to this theme are SpaceX and OpenAI. His company conducts research in the field of AI with the stated goal of promoting and developing friendly AI in a way that benefits humanity as a whole.

Bill Gates

He is the co-founder of Microsoft and is considered the main proponent for the micro-computer revolution. He left Microsoft to become a philanthropist.

Margaret Hamilton

An American computer scientist, systems engineer, and business owner, she was director of the Software Engineering Division of the MIT Instrumentation Laboratory, which developed on-board flight software for NASA's Apollo program. She is often credited with creating the term *software engineering*.

Further Resources

A Robot Friend (video)

Meet Honda's Asimo. This robot can dance, make our drinks, and kick a ball at the net. *Dialogueworks/stimulus-suggestions/* (accessed 21/09/2020); suitable for (3–7 year-olds)

Changing Batteries (video)

A story about an old lady who gets a robot sent to her by her son. They create a bond, and it reveals the dependency of a robot upon a person and vice versa.

Dialogueworks/stimulus-suggestions/ (accessed 21/09/2020); suitable for KS1 and KS2

Toy Story 2 (film)

This film explores the story of toys and are of a certain time who find that they are being replaced with new technical toys and robots.

The Wrong Trousers – Wallace and Gromit (film)

This is a story about Wallace, who loves to invent things. He creates his fantastic Techno Trousers, but when his boarder, a mute penguin, tampers with them, things take a different turn.

Coding – First LEGO Challenge

Get involved with the First LEGO Challenge! Children across the world will be given a challenge, and you must solve it. As participants progress into Explore, children will take their background knowledge of STEM and put it into practice as they work in teams to design and build robots using the LEGO Education WeDo 2.0 system. Once they are ready to move into a competitive setting, they join Challenge and apply their STEM skills combined with critical thinking to work with a team, build a robot, and compete in an exciting, mission-based robotics game. www.firstlegoleague.org/ (accessed 10/11/2020)

The Book Corner

WaR: wizards and robots by Brain David Johnson and Will.I.Am
When a wizard travels back in time to find the scientist Ada Luring, he asks her to create the first robot. Ada may be the key to the Earth's future and preventing its destruction. This is a fast action story. Suitable for KS2.

The Iron Man by Ted Hughes
Iron Man appears in a rural farming community, where people are scared of him and are plotting to get rid of him – until there is another threat. This classic story is about how friendship and community come together in adversity. Suitable for KS2.

Wild about robots by Peter Brown
Roz, the robot, wakes up on an island and doesn't know how he got there. Roz knows he must survive, so he befriends the wildlife to learn how to live. It is a heart-warming story about when nature and technology collide. Suitable for KS2.

Curiosity: the story of a space rover by Markus Motum
This is a retro-illustrated true story that shares how Curiosity the space rover was created and its space mission to the red planet Mars to search for signs of life. It will make young space lovers' minds come alive. Suitable for KS2.

How to build robots by Louise Derrington
This non-fiction book will provide insight and reveal to curious minds how to build real robots. It has lots of detailed illustrations and explains in depth to the reader how the process works. Suitable for upper KS2.

NC subject	Activity	Curriculum connections
English	STEM Ambassador	Spoken language – Pupils should be able to ask relevant questions to extend their understanding and knowledge.
English	Definition of artificial intelligence	Spoken language – Pupils should consider and evaluate difference viewpoints, attending to and building on the contributions of others. Spoken language – Pupils should be able to articulate and justify answers, arguments, and opinions.
Maths	Maths in AI	The purpose of the curriculum is to deliver a high-quality computing education which equips pupils to use computational thinking and creativity to understand and change the world. Computing has deep links with mathematics, science, and design and technology, and it provides insights into both natural and artificial systems.
Science	Famous computer scientists	Spoken language – Pupils should participate in presentations. Computing – Pupils should use search technologies effectively.
Science	"10 Amazing Robots that Will Change the World"	Computing – Pupils should be able to recognise common uses of IT beyond school.
History	The recent history of computers	History – Pupils should have learning links to change since 1948 in Year 6. D & T – KS2 – Pupils should understand how key events and individuals in design and technology have helped shape the world.
Geography	Geo-caching	KS1 – Pupils should learn to use aerial photographs and plan perspectives to recognise landmarks and basic human and physical features; devise a simple map; and use and construct basic symbols in a key. KS2 – Pupils should learn to use maps, atlases, globes, and digital/computer mapping to locate countries and describe features studied.
Music	Computers making music	Pupils should learn to sing and to use their voices, to create and compose music on their own and with others, have the opportunity to learn a musical instrument, use technology appropriately, and have the opportunity to progress to the next level of musical excellence.
Art and Design	The art of binary	Pupils should develop a wide range of art and design techniques in using colour, pattern, texture, line, shape, form, and space. The pupils produce creative work, exploring their ideas. KS1 – Pupils should learn about a range of artists. KS2 – Pupils should learn to use charcoal or pen and ink to explore their mastery of art and design techniques.
Design and Technology	The future of design	Pupils should learn to generate, develop, model, and communicate their ideas through discussion, annotated sketches, cross-sectional and exploded diagrams, prototypes, pattern pieces, and computer-aided design.

NC subject	Activity	Curriculum connections
Computing	Codes and how to use them	KS1 and 2 – Pupils should understand and apply the fundamental principles and concepts of computer science including . . . data representation. Pupils should understand computer networks including the internet – how they provide multiple services, such as the WWW, and the opportunities they offer for communication and collaboration.
Religious education	Tower of Babel	KS1: Why are some stories special? Theme: Believing/Story. This enquiry explores how religions and beliefs express values and commitments in a variety of creative ways. KS2: Pupils consider the beliefs, teachings, practices, and ways of life central to religion. They learn about sacred texts and other sources and consider their meanings.
Physical education	Sport and artificial intelligence	The purpose of study is to deliver a high-quality physical education curriculum which inspires all pupils to succeed and excel in competitive sport and other physically demanding activities.
PSHE	Using our devices safely	KS1: Keeping Safe H34. Pupils should be taught the basic rules to keep safe online, including what is meant by personal information and what should be kept private; the importance of telling a trusted adult if they come across something that scares them. KS2: Keeping Safe H42. Pupils should learn about the importance of keeping personal information private; strategies for keeping safe online, including how to manage requests for personal information or images of themselves and others; what to do if frightened or worried by something seen or read online, and how to report concerns or inappropriate content and contact.
Citizenship	Robots that can think	A high-quality computing education equips pupils to use computational thinking and creativity to understand and change the world. Computing has deep links with mathematics, science, and design and technology, and it provides insights into both natural and artificial systems.

Science

What is biodiversity?

Finding out about biodiversity
Explore what biodiversity means in depth. Think about the key concepts words, such as safeguard, survival, protect and more.

Should humans intervene to preserve all species?

Collecting the world's seeds
The Millennium Seed Bank has all of the world's seed and are collected for the Earth's preservation. Explore a local wildlife patch and catalogue what seeds you find by taking photos and drawing sketches.

English

Do all animals matter?

A day in the life of an unusual animal
We tend to like animals that look cute, or know about life cycles in which animals change dramatically. Pick an animal that you don't know anything about and research its life cycle. Draw the life cycle and make annotations around it.

Biodiversity

R.E.

Should we build an ark like Noah to save all the animals?

Noah's Ark
In The Old Testament Genesis (chapter 6 -9) Noah creates an ark into which he put two of each animal. Explore the meaning of the story.

Music

Are museums good?

A tree museum
Sometime songs' lyrics address how we live. For example, Big Yellow Taxi by Joni Mitchell tells us that we need to look after our natural environment. Create your own song with lyrics about how to look after the environment.

Computing

Can computers replace animals?

Create your own moving animal
Using Scratch software create ten movements in a sequence for an animal you have selected.

History

Is extinction part of life?

Animals that have gone extinct
Explore the theory of evolution by Charles Darwin and how animals have changed over thousands of years by natural selection. Discuss extinction and explore how some animals have gone extinct.

Geography

Is biodiversity important?

Large and small populations
Research animals that have large population sizes and say why they have been so successful. Then research some of the animals that have very low population sizes and say why they have not been successful.

PSHE

How should we best live with other animals?

Ethics and biodiversity
Read the 2012 Convention on Biological Diversity. Think about what you believe is important for animal welfare.

Maths

Should we prevent animals going extinct?

Stop animals going extinct
Environmentalists have been concerned for years about the decline in numbers of some animal populations around the world. Learn how to calculate animal population sizes using mathematical calculations.

Art

Is it possible to look after everything?

Animal collage
There are many types of each species. For example, there are around 200 dog breeds. Select a type of animal and research all the types of them to create a collage.

Design and Technology

Are we all designed to survive?

Origami animals
Animals move in so many different ways. Create an origami moving animal. Think about which animals use these movements.

Citizenship

Do all species of animal have the right to exist?

Life on land
The United Nations 17 Sustainable Development Goals address the issues across the world. Goal 15 is about looking after our environment above land. Explore this statement and create in a poster.

P.E.

Do we have move to survive?

How we move. How other animals move.
Create a ten-movement program. Work on your sequence and practise the moves until you feel you have created a good piece.

7 Biodiversity

Concept stretchers   **SPEC grids**

As part of a P4C enquiry, children brainstorm synonyms, phrases, connections, and examples (SPEC) in a SPEC grid, as in these examples.

Biodiversity

Synonyms	Phrases
• Difference • Diverse • Change • Assorted • Variance/Varied • Miscellaneous/Miscellany • Range	• Wild flora and fauna • It takes all sorts • It would be dull if we were all the same • Variety is the spice of life • All things bright and beautiful • God's creations/creatures
Connections	**Examples**
• Zoos • Wildlife parks • Noah's Ark • Sea aquariums • Ecosystem • Interdependence	• Rain forests • Madagascar • Birds of paradise • Back garden • Local park • School wildlife garden • Nature reserve

Uniform (antonym)

Synonyms	Phrases
• Unchanging • Even • Unvarying • Constant • Unbroken • Identical	• Keep in line • The human race is a herd
Connections	**Examples**
• The army • School • Sports clubs • Fashion culture • Cubs/Brownies/Scouts	• School uniform • Sports kits • School rules of behaviour • Clothes choices

DOI: 10.4324/9780429263033-7

Curriculum connections

Years 1–6 Spoken language – Pupils should learn to articulate and justify answers, arguments, and opinions.

SPEC grids are the work of Roger Sutcliffe, Director and Programme Designer of P4C Plus and Thinking Moves A – Z at Dialogue Works, Philosophical Teaching and Learning. www.dialogueworks.co.uk

Concept sorting   **P4C**

Using a 'concept line' or 'Venn diagram rings', pupils sort examples into the categories of:

IMPORTANT	LESS IMPORTANT

Use these examples or some of your own.

Work in pairs or groups to encourage discussion. This will elicit the children's starting point. Ask them to give reasons why. Can the children add any of their own?

Mushrooms	Coral reef
Birds	Dogs
Worms	Cats
Alpine plants	Wildflowers
Trees	Orchids
Bees	Wasps
Flies	Beetles
Elephants	Lions
Turtles	Sloths
Whales	Dolphins

Curriculum connections

Years 1–6 Spoken language – Pupils should also be taught to understand and use the conventions for discussion and debate.

Biodiversity

Quotes to explore P4C Stimuli

Here are some quotes for you to explore with your children within a P4C enquiry. P4C practitioners often ask the children to carry out a blind vote for which one interests then the most.

> "We cannot win this battle to save species and environments without forging an emotional bond between ourselves and nature as well – for we will not fight to save what we do not love."
> – Stephen Jay Gould, 1993,
> *Eight Little Piggies' Reflections in natural history.* – Vintage

> "Uniformity is not nature's way; diversity is nature's way."
> – Vandana Shiva

> "The question is, are we happy to suppose that our grandchildren may never be able to see an elephant except in a picture book?"
> – David Attenborough

Curriculum connections

Spoken language – Pupils should learn to maintain attention and participate actively in collaborative conversations, staying on topic and initiating and responding to comments.

Spoken language – Pupils should participate in discussions, presentations, performances, role play, improvisations, and debates.

Spoken language – Pupils should be able to consider and evaluate different viewpoints, attending to and building on the contributions of others.

Do all animals matter? English

A day in the life of an unusual animal

We tend to like animals that look cute, such as baby elephants, or know about life cycles that have huge metamorphosis, such as tadpoles and frogs.

Pick an animal that you don't know anything about from the following list and research its life cycle. Draw the life cycle and make annotations around it.

 **Bats**

Read *The Secret Life of a Little Brown Bat* by Lawrence Pringle.

Bats are very clever. For example, they have a crèche where they keep all their young together while others go and hunt.

 **Octopus**

Read *The Bizarre Life Cycle of the Octopus* by Therese Shea.

An octopus has three hearts. Do you know how many babies an octopus has?

 **Eels**

Read *Think of an Eel* by Karen Wallace.

Scientists still don't know why eels go the Sargasso Sea to spawn. They swim miles!

 **Turtles**

Read *One Tiny Turtle* by Nicola Davies.

This story chronicles the journey of a tiny, endangered loggerhead turtle from birth to adulthood.

Curriculum connections

Year 5 Science – Pupils should be able to describe the differences in the life cycles of a mammal, an amphibian, an insect, and a bird.

Year 5 Science – Pupils should be taught to describe the life process of reproduction in some plants and animals.

Should we prevent animals going extinct?   Maths

Stop animals going extinct

Environmentalists have been concerned for years about the decline in numbers in some animal populations around the world. It is known that there is only one Northern White Rhino left in the world, and he is called Sudan. You can meet him on this video.

www.youtube.com/watch?v=BgGtzDwJRD0 (accessed 29/09/2021)

We can determine animal population sizes by using mathematics calculations. Watch a video, such as this one to explain how we do this.

www.youtube.com/watch?v=fYAXS6-uhEQ (accessed 29/09/2021)

Using population sampling methods

Go outside into your school field or garden and decide what you are going to count. This might be dandelions, ants, daisies, or whatever is growing there. Make a one-metre by one-metre square frame. Place this anywhere on the ground. Start your count.

P = Total population

N = Total number of plants or animals counted

A = Total area of field or school garden (you can ask your teacher)

Aq = Area of your measuring quadrants

$$P = NA / Aq$$

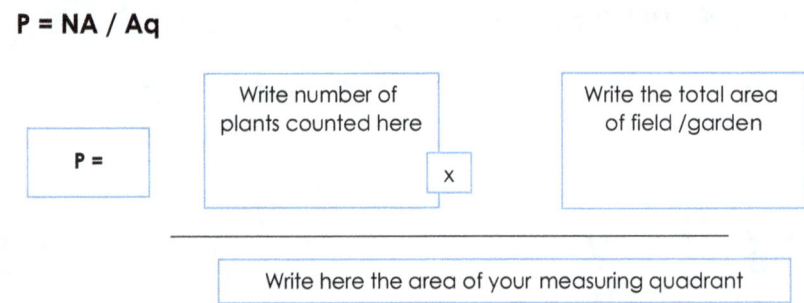

Think about the reasons why animals' population sizes change using some of these concepts.

Migration	Food	Habitat
Weather	Human need	Dependency
Global warming	Water	Disease

Curriculum connections

Year 4 – Pupils should be taught to recall multiplication and division facts for multiplication tables up to 12 × 12.

Year 5 – Pupils should learn to multiply and divide whole numbers and those involving decimals by 10, 100, and 1000.

Year 5 – Pupils should be able to calculate and compare the area of rectangles (including squares) using standard units, square centimetres (cm2), and square metres (m2) and to estimate the area of irregular shapes.

Year 6 – Pupils should be taught to find pairs of numbers that satisfy an equation with two unknowns.

What is biodiversity? Science

Finding out about biodiversity

The word *biodiversity* has been used often. Explore in more depth what the word means. Watch this video, which explains what biodiversity is.

www.youtube.com/watch?v=GK_vRtHJZu4 (accessed 21/09/2020)

> Write here some phrases, words, and sentences that describe what biodiversity means.

This video concludes with "we should safeguard our survival". This seems to assume that we only protect biodiversity for our own survival. Select one of these questions that interests you. This could be for a P4C enquiry or in pairs.

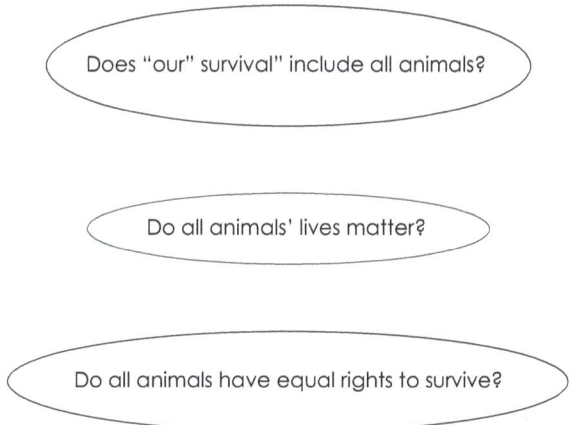

Curriculum connections

Year 2 – Pupils should learn to identify that most living things live in habitats to which they are suited and describe how different habitats provide the basic needs of different kinds of animals and how they depend on each other.

Year 4 – Pupils should explore examples of human impact (both positive and negative) on environments, for example, the positive effects of nature reserves, ecologically planned parks, or garden ponds and the negative effects of population and development, litter, or deforestation.

Should humans intervene to preserve all species? Science

Collecting the world's seeds

The Millennium Seed Bank at Kew Gardens Royal Botanical Gardens started in 2009. The world's seed are to be collected for the earth's preservation.

www.kew.org/science/collections-and-resources/research-facilities/millennium-seed-bank (accessed 21/09/2020)

Seed search – your local environment

Explore a local wildlife patch and catalogue what seeds you find by taking photos and drawing sketches. Can you identify them?

The Cat in the Hat explains how seeds travel

Watch this video clip, which explains how plants and trees know how to travel as their seeds manage to scatter. www.youtube.com/watch?v=nqaPC-SqGE0 (accessed 06/10/2020)

Go on a seed hunt or research seeds. Draw some seeds in the box provided.

What seeds have you found? How do seeds disperse?

My seed search

Curriculum connections

Year 1 – Pupils should use the local environment throughout the year to explore and answer questions about plants growing in their habitat (non-statutory).

Year 2 – Pupils should be able to identify and name a variety of plants and animals in their habitats, including microhabitats.

Year 3 – Pupils should learn to explore the part that flowers play in the life cycle of flowering plants, including pollination, seed formation, and seed dispersal.

Year 4 – Pupils should be able to explore and use classification keys to help group, identify, and name a variety of living things in their local and wider environment.

Is extinction part of life?   History

Animals that have gone extinct

Charles Darwin wrote *The Origin of the Species* in 1859 in which he introduced the idea of evolution, and this has changed the way we understand animals. Evolution is the belief that animals have been changing for 500 million years and that they adapt by natural selection, which means that the better aspects of their bodies survive to the next generation.

Over many years some animals have gone extinct, and we know lots about dinosaurs as their bones have been found all over the world. Read about some of them at the following link.

https://kids.britannica.com/kids/browse/animals/2173176 (accessed 31/08/2021)

> Select one of the dinosaurs or animals from the list. Write some facts about them here.

Theories about extinction

There are many reasons people believe dinosaurs became extinct. Find out about some of the theories using a website such as this one. You could work in expert groups or individually.

www.kids-dinosaurs.com/dinosaur-extinction.html (accessed 31/08/2021)

Volcano theory	**Disease theory**
Meteorite Impact theory	**Ice Age theory**

Do you think that extinction is a natural part of life? Write your thoughts here.

Curriculum connections

A high-quality history education will help pupils gain a coherent knowledge and understanding of Britain's past and that of the wider world. It should inspire pupils' curiosity to know more about the past. Teaching should equip pupils to ask perceptive questions, think critically, weigh evidence, sift arguments, and develop perspective and judgement.

Is biodiversity important?   **Geography**

Large and small populations

To learn about large and small populations, you may want to watch this video. www.youtube.com/watch?v=GK_vRtHJZu4 (accessed 21/09/2020)

Research some of the animals listed that have **large population** numbers and say why these animals have been so successful. Think of the challenges they **have** overcome. Note where they live and think about why this may have an impact on their numbers.

Domestic chickens	Lionfish in Florida	Humans
Rabbits	Krill	Ants
Bacteria	Sheep	Cattle

Research some of the animals listed that have very **low population numbers** and say why these animals have not been successful. Think of the challenges that they **cannot** overcome. Again, note where they live and think about whether this has an influence on their low population.

Black Rhino	Sumatran Orang-utan	Blue Whale
Pangolin	Fin Whale	Siberian Tiger
Artic Fox	Tasmanian Devil	Polar Bears

Can you have too many of one animal?

Write some more questions that you have thought of whilst researching these animals.

Curriculum connections

Year 4 – Pupils should be able to recognise that environments can change and that this can sometimes pose dangers to living things.

Year 6 – Pupils should be able to recognise that living things produce offspring of the same kind, but normally offspring vary and are not identical to their parents.

Year 6 – Pupils should learn to identify how animals and plants are adapted to suit their environment in different ways and that adaptation may lead to evolution.

Are museums good?   **Music**

A tree museum

Many songs have lyrics about the world and how we live. For example, "Big Yellow Taxi" by Joni Mitchell tells us that we need to look after our natural environment.

Listen to the words carefully. Discuss the lyrics you have noticed with a partner.

www.youtube.com/watch?v=2595abcvh2M (accessed 23/09/2020)

Now in pairs select two words from the following list and say how they are different and how they are the same.

Museum	Zoo	Garden	Tree	Car park
Cage	Tank	Fence	Park	Freedom
Forest	Field	Meadow	Wood	Prison

Curriculum connections

Year 4 – Recognise that environments can change and that this can sometimes pose dangers to living things. Notes and guidance – Pupils should explore examples of human impact (both positive and negative) on environments, for example, the positive effects of nature reserves, ecologically planned parks, or garden ponds and the negative effects of population and development, litter, or deforestation.

Is it possible to look after everything?   **Art and Design**

Animal collage

There are many types of each species. For example, there are hundreds of breeds of dog. You may not know, but there are many types of oak tree. We often oversimplify what things are.

Select a type of animal from the list or choose your own. Research all the types of the animal and create a collage of as many as you can. You could draw or cut out pictures and photographs to create this piece.

Dogs	Cats	Frogs	Fish	Chameleons
Birds	Cows	Mice		

Curriculum connections

The national curriculum for art and design aims to ensure that all pupils produce creative work, exploring their ideas and recording their experiences.

Should we build an ark like Noah to save all the animals?   **Religious education**

Noah's Ark

In the Old Testament book of Genesis (chapters 6–9) Noah builds an ark, into which he put two of each animal.

Read the story in the Bible together, or you could watch a video like this one.

www.youtube.com/watch?v=_vjjhMWJ2wE (accessed 23/07/2021)

Write some words in the boxes that capture some of the meaning of the story.

Care	Preserve	Love	

Animal rights explored in the Bible

The Bible talks about caring for animals and tells us the way to behave with them. See some of those ways on this website.

www.bbc.co.uk/bitesize/guides/zgvrq6f/revision/5 (accessed 23/07/2021)

> Now write some of your own principles. Use your own phrases and sentences that promote the care of animals.

Curriculum connections

Religious education contributes dynamically to children and young people's education in schools by provoking challenging questions about meaning and purpose in life, beliefs about God, ultimate reality, issues of right and wrong, and what it means to be human.

Can computers replace animals?   **Computing**

Create your own moving animal

Using Scratch software, create ten movements in a sequence from an animal you have selected. For example, if you choose a tiger then make it jump, run, or lie down.

https://scratch.mit.edu/projects/editor/?tutorial=getStarted (accessed 23/07/2021)

Curriculum connections

KS1 – Pupils should be taught to understand what algorithms are, how they are implemented as programs on digital devices, and that programs execute by following precise and unambiguous instructions.

KS2 – Pupils should be taught to use sequence, selection, and repetition in programs and to work with variables and various forms of input and output.

Do we have to move to survive?   **Physical education**

How we move

Can we move like other animals? They have learnt to move in a variety of ways to survive. Using the work you have done on Scratch to create a ten-movement programme, see if you can copy this yourself.

Work on your sequence and practise the moves until you feel you have created a good piece.

Curriculum connections

KS1 – Pupils should develop fundamental movement skills, become increasingly competent and confident, and access a broad range of opportunities to extend their agility, balance, and coordination, individually and with others.

KS2 – Pupils should continue to apply and develop a broader range of skills, learning how to use them in different ways and to link them to make actions and sequences of movement.

Are we all designed to survive? **Design and Technology**

Origami animals

Animals move in so many different ways. Which animals make these movements?

Fly	Crawl	Run	Gallop
Pounce	Slide	Flip	Bend
Hop	Curl	Swing	Roll

Think about which animals are the best at each of these movements.

Now try and make some paper animals that have some moving parts.

Make an origami fish.

www.youtube.com/watch?v=btxMOUyAKhU (accessed 02/09/2021)

Now make an origami paper jumping rabbit.

www.youtube.com/watch?v=Dn2AN_uAXqc (accessed 02/09/2021)

Next make an origami paper jumping frog.

This one is more challenging. Try making this frog. You'll need to take your time and think about how the moving parts work together.

www.youtube.com/watch?v=DPdrU63H2VQ (accessed 02/09/2021)

Challenge – Can you make it into another animal which moves in the same way?

Curriculum connections

KS1 – Pupils should explore and use mechanisms (for example, levers, sliders, wheels, and axles) in their products.

KS2 – Through a variety of creative and practical activities, pupils should be taught the knowledge, understanding, and skills needed to engage in an iterative process of designing and making.

How should we best live with other animals?   **PSHE**

Ethics and biodiversity

Ethics is the question of how one should best live and act. To treat the natural world ethically means loving and respecting it for its own sake, not just ours.

Read the 2012 Convention on Biological Diversity. Think about what you believe is important for animal welfare.

www.un.org/en/observances/biological-diversity-day/convention (accessed 22/06/2021)

Write your own ten principles about biodiversity here.
1
2
3
4
5
6
7
8
9
10

Curriculum connections

Year 4 – Pupils should be able to recognise that environments can change and that this can sometimes pose dangers to living things. Notes and guidance – Pupils should explore examples of human impact (both positive and negative) on environments, for example, the positive effects of nature reserves, ecologically planned parks, or garden ponds and the negative effects of population and development, litter, or deforestation.

Do all species of animal have the right to exist? Citizenship

Life on land

The United Nations has created 17 Sustainable Development Goals that address the issues across the world. Explore these in a poster. www.un.org/sustainabledevelopment/

> **Goal 15: Life on land** https://sdgs.un.org/goals/goal15 (accessed 08/10/2020)
>
> "Protect, restore and promote sustainable use of terrestrial ecosystems, sustainably, manage forests to combat deforestation, and halt and reverse land degradation and halt biodiversity loss."

Goal 15 is about looking after our environment above land. There are many words in this statement that need more exploration.

From the grid, select one word and write down all the words, thoughts, phrases, and basically any associations that you have with it.

Protect	Restore	Promote	Sustainable	Terrestrial
Ecosystem	Manage	Deforestation	Reverse	Degradation

Now share your thoughts with your group. Once you have heard people talk about all the words, write your own statement (it can be more than one sentence) that captures what you think this goal is saying to do.

My UN Goal 15 statement

Curriculum connections

KS1 L3 – Pupils should learn about things they can do to help look after their environment.

KS2 L3 – Pupils should learn about things they can do to help look after their environment.

Inspirational people

David Attenborough

Attenborough is a British naturalist who has a broadcasting career over six decades. He advocates that we put nature at the heart of our decisions.

https://attenboroughfilm.com (accessed 23/07/2021)

Midori prize for biodiversity 2020

Each year this prize honours three individuals who have made outstanding contributions to conservation and sustainable use at local and global levels. www.cbd.int/cooperation/midori/ (accessed 22/06/2021)

Young champions of the Earth

This is a forward-looking prize designed to breathe life into the ambitions of young environmentalists. www.unep.org/youngchampions/ (accessed 25/10/2021)

Further resources

RSPB
This resource has top tips for schools and how to engage with biodiversity.

www.rspb.org.uk/globalassets/downloads/documents/positions/education/top-tips-for-schools-to-engage-with-biodiversity.pdf (accessed 22/06/2021)

Dialogue Works
Dialogue Works produces Home Talk packs to discuss each concept in depth, such as this one about life cycles. https://dialogueworks.co.uk/wp-content/uploads/2021/06/HomeTalk-Life-Cycles.pdf

UN Convention on Biodiversity
This website captures the programmes and issues across the world and provides in detail where help is needed about the world. https://cbd.int/ (accessed 25/10/2021)

The Wildlife Trust
Read their reports about wildlife and the Every Child Wild report in particularly.

www.wildlifetrusts.org/about-us/publications (accessed 25/10/2021)

World Wildlife Fund for Nature
This website has lots of information about how to protect our wildlife and how others are doing it.

www.wwf.org.uk/what-we-do/protecting-our-natural-places (accessed 22/06/2021)

www.wwf.org.uk/get-involved/schools/resources/species-resources

2050 – What a garden may be like
Explore what a future garden will look like in 2050 and design your own!

www.kew.org/about-us/press-media/surviving-or-thriving-exhibition

Coding Scratch
This website has lots of free Scratch coding projects that are wildlife-based.

https://scratch.mit.edu/search/projects?q=wildlife

The Book Corner

Think of an eel by Karen Wallace
Learn about the fascinating life cycle of an eel with fiction and non-fiction text running alongside each other. Read about how the eels undertake an enormous journey and overcome many challenges. Suitable for KS1/2.

The variety of life by Nicola Davies
Davies is a well-known naturalist from *The Really Wild Show*, who has written a wide variety of books to engage children in wildlife. This book explores the extraordinary diversity of the natural world and profiles some of its most surprising creatures. Suitable for KS1/2.

Life on Earth by David Attenborough
This fascinating book has 60 full-colour photographs to engage young readers to learn more about animal and plant life. It is destined to enthral the next generation. Suitable for KS1/2.

Planet ark: preserving Earth's biodiversity by Adrienne Mason
This illustrated non-fiction book compares Earth today to Noah's Ark and explores why having a healthy biodiversity is needed like a leak-proof hull. Suitable for KS2.

Tree of life: the incredible biodiversity of life on Earth by Rochelle Strauss
A very well-illustrated book about the diversity of life on our planet which uses the analogy that humans are just one leaf on the tree of life. It shows how all living things are interconnected and have a name. Suitable for KS2.

NC subject	Activity	Curriculum connections
English	A day in the life of an unusual animal	Year 5 – Science – Pupils should be able to describe the life process of reproduction in some plants and animals and to describe the differences in the life cycles of a mammal, an amphibian, an insect, and a bird.
Maths	Stop animals going extinct	Year 4 – Pupils should be taught to recall multiplication and division facts for multiplication tables up to 12 × 12. Year 5 – Pupils should learn to multiply and divide whole numbers and those involving decimals by 10, 100, and 1000. Year 5 – Pupils should be able to calculate and compare the area of rectangles (including squares) using standard units, square centimetres (cm2), and square metres (m2) and to estimate the area of irregular shapes. Year 6 – Pupils should be taught to find pairs of numbers that satisfy an equation with two unknowns.
Science	Finding out about biodiversity	Year 2 – Pupils should identify that most living things live in habitats to which they are suited and describe how different habitats provide the basic needs of different kinds of animals and how they depend on each other. Year 4 – Pupils should explore examples of human impact (both positive and negative) on environments, for example, the positive effects of nature reserves, ecologically planned parks, or garden ponds and the negative effects of population and development, litter, or deforestation.
Science	Collecting the world's seeds	Year 1 – Pupils should use the local environment throughout the year to explore and answer questions about plants growing in their habitat. (non-statutory) Year 2 – Pupils can identify and name a variety of plants and animals in their habitats, including microhabitats. Year 3 – Pupils should explore the part that flowers play in the life cycle of flowering plants, including pollination, seed formation, and seed dispersal. Year 4 – Pupils should explore and use classification keys to help group, identify, and name a variety of living things in their local and wider environment.
Geography	Large and small populations	Year 4 – Pupils should recognise that environments can change and that this can sometimes pose dangers to living things. Year 6 – Pupils should recognise that living things produce offspring of the same kind, but normally offspring vary and are not identical to their parents. Year 6 – Pupils should identify how animals and plants are adapted to suit their environment in different ways and that adaptation may lead to evolution.

NC subject	Activity	Curriculum connections
History	Animals that have gone extinct	A high-quality history education will help pupils gain a coherent knowledge and understanding of Britain's past and that of the wider world. It should inspire pupils' curiosity to know more about the past. Teaching should equip pupils to ask perceptive questions, think critically, weigh evidence, sift arguments, and develop perspective and judgement.
Music	A tree museum	Year 4 – Pupils should recognise that environments can change and that this can sometimes pose dangers to living things. Notes and guidance – Pupils should explore examples of human impact (both positive and negative) on environments, for example, the positive effects of nature reserves, ecologically planned parks, or garden ponds and the negative effects of population and development, litter, or deforestation.
Art and Design	Animal collage	The national curriculum for art and design aims to ensure that all pupils produce creative work, exploring their ideas and recording their experiences.
Design and Technology	Origami animals	KS1 – Pupils should explore and use mechanisms (for example, levers, sliders, wheels, and axles) in their products. KS2 – Through a variety of creative and practical activities, pupils should be taught the knowledge, understanding, and skills needed to engage in an iterative process of designing and making.
Computing	Create your own moving animal	KS1 – Pupils should be taught to understand what algorithms are, how they are implemented as programs on digital devices, and that programs execute by following precise and unambiguous instructions. KS2 – Pupils should be taught to use sequence, selection, and repetition in programs and to work with variables and various forms of input and output.
Religious education	Noah's Ark	Religious education contributes dynamically to children and young people's education in schools by provoking challenging questions about meaning and purpose in life, beliefs about God, ultimate reality, issues of right and wrong, and what it means to be human.
PE	How we move How other animals move	KS1 – Pupils should develop fundamental movement skills, become increasingly competent and confident, and access a broad range of opportunities to extend their agility, balance, and coordination, individually and with others. KS2 – Pupils should continue to apply and develop a broader range of skills, learning how to use them in different ways and to link them to make actions and sequences of movement.

NC subject	Activity	Curriculum connections
PSHE	**UN sustainability goals**	PSHE Association Curriculum KS1 L3 – Pupils learn about things they can do to help look after their environment. KS2 L3 – Pupils learn about things they can do to help look after their environment.
Citizenship	**Ethics and biodiversity**	Year 4 – Pupils should be taught to recognise that environments can change and that this can sometimes pose dangers to living things. Notes and guidance – Pupils should explore examples of human impact (both positive and negative) on environments, for example, the positive effects of nature reserves, ecologically planned parks, or garden ponds and the negative effects of population and development, litter, or deforestation.

Heart and Lungs

Science

Is it true that because I breathe, therefore I am?

The functions of the heart and lungs
Research what your heart and lungs do through experiments and scientific activities. Explore the comparison of your lungs to a sponge. Find out how to capture your heart rate.

Can we always choose to be healthy?

Smoking
Research the side effects of smoking on heart and lung health. Capture the main effects and the side effects in a diagram.

R.E.

Can your breath influence your mind?

Breathing and meditation
Explore breathing exercises for mindful meditation and as a stimulus for philosophical enquiry. Think about the ways that breathing techniques are used in religious contexts.

Music

Is breathing a musical rhythm?

Circular breathing
Some people are able to breathe out and breathe in at the same time. This technique is called circular breathing and is used for playing instruments, such as the didgeridoo and the bagpipes. Explore how to do this.

History

Have people's views of tobacco changed over time?

Tobacco's past and present
Research how attitudes to smoking have changed over time. Interview your parents and grandparents about their own experiences of smoking. Find out where tobacco originated. Research the relationship between the tobacco and slave trade.

Maths

Can you put a value on your lungs?

The cost of vaping
Calculate the total cost of one parent smoking or vaping for one year. Investigate and calculate how a parent might spend their money instead. Explain and justify your reasoning. Investigate how you can spend the money without spending it in a way that benefits you directly.

Computing

Should computers be used to improve your health?

Computers in the heart
Medical experts are using computers in human's hearts to detect how their heart behaves. Use the Scratch programme to create a card with a heart.

English

> Should we give a heart transplant?

Pig-heart boy
Read Pig-heart Boy by Malorie Blackman. Discuss the arguments presented in the book for and against heart transplants.

Geography

> Do we all breathe the same air?

The air we breathe
All around and above us there is air that we breathe. Wind is the movement of air and can be strong enough to cause damage and destruction to homes. Research the Beaufort Wind Scale. Explore the air quality of the countries around the world.

Art

> Why is love linked to the heart?

Diagrams of organs
Leonardo De Vinci produced anatomical (body) drawings and, in particular, Vitruvian Man. Explore this work together.

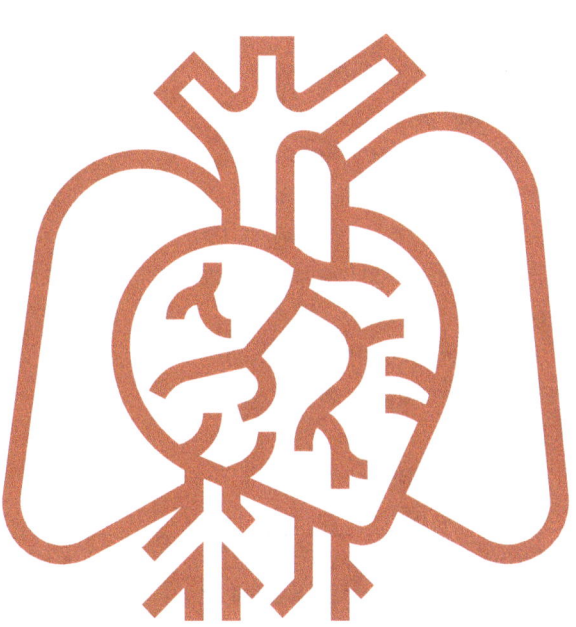

Design and Technology

> Should we design new musical instruments?

Make your own wind instrument
Research how to make a wind instrument. Design it, make it, and try it. Your challenge is to make it sound better.

Citizenship

> Who should educate all children about good health?

Children's health
Article 24 from the UN Convention of the Rights of the Child states that every child has the right to the best health. Explore the full statement in depth and discuss.

PSHE

> Do we have a responsibility to look after the health of our heart?

Healthy hearts
Learn how to keep your heart healthy. Categorise foods into how salty they are and create a wall poster for your local community centre.

P.E.

> What does it mean to take a breath?

Take a breath!
Learn how to measure your resting and post-exercise heart rate. Explore how to measure this over time and create a comparison test of different movements and exercises.

8 Heart and lungs

Concept stretchers **SPEC grid**

As part of a P4C enquiry, children brainstorm synonyms, phrases, connections, and examples (SPEC) in a SPEC grid, as in this example.

Synonyms	Phrases
• Pump • Muscle • Organ • Ticker • Love • Compassion • Feelings • Sympathy • Humaneness • Consideration • Goodness • Beneficence • Soul/Spirit • Courage/Bravery • Willpower	• In a heartbeat • My heart was in my mouth • My heart stopped • She gets heartburn all the time • Cross my heart and hope to die • He's totally stolen her heart away • He wears his heart on his sleeve • It makes my heart bleed/sink • What a heart-breaking/warming story • Heart of gold • He didn't carry any hate in his heart • With all my heart and soul • Don't lose heart • Don't take it to heart • The heart of the matter
Connections	**Examples**
• Anatomy • Organs (interdependence) • Muscle (contract/contraction, atria, ventricles) • Blood/blood vessels: veins, arteries, capillaries (dilate/dilation) • Circulation, oxygen • Beat, rhythm • Soul • Emotions, feelings, sentiment • Kindness, goodwill, love, compassion • Hurt • Courage, determination	• The place where emotions are felt: a broken heart, heartbreak • Soul/life-force/source of life • Anatomical heart: the organ in your chest that pumps blood through your veins and arteries • Medical: heart disease, heart murmur, heart monitor, heart attack, heart surgery • Love-heart shape ♥ • Symbolic of love • The ace of hearts

Curriculum connections

Years 1–6 Spoken language – Pupils should be taught to articulate and justify answers, arguments, and opinions.

SPEC grids are the work of Roger Sutcliffe, Director and Programme Designer of P4C Plus and Thinking Moves A – Z at Dialogue Works, Philosophical Teaching and Learning. www.dialogueworks.co.uk

Concept stretchers **SPEC grid**

As part of a P4C enquiry, children brainstorm synonyms, phrases, connections, and examples (SPEC) in a SPEC grid, as in this example.

Breath/Breathe

Synonyms		Phrases
Breath (n): • Life • Rest • Pause • Life force	**Breathe (v):** • Inhale/Inhalation • Exhale/Exhalation • Live • Gasp • Pant • Wheeze • Sigh • Breathing space • Respiration	• She held her breath. • I breathe life in it. • She is a breath of fresh air. • Do not breathe a word. • Stop breathing down my neck! • Breathe easy.
Connections • Being out of breath • Listening to own breathing • Hearing people snore • Choking on food • Laughing so much you can't breathe		**Examples** • Looking at your breath on a cold day • Being nervous and unable to breathe

Curriculum connections

Years 1–6 Spoken language – Pupils should be taught to articulate and justify answers, arguments, and opinions.

Heart and lungs

Quotes to explore **P4C enquiry**

Here are some quotes for you to use to start a philosophical enquiry. Which one do you like? Discuss with a partner.

Share your thoughts about the concept words in the quotes, such as *home*, with your group or class. Maybe you would like to change a word or two before you decide to offer it as a question to be explored in a P4C enquiry.

> "Sometimes the heart sees what is invisible to the eye."
> – H. Jackson Brown, Jr.

> "Tears come from the heart and not from the brain."
> – Leonardo da Vinci

> "The most beautiful things in the world cannot be seen or even touched, they must be felt with the heart."
> – Helen Keller

> "Home is where the heart is."
> – Pliny the Elder

Curriculum connections

Spoken language – Pupils should learn to consider and evaluate different viewpoints, attending to and building on the contributions of others.

Concept stretchers   **Decision pairs**

Would you rather?

Read these options and choose one out of each pair. Discuss with a partner or in a group why you have chosen it. Take questions from your audience and justify your reasons.

Have a healthy heart	Have healthy lungs
Choose one of the options and give your reason.	
To give love	To receive love
Choose one of the options and give your reason.	
To know love and lose it	To never know love
Choose one of the options and give your reason.	
To breathe under water	To breathe in space
Choose one of the options and give your reason.	
Now create one of your own.	
Choose one of the options and give your reason.	

Curriculum connections

Spoken language – Pupils should learn to maintain attention and participate actively in collaborative conversations, staying on topic and initiating and responding to comments.

Spoken language – Pupils should participate in discussions, presentations, performances, role play/improvisations, and debates.

68 *Heart and lungs*

Should we give a heart transplant?   English

Pig-heart boy

Read *Pig-heart boy* by Malorie Blackman.

1. Discuss the arguments presented in the book for and against heart transplants. Write notes in the spaces provided.

PROS	CONS

2. In chapter 3 of the book, Cameron's parents argue. What different arguments do his mum and dad make? Summarise the points of their debates which support their reasoning.

PROS	CONS

3. If you were in Cameron's situation, what would you do and why?

Curriculum connections

Years 1–6 Spoken language – Pupils should be taught to articulate and justify answers, arguments, and opinions.

Year 3/4 Writing – The curriculum involves teaching pupils to enhance the effectiveness of what they write as well as increasing their competence.

Year 5/6 Spoken language – Pupils' confidence, enjoyment, and mastery of language should be extended through public speaking, performance, and debate.

Can you put a value on your lungs? Maths

The cost of vaping

Calculate the total cost of one parent smoking or vaping for one year. Investigate and calculate how a parent might spend their money instead. Explain and justify your reasoning.

The cost of a packet of 20 cigarettes was £11 in 2020. Find out how much they cost today.

KS2 Challenge – Can you make it to the nearest pence as possible?

If they smoke 5 a day . . .   **It could be spent on . . .**

If they smoke 10 a day . . .   **It could be spent on . . .**

If they smoke 20 a day . . .   **It could be spent on . . .**

Challenge – Can you think of something that it is not a physical object to spend the money on?

Challenge – Investigate how you can spend the money without spending it on yourself, your family, or in a way that benefits you directly.

Curriculum connections

KS1 – Multiplication and division – Pupils should be able to solve problems involving multiplication and division, using materials, arrays, repeated addition, mental methods, and multiplication and division facts, including problems in contexts.

KS2 – Pupils should learn to solve problems, including missing number problems, involving multiplication and division.

Heart and lungs

I breathe, therefore I am. **Science**

The functions of the heart and lungs

What do your heart and lungs do? Follow these activities to find out.

What happens when you breathe in and out?

1. Partner breathing

Sit back-to-back on the floor (ideally with a similar-sized partner) with your legs out in front of you. Can you feel or see your partner breathing?

Now, try to take the next 10 breaths slowly. What do you notice? What do you think is happening?

Experiment or watch a video of a sponge.

What happens when you put a dry sponge into water?

Can you explain how the sponge behaves in a similar way to your lungs?

Heart function

Identify and name the main parts of the human circulatory system and describe the functions of the heart, blood vessels, and blood.

a) Watch explanatory video clips.

b) Work as a pair/team to label the circulatory system correctly.

c) Explain the diagram to a different friend.

d) Make a model (group work) to show and explain how the circulatory system works.

Learn how to take someone's heart rate.

> In preparation for PE circuit training sessions, pupils make predictions and design experiments to test and compare heart rate changes over time or between different groups of pupils relating to, for example, age (month of birth), sex, or height of pupil.
>
> Which variables do they predict will make a difference?
>
> How can you ensure tests are as fair as possible?

Curriculum connections

Year 6 – Pupils should identify and name the main parts of the human circulatory system and describe the functions of the heart, blood vessels, and blood. They should recognise the impact of diet, exercise, drugs, and lifestyle on the way their bodies function.

Pupils might work scientifically by scientific research about the relationship between exercise and health.

Can we always choose to be healthy? Science

Smoking

1. What do you know about any substances or drugs that might impact on heart and lung health?

2. Research the side effects of smoking on human heart and lung health.

3. Research lung cancer and write a paragraph about it.

4. Watch a video about the effects of smoking on your lungs. Capture words that tell you what the damage and effects of smoking.

www.youtube.com/watch?v=sVrb3B5m99M (accessed 13/01/2021)

www.youtube.com/watch?v=Y18Vz51Nkos (accessed 13/01/2021) (KS2)

Curriculum connections

Year 6 – Pupils should learn how to keep their bodies healthy and how their bodies might be damaged – including how some drugs and other substances can be harmful to the human body.

Working scientifically – Plan scientific enquiries to answer questions, including reporting and presenting findings from enquiries, including conclusions, causal relationships, and explanations of and degrees of trust in results, in oral and written forms such as displays and other presentations.

Heart and lungs

Have people's views of their lungs and heart changed over time? History

Tobacco's past and present

Group research projects:

1. Research how attitudes towards smoking have changed over time. Interview your parents and grandparents about their own experiences of smoking. Make notes here.

2. Where did tobacco originate? Research the relationship between the tobacco and slave trades. Write your notes here.

3. Research the history of lung transplants. You could use this BBC Newsround article: www.bbc.co.uk/newsround/43963798 (accessed 02/07/2021) Makes notes here.

4. What rules about smoing have changed since we have learnt what it does to our bodies? Make notes here.

Curriculum connections

KS1 – Pupils should be taught about changes within living memory. Where appropriate, these should be used to reveal aspects of change in national life.

KS2 – Pupils should regularly address and sometimes devise historically valid questions about change, cause, similarity and difference, and significance.

Why is love linked to the heart? Art

Diagrams of organs

Leonardo da Vinci drew the great picture chart of the human body through his anatomical (body) drawings and *Vitruvian Man* as a *cosmografia del minor mondo* ("cosmography of the microcosm"). He believed the workings of the human body to be an analogy, in microcosm, for the workings of the universe.

Go to alamy.com and search for "Leonardo da Vinci lungs and heart" to see his anatomical drawings of these organs.

Research diagrams of the heart. Select one and carefully sketch it here.

Whilst drawing, think about why the heart is often connected to falling in love.

Curriculum connections

Pupils should know about great artists, craft makers, and designers, and should understand the historical and cultural development of their art forms.

Is breathing a musical rhythm?   **Music**

Wind instruments – Circular breathing

Some people can breathe out and breathe in at the same time. This technique is called circular breathing, and it is used for playing the instruments such as the didgeridoo, which is an Aboriginal instrument, and the bagpipes.

What is circular breathing?

It is good to watch someone doing the technique. Watch a video such as this one.

www.youtube.com/watch?v=xdaj3D-u9TA (accessed 12/10/2021)

How to play a didgeridoo

Watch this video of Xavier Rudd playing a didgeridoo.

www.youtube.com/watch?v=QRBCzUPDUVA (accessed 12/10/2021)

Using a didgeridoo, the bagpipes, or a recorder have a go at circular breathing. See if you can build up the length of note that you can play the instrument for.

Curriculum connections

KS1 – Pupils should be taught to play tuned and untuned instruments musically.

A high-quality music education should engage and inspire pupils to develop a love of music.

Should we design new musical instruments?   **Design and Technology**

Make your own wind instrument

Now that you have learnt about wind instruments, you are going to make one. Do some research about how to make one. You could use how-to videos, such as those that follow.
Your challenge is to make a wind instrument. Design it, make it, and try it. If it doesn't work, what can you do to change it or make it sound better?

How to make bagpipes

www.youtube.com/watch?v=y95l0rb1JoU&t=236s (accessed 12/10/2021)

How to make a pan flute

www.youtube.com/watch?v=zKFyiA4lklY (accessed 12/10/2021)

Curriculum connections

Pupils should be taught to make, select from, and use a wider range of tools and equipment to perform practical tasks (for example, cutting, shaping, joining, and finishing) accurately.

Should computers be used to improve your health? **Computing**

Computers in the heart

Medical experts are using computers in human hearts to detect how their hearts behave and to send out information that could be life-saving for people with heart problems.

www.bhf.org.uk/informationsupport/heart-matters-magazine/research/artificial-intelligence (accessed 12/10/2021)

Heart monitors

If you can access a heart monitor on a smart watch or a computer, have a go a counting your heart beats with the monitor.

Scratch coding

As we can't play with the coding for the programming of heart monitors, you could use the Scratch programme to create a card with a heart for Valentine's Day or just give a card to someone you care about. You can add a hidden message.

Curriculum connections

A high-quality computing education equips pupils to use computational thinking and creativity to understand and change the world. Computing has deep links with mathematics, science, and design and technology, and it provides insights into both natural and artificial systems.

76 *Heart and lungs*

Do we all breathe the same air? Geography

The air we breathe

All around us and above us there is air that we breathe. Wind is the movement of air. The wind can be very strong. Research the Beaufort Wind Scale.

Complete the following force chart from 1–12.

Force	Wind speed (knots)	WMO classification
1		Calm
2		
3		
4		
5		
6		
7		
8		
9		
10		
11		
12		Hurricane

Air quality

Air quality varies around the world and in different parts of each country. Research how where you live affects the air quality. Using an air quality index, such as https://waqi.info/, find where you live and see what rating your area has.

Write down places that you find which are in the following categories.

Good	Moderate	Unhealthy for sensitive groups	Unhealthy	Very unhealthy	Hazardous

What affects the quality of the air? Discuss with your friends what you know.

Curriculum connections

Teaching should equip pupils with knowledge about diverse places, people, resources, and natural and human environments, together with a deep understanding of the earth's key physical and human processes.

Do we have a responsibility to look after the health of our heart? **PSHE**

Healthy hearts

There are many ways to keep your heart healthy, and as you get older it is important to know how. Here are some important ways to do it.

www.heartfoundation.org.au/heart-health-education/keeping-your-heart-healthy

What could you do to help with other people understand the effects of salt? Categorise the following foods according to how salty they are.

Write some foods here.

Now put them into categories according to how much salt they have.

High	Moderate	Low

Now create a poster that can go on the wall of your local community centre or on an online computer programme. Make it factual. Design it so people will look at it.

Curriculum connections

KS1 H1 – Pupils learn about what keeping healthy means; different ways to keep health.

KS2 H3 – Pupils learn about choices that support a healthy lifestyle and recognise what might influence these.

What does it mean to take a breath?   **Physical education**

Take a breath

1. Explore: rest, pauses in music, silence.
   Play your class a piece of silence.

2. Body percussion.
   Experiment with beat, pace, keeping time and rhythm, using body percussion.

The impact of exercise

1. Circuit training stations – How could I measure improvement across a half term?
   Time, form, heart rate from resting to after exercise activity.

Who is the fittest?

2. Design and carry out an experiment to show who is fittest, boys or girls?
   Work scientifically to compare resting/active heart rates or running speed, for example.

Using apps

Try exploring how to use applications to monitor your heart or show you ways to stay healthy.

You could try some yoga.

www.unicefkidpower.org/yoga-poses-for-kids/ (accessed 02/07/2021)

https://seewhatgrows.org/10-best-health-nutrition-apps-kids/

Curriculum connections

KS2 – Year 6 Science – Recognise the impact of exercise on the way bodies function.

PE – A high-quality physical education curriculum inspires all pupils to succeed and excel in competitive sport and other physically demanding activities. It should provide opportunities for pupils to become physically confident in a way which supports their health and fitness.

Can your breath influence your mind? **Religious education**

Breathing and meditation

- Why is breathing or meditation considered an important practice in some faiths?
- Can breathing or meditation quiet or still the mind – or change your thinking?
- Prayer is sometimes also considered quiet contemplation time – how do prayer and meditation compare?
- How do different faith practitioners prepare themselves for prayer?

Explore exercises for mindful meditation (as a stimulus for philosophical enquiry).

1. **Is it possible to think nothing at all?**
   Ask the class to close their eyes, be still, and try to think of nothing for 1 minute.
   In pairs, discuss experiences. Share findings in a philosophy circle.

2. **Can 'listening' to your breath affect your mind?**
   Ask your class to find a place to lie on their backs – or to sit cross-legged if they prefer.
   Make a triangular heart (touching thumbs and forefingers) and place your heart-hands on your belly, with your bellybutton in the centre of the heart.
   If it helps you to concentrate, you can close your eyes.

   a. Breathe normally – notice what happens.
   b. Next, try and keep your belly still so your thumbs and fingers stay touching – fill your **chest** with air to make it bigger. Take 5–10 big breaths this way.
   c. Now, fill your belly with air to make it as big as possible each time – what happens to your hands? Can you make your thumb and fingers move apart by expanding your belly? (belly breathing or diaphragm breathing) Take 5–10 big breaths this way.
   d. What does it feel like to breathe faster? Or slower? Or make bigger or smaller chests or bellies? Have a play!
   e. Finally, having spent a short time exploring and playing with breath, spend **1 minute** using your heart-hands to listen to your breathing.
   Try not to change your breathing – just breathe normally.
   What do you notice?

It can be hard to think of nothing and can feel impossible. Your mind makes all sorts of noisy thoughts. Focusing on your breathing helps quiet your mind and I wonder what you might discover.

Curriculum connections

Compare and contrast the meditation practices of different faiths – for example, Buddhist, Christian, or Hindu meditation. Recognise and explain the practices involved in belonging to different faith communities.

80 *Heart and lungs*

Who should educate all children about health and well-being?　　　　　　　　　　**Citizenship**

Children's health

Here is Article 24 from the UN Convention of the Rights of the Child (see appendix for full list).

Read and discuss with a partner or group.

> Every child has the right to the best possible health. Governments must provide good health care, clean water, nutritious food, and a clean environment and education on health and well-being. Richer countries must help poorer countries achieve this.

Circle any words in the statement that need to be explored in more depth to make sure that you all have the same understanding of these words. Write them here.

Nutritious	Richer			

Use the space provided to write any new questions that you have since exploring these words.

Do you know how many countries have signed up to the UNCRC? Do some research and see whether your country has.

Curriculum connections

Living in the wider world

KS1 L5 – Pupils learn about the different roles and responsibilities people have in their community.

KS1 L6 – Pupils learn to recognise the ways they are the same as, and different from, other people.

KS2 L2 – Pupils learn to recognise that there are human rights in place to protect everyone.

KS2 L3 – Pupils learn about the relationship between rights and responsibilities.

Inspirational people

Edward Jenner (1796)

Jenner was an English doctor who discovered the benefits of vaccines by experimenting with cowpox to prevent smallpox. Jenner coined the word *vaccine*.

www.bbc.co.uk/history/historic_figures/jenner_edward.shtml (accessed 20/09/2021)

Dr. Joseph Murray and Dr. David Hume (1954)

The first living-related successful kidney transplant was led by Murray and Hume. Murray was awarded the Nobel Prize in 1990.

www.nobelprize.org/prizes/medicine/1990/murray/facts/ (accessed 19/09/2021)

Helen Brooke Taussig (1898–1986)

Among many other amazing achievements, Taussig wrote a book on *Congenital malformations of the heart* and went on to found "Paediatric Cardiology", which is the study of children's hearts.

https://en.wikipedia.org/wiki/Helen_B._Taussig (accessed 19/09/2021)

Donnal Thomas (1920–2012) and Joseph Murray (1919–2012)

Thomas and Murray jointly won the Nobel Prize 1990 for their work in organ and cell discovery, in particularly, how to provide new bone marrow through transplants.

www.nobelprize.org/prizes/medicine/1990/thomas/facts/ (accessed 21/09/2021)

Further resources

CBBC
The twin Van Tulleken doctors explore the heart and have a quiz for the children to complete.

www.bbc.co.uk/cbbc/quizzes/operation-ouch-quiz-quiz-heart (accessed 02/07/2021)

Cbeebies
Dr. Ranj sings a song about what an echocardiogram is, aimed at young children.

www.bbc.co.uk/cbeebies/watch/get-well-soon-echocardiogram-song (accessed 02/07/2021)

Your Happy Heart
There are lots of lesson ideas here for how to keep your heart healthy.

https://healthpoweredkids.org/lessons/your-happy-heart/ (accessed 19/09/2021)

We Are Teachers
This website has many activities to help with your planning.

www.weareteachers.com/circulatory-system-activities/ (accessed 12/09/2021)

Respiratory System
This website has lots of ideas and lesson plans.

https://classroom.kidshealth.org/classroom/prekto2/body/systems/respiratory.pdf (accessed 19/09/2021)

The Book Corner

The quiet at the end of the world by Lauren James
This story explores the dilemma placed upon the youngest people left alive when a global virus has caused global infertility. A young pair of friends must make impossible decisions. Suitable for KS2.

Eating the alphabet by Lois Ehlerd
This book introduces lots of fruits from all around the world and goes through all the letters of the alphabet. It is a good look at the array of food we can eat for a varied diet. Suitable for KS1.

My heart by Corinna Luyken
This is a simple ode to love and what the heart can feel. It is simply illustrated to create space for the reader to think and reflect. Suitable for KS1.

Your heart and lungs (Science in Action series) by Sally Hewitt
This colourful, illustrative, non-fiction text is a comprehensive introduction to how our lungs and heart work to keep us alive. Suitable for KS2.

Your hard-working heart and spectacular circulatory system
This is from the *Your brilliant body* series and takes readers on an entertaining tour of the body's heart and circulatory system. Suitable for KS2.

84 *Heart and lungs*

NC subject	Activity	Curriculum connections
English	*Pig-heart boy*	Years 1–6 Spoken language – Pupils should be taught to articulate and justify answers, arguments, and opinions.
Maths	The cost of vaping	KS1 – Multiplication and division – Pupils should be able to solve problems involving multiplication and division, using materials, arrays, repeated addition, mental methods, and multiplication and division facts, including problems in contexts. KS2 – Pupils should learn to solve problems, including missing number problems, involving multiplication and division.
Science	The function of the heart and lungs	Pupils should identify and name the main parts of the human circulatory system and describe the functions of the heart, blood vessels, and blood. They should recognise the impact of diet, exercise, drugs, and lifestyle on the way their bodies function. Pupils should build on their learning from Years 3 and 4 about the main body parts and internal organs (skeletal, muscular, and digestive system) to explore and answer questions that help them to understand how the circulatory system enables the body to function. Pupils might work scientifically by exploring the work of scientists and scientific research about the relationship between diet, exercise, drugs, lifestyle, and health.
Science	Smoking	Year 6 – Pupils should learn how to keep their bodies healthy and how their bodies might be damaged – including how some drugs and other substances can be harmful to the human body. Working scientifically – Plan scientific enquiries to answer questions, including reporting and presenting findings from enquiries, including conclusions, causal relationships, and explanations of and degrees of trust in results, in oral and written forms such as displays and other presentations.
History	Tobacco's past and present	KS1 – Pupils should be taught about changes within living memory. Where appropriate, these should be used to reveal aspects of change in national life. KS2 – Pupils should regularly address and sometimes devise historically valid questions about change, cause, similarity and difference, and significance.
Geography	The air we breathe	Teaching should equip pupils with knowledge about diverse places, people, resources, and natural and human environments, together with a deep understanding of the Earth's key physical and human processes.
Music	Circular breathing	Pupils should be taught to play tuned and untuned instruments musically. A high-quality music education should engage and inspire pupils to develop a love of music.
Art and Design	Diagrams of organs	Pupils should know about great artists, craft makers, and designers, and should understand the historical and cultural development of their art forms.

NC subject	Activity	Curriculum connections
Design and Technology	Make your own wind instrument	Pupils should be taught to make and select from and use a wider range of tools and equipment to perform practical tasks (for example, cutting, shaping, joining, and finishing) accurately.
Computing	Computers in the heart	A high-quality computing education equips pupils to use computational thinking and creativity to understand and change the world. Computing has deep links with mathematics, science, and design and technology, and it provides insights into both natural and artificial systems.
Religious education	Breathing and meditation	Compare and contrast the meditation practices of different faiths – for example, Buddhist, Christian, or Hindu meditation. Recognise and explain the practices involved in belonging to different faith communities.
Physical education	Take a breath!	Recognise the impact of exercise on the way bodies function (Y6). Year 6 Cross-curricular 'working scientifically' objectives: planning different types of scientific enquiries to answer questions, including recognising and controlling variables where necessary, taking measurements, using a range of scientific equipment with increasing accuracy and precision, taking repeat readings when appropriate, recording data and results of increasing complexity using scientific diagrams and labels, classification keys, tables, scatter graphs, bar and line graphs, using test results to make predictions to set up further comparative and fair tests, reporting and presenting findings from enquiries, including conclusions, causal relationships, and explanations of and degree of trust in results, in oral and written forms such as displays and other presentations.
PSHE	Healthy hearts	PSHE Association Curriculum KS1 H1 – Pupils learn about what keeping healthy means; different ways to keep healthy. KS1 H3 – Pupils learn about how physical activity helps us to stay healthy and ways to be physically active every day. KS2 H6 – Pupils learn about what constitutes a healthy diet; how to plan healthy meals; benefits to health and wellbeing of eating nutritionally rich foods; risks associated with not eating a healthy diet, including obesity and tooth decay. KS2 H5 – Pupils should learn about what good physical health means; how to recognise early signs of physical illness.
Citizenship	Children's health	Living in the wider world KS1 L5 – Pupils learn about the different roles and responsibilities people have in their community. KS1 L6 – Pupils learn to recognise the ways they are the same as, and different from, other people. KS2 L2 – Pupils learn to recognise there are human rights that are there to protect everyone. KS2 L3 – Pupils learn about the relationship between rights and responsibilities.

Journeys

Science

What other things have journeys?

Journeys inside our bodies
Think about things that have journeys, such as water or blood. Explore their journeys. Compare two closely and say how they are similar and dissimilar.

Do possessions matter on a journey?

Taking a long trip
Explore what you would pack for a long journey. Think about the obstacles, such as their weight. Consider what you need and what you want. Some items may be essential for their waterproof qualities. Create a test to see how waterproof materials are.

R.E.

Do all journeys have a purpose?

Journeys people make to show their faith
Find out about the journeys people make for their faith.

Music

Can music take you on an emotional journey?

Musical journeys
Explore a piece of music that takes you on an emotional journey and notice your thoughts about colour, images and feelings. Discuss with a friend. Consider whether you all responded the same.

History

Are we all refugees?

Refugees from the past
Explore stories from the past that tell us of the journeys that people have had to make, such as the Nativity from The Bible. Find out about other well-known journeys.

Citizenship

Should we look after refugee children?

Refugee children
The UN Convention on the Rights of the Child article 222 states that if a child is seeking refuge or has refugee status, governments must provide them with appropriate protection and assistance. Consider their needs in depth. Write a short letter to the government about how they can help.

Computing

Should computers control vehicles?

Smart cars
Driverless vehicles are programmed to be automatic. They do not need a human driver as they are programmed by a computer. Explore the advantages and disadvantages of them.

Maths

Are we always on a journey?

Mapping journeys with coordinates
You can look at maps to find your way on a journey. Learn how to use co-ordinates to locate particular places.

English

What reason do people make journeys for?

Journeys
Think about a time when you went on a journey. Explore the reasons people go on journeys. Retell a journey you have had and focus on your feelings.

Are decisions part of a journey?

The road not taken
The Road Not Taken by Robert Frost is a poem which examines paths we take in life. Some paths are easy to walk and others are harder. It may feel that you are the only person taking your path or the path seems difficult. Explain the poem in depth.

Geography

Are two journeys ever the same?

Collage of a journey
Create a visual journey with waypoints from A to B. Select images from holiday catalogues, internet, and brochures, or pictures you have drawn create a collage with notable features of the cities and area.

Art and design

Do we need voices to tell a story of a journey?

Pebble art
Imagine you have nothing to use but natural resources and you want to leave an image of your journey for others to see afterwards. Create a piece using natural resources.

Design and Technology

Are wheels for traveling?

Have wheels will travel
Explore vehicles that have wheels and ones that don't. Your challenge is to design a moving vehicle.

P.E.

Can you have a health journey?

A health journey
Discuss ways in which your body goes on a journey. For example, you could become fitter and healthier. Take the challenge to make yourself go on a development journey.

PSHE

Are we constantly on an emotional journey?

Emotional journeys
Track your day at school and record what you are feeling at different times. Consider if and how they vary.

9 Journeys

Concept stretchers   **SPEC grids**

As part of a P4C enquiry, children brainstorm synonyms, phrases, connections, and examples (SPEC) in a SPEC grid, as in these examples.

Belonging

Synonyms	Phrases
• Connect • Membership • Fit in • Ownership • Identity	• Go home, you don't belong here • 'I belong to you; you belong to me.' (The Lumineers, "Ho Hey") • Where are your belongings • 'By building relations, we create a source of love, personal pride and belonging that makes living in a chaotic world easier.' (Susan Lieberman) • 'Language, identity, place, home: these are all of a piece – just different elements of belonging and not belonging.' (Jhumpa Lahiri)
Connections	**Examples**
• Home, place • Refugee • Migration – Immigration • Strangers • Type, classification, stereotype • Relationship • Loyalty • Slavery • Citizenship	• Club, group • Church, religion, faith • Family • Gang • Nationality • School • Peers • Citizen

Journey

Synonyms	Phrases
• Trip/tour • Path • Way • Travel • Holiday • Progression • Movement • Voyage/quest • Voyage	• Life is a journey • You've come a long way • 'A journey of 1000 miles begins with a single step.' (Lao Tzu) • Don't go there • 'Success is a journey, not a destination.' (Arthur Ashe) • 'Sometimes it's the journey that teaches you a lot about your destination.' (Drake) • 'Every day is a journey, and the journey itself is home.' (Matsuo Basho)

DOI: 10.4324/9780429263033-9

Connections	Examples
• Travel • Life • Learning • Growth mind-set, perseverance	• Walking to school • Holiday travel • Getting stuck in a traffic jam • Climbing Mt. Everest • Sailing around the world • Learning a language

SPEC grids are the work of Roger Sutcliffe, Director and Programme Designer of P4C Plus and Thinking Moves A – Z at Dialogue Works, Philosophical Teaching and Learning. www.dialogueworks.co.uk

Concept stretchers **Concept sorting**

Using a concept line or Venn diagram rings, pupils sort examples into the categories of:

Journey	Not a journey

Cut out the examples below. Work in pairs or groups to encourage discussion, as appropriate.

Mary and Joseph travelling to Bethlehem	Walking to the shop
Life	Getting stuck in a traffic jam
Going on holiday in the UK	Crossing a busy road
Going on holiday abroad	Collecting your English book
Catching a train to London	Catching the bus to school
Climbing Mt. Everest	Walking up a hill
Flying somewhere on an aeroplane	Jogging a parkrun
Hiking across the Scottish Highlands	Walking to the toilet
Sailing around the world	Rowing a boat
Learning a language	Failing a maths test
The death of a pet	Going downstairs
Sprinting 100m	Running a marathon

Curriculum connections

Spoken language – Pupils can consider and evaluate different viewpoints, attending to and building on the contributions of others.

90 *Journeys*

Concept stretchers   **Concept web**

Think about how these concepts can be connected. Draw a line between the two ideas, and write a sentence along it explaining how they connect.

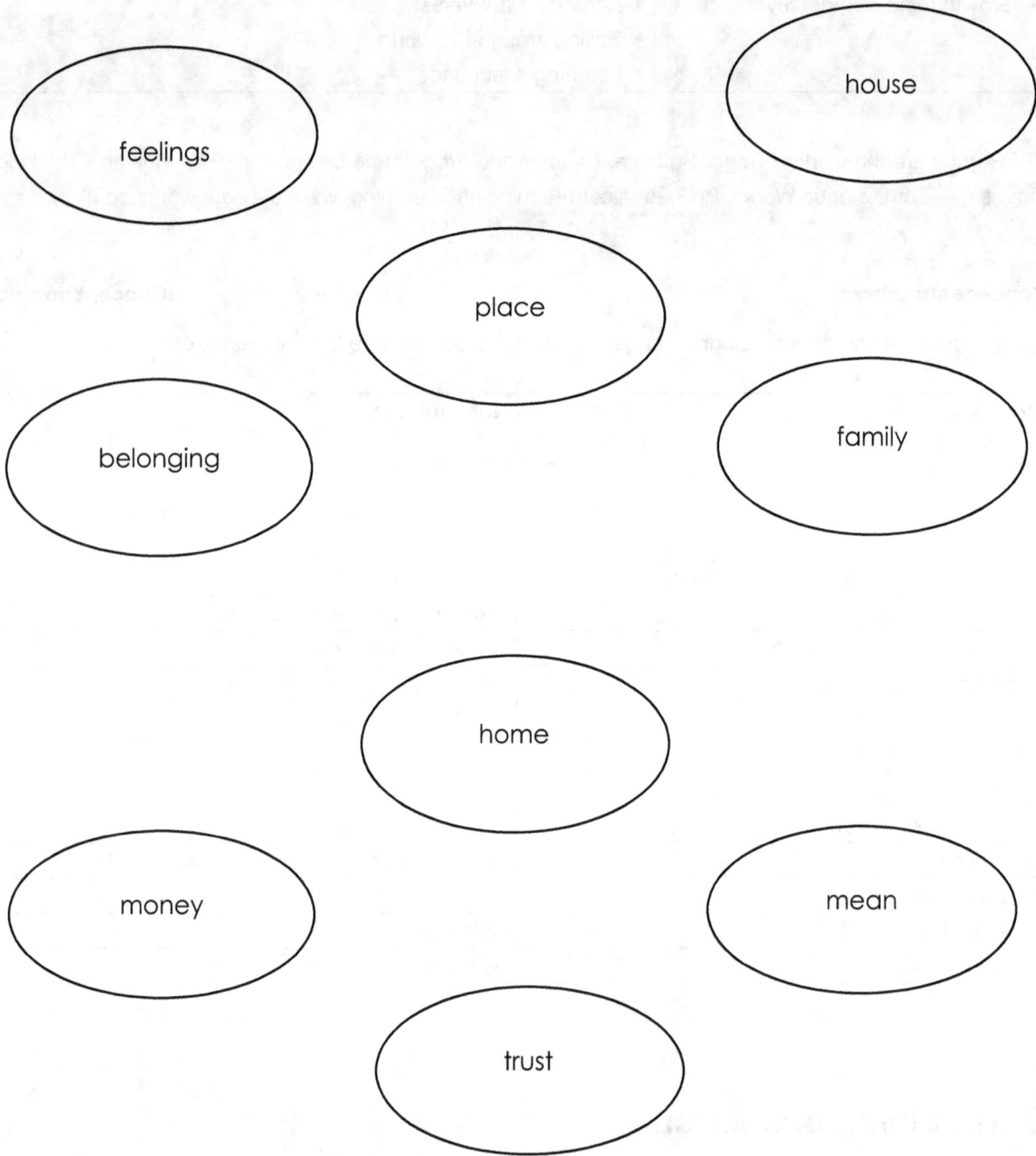

Curriculum connections

Spoken language – Pupils should consider and evaluate different viewpoints, attending to and building on the contributions of others.

Quotes to explore   **P4C enquiry**

"The only impossible journey is the one you never begin."
— Tony Robbins

"It is good to have an end to journey toward; but it is the journey that matters, in the end."
— Ursula K. Le Guin, *The Left Hand of Darkness*

"The only journey is the one within."
— Rainer Maria Rilke

"Some beautiful paths can't be discovered without getting lost."
— Erol Ozan

Curriculum connections

Spoken language – Pupils should learn to gain and monitor the interest of the listener.

Concept stretchers   **Question chain**

Belonging

What does it mean to belong?
What makes you belong to a family?
What makes you belong to your faith?
Where would you go if you had no faith or family?
Can you belong to a place?
What makes you belong to a place?
What makes you belong to a nation?
Does everyone belong to something?
Do you have to belong to something?
Does belonging last forever?
What happens if what you belong to disappears?
Where do refugees belong?
What defines a refugee?

Why do people make journeys? English

Journeys

Think about a time when you went on a journey. It may have been to go to a family member's home a long way away or to see something, such as going to London for a day out. Focus on the words you have used to describe your feelings. Write them in the box.

Now tell the story of your journey focussing on the words you listed.

What reasons can you think of for why people go on journeys?

Work with a partner or group and write your ideas below.

Holiday	To go shopping			

What other variations of a journey can you have? Think of opposites.

Long	Short

Curriculum connections

Pupils should give well-structured descriptions, explanations, and narratives for different purposes, including for expressing feelings.

Pupils should use spoken language to develop understanding through speculating, hypothesising, imagining, and exploring ideas.

Are decisions part of a journey? **English**

'The road not taken'

'The road not taken' by Robert Frost (https://vimeo.com/53740755) is a poem that helps us think about the paths we take in life. Some paths are easy to walk, and others are harder as you are the only person taking that path or it seems difficult.

The poem starts with 'Two roads diverged in a yellow wood, And sorry I could not travel both . . .'

Read it with your class and think about the words and phrases that come into your mind. List them here, such as *decisions*, *challenge*, etc.

Write down any questions that you now have. For example – How many paths are there?

In your class/group discuss your favourite question from the list. Explain the concept words in your question in more depth. Take questions from your peers.

Think about these words and say how they could connect to a pathway through life.
Look at these words. Select two that have something in common, and also say how they are different.

Home	Shelter	Sanctuary	Refugee	Weight	Distance
Relationship	Group	Family	Belonging	Feelings	Scale
Belief	Same	Division	Barriers	Story	Measure

Curriculum connections

Spoken language – Pupils should use spoken language to develop understanding through speculating, hypothesising, imagining, and exploring ideas.

Are we always on a journey? Mathematics

Mapping journeys with coordinates

You can look at maps to find your way on a journey and use the coordinates to locate particular places.

	A	B	C
1			
2			
3			
4			
5			
6			
7			

As in 'The Road Not Taken', there are many paths in life. Your challenge is to find out the number of ways to get from A1 to C7. For example, A2, A3, A4, B4, C4, C5, C6, C7. You can only go horizontally or diagonally. List your answers in these boxes.

Path 1	A1	A2	A3	A4	B4	C4			
Path 2									
Path 3									
Path 4									
Path 5									
Path 6									

Use this exercise as a metaphor for something in your life. When might a long path be the best option? Can you give an example?

Use this exercise as a metaphor for something in your life. When might the short path be the best option? Can you give an example?

Curriculum connections

Year 1–2 Pupils use the language of position, direction, and motion, including: left and right; top, middle, and bottom; on top of; in front of; above; between; around; near; close and far; up and down; forwards and backwards; inside and outside.

Year 3–4 Pupils should be taught to describe positions on a 2D grid as coordinates in the first quadrant.

What other things have journeys? **Science**

Journeys inside our bodies

Think about other things that go on journeys. Do these things go on a journey?

Blood	Food	Oxygen	Water	Rocks
Sand	Clouds	Flowers	Seeds	Elephants
Ironing boards	Chairs	Tables	Flotsam	

Can you add some more of your own to the table?

Now pick two and say how they are the same.

Now, say how they are different.

Now pick one that goes on a journey which interests you. Think about where it goes and write a list of those places here.

Curriculum connections

Year 2 – Pupils might work scientifically by sorting and classifying things.

Year 3–4 Pupils should do this through exploring, talking about, testing, and developing ideas about everyday phenomena and the relationships between living things and familiar environments, and by beginning to develop their ideas about functions, relationships, and interactions.

Year 5–6 At upper key stage 2, pupils should encounter more abstract ideas and begin to recognise how these ideas help them to understand and predict how the world operates.

Do possessions matter on a journey?   **Science**

Taking a long trip

What would you pack for a long journey? Write the items here.

Now tick the things that you **need** and circle the ones that you **want**.

How would you carry them? Revise the list and think again about what you would take.

Backpack investigation: How waterproof is it?

Aim: To test different materials and find out which have waterproof properties

Equipment:
Container
Water
Small, soft toy
Materials to test, such as tinfoil, paper, sandwich bag, fabric tea towel (pupils can help choose)
Waterproof tape (or Sellotape)

Method:
Half fill a container with water.
Wrap a dry, soft toy in one of your materials.

1. Check for gaps where water could seep in.
2. Carefully place the wrapped toy in the water for a few seconds.
3. Remove the toy. Is it dry?

Questions:

1. How can we make it a fair test?
   What things do should we keep the same (constant)? For example, use the same amount of material for each test. Keep the toys in the water for the same amount of time. Can you think of other ideas?

2. How will you know if water got through the material?
   Can you feel the toy?
   Or can you weigh it before and after?

Challenge

You need to keep a bottle of water hot, but you need to work out how to keep it hot as long as you can using a thermal flask. What can you use? Plan what you will use from the list of materials.

Curriculum connections

Year 1 – Pupils identify and compare the suitability of a variety of everyday materials, including wood, metal, plastic, glass, brick, rock, paper, and cardboard for particular uses.

Year 2 – Pupils should ask relevant questions and use different types of scientific enquiries to answer them.

Year 5 – Pupils should be taught to compare and group together everyday materials based on their properties, including their hardness, solubility, transparency, conductivity (electrical and thermal), and response to magnets.

Are two journeys ever the same? Geography

Collage of a journey

You are going to create a visual journey with waypoints from A to B. By selecting images from holiday catalogues, internet, and brochures (or pictures you have drawn), create a collage with notable features of the cities and area. You could work in pairs or in groups.

Use well-known and obvious geographical features, such as a mountain or a waterfall. Select buildings that are specific to the city, such as the Eiffel Tower if you are going to travel through France. For example, if you live in the United Kingdom, plan your journey to the four countries (Wales, England, Scotland, and Northern Ireland) and their capital cities.

Research the area and its notable features. On large paper place the images along a wandering line.

Think about whether two journeys are ever the same. What can make them different?

KS2 Challenge – Draw a map on a large piece of paper, trying as best as you can to draw the country's outline and place the capital cities where they are. Use zoom-out lines to point to where the images are.

Curriculum connections

KS1 – Pupils should be able to name, locate, and identify characteristics of the four countries and capital cities of the United Kingdom and its surrounding seas.

KS2 – Pupils should be able to name and locate counties and cities of the United Kingdom, geographical regions and their identifying human and physical characteristics, key topographical features (including hills, mountains, coasts, and rivers), and land-use patterns; and understand how some of these aspects have changed over time.

KS2 – Pupils should be able to locate the world's countries, using maps to focus on Europe (including the location of Russia) and North and South America, concentrating on their environmental regions, key physical and human characteristics, countries, and major cities.

Are wheels for traveling?   **Design and Technology**

Have wheels will travel

Most vehicles have wheels. Think of ones that do have wheels and ones that don't.

Has wheels	Does not have wheels

> Think of things that have wheels but are not vehicles. Write them below.

Design and make a LEGO moving car

Create a LEGO car with four wheels.

Technology

Create a way to secure a balloon to the vehicle. Watch how to make the vehicle move by using air. https://littlebinsforlittlehands.com/building-vehicle-stem-activities-kids/ (accessed 30/09/21)

Consider/reflect

Is this an effective design for a vehicle?

Curriculum connections

Technical knowledge – Pupils should understand and use mechanical systems in their products (for example, gears, pulleys, cams, levers, and linkages).

Can music take you on an emotional journey? Music

Music that can take you away

Musical appreciation

Explore one of these pieces of music or choose some 'journey' pieces of your own. Write the title of the piece and composer in the middle of the star below. Play the piece four separate times, and then respond to these questions.

> Listen to and compare:
>
> · 'Flight of the Bumble Bee', Rimsky-Korsakov
> · 'Moonlight Sonata', Beethoven
> · 'Spring Waltz', Chopin

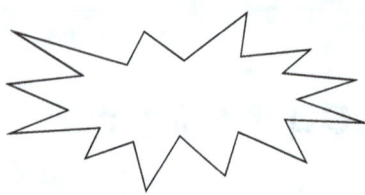

1. Colours: What colours does the piece of music make you think of?

2. Images: Can you draw what you hear?

3. Places: Does it make you think of a place?

4. Feelings/Emotions: How does the piece make you feel?

Share your responses with a friend or group. Did all pupils respond similarly to the music?

Curriculum connections

All pupils perform, listen to, review, and evaluate music across a range of historical periods, genres, styles, and traditions, including the works of the great composers and musicians.

Do all journeys have a purpose?   **Religious education**

Journeys people make to show their faith

Use the internet or research from your teacher to find out about the journeys people make for their faith.

Write in the boxes the key features of why they make these journeys. How are the journeys different? What are the similarities?

Christians Jerusalem in Israel	**Buddhists** Mahabodhi Temple in India
Hindus Kumbh Mela by the River Ganges, India www.bbc.co.uk/teach/class-clips-video/religious-studies-ks2-my-life-my-religion-hinduism-pilgrimage-hinduism/z4ghf4j (accessed 19/07/2021)	**A Pagoda (Buddhist)**
Islam Mecca in Saudi Arabia	**Sikh** The Golden Temple, called *Harimandir Sahib* www.bbc.co.uk/teach/class-clips-video/religious-studies-ks2-what-is-sikhism/zn4h382 (accessed 19/07/2021)

Curriculum connections

The principal aim of religious education is to explore what people believe and what difference this makes to how they live, so that pupils can gain the knowledge, understanding, and skills needed to handle questions raised by religion and belief, reflecting on their own ideas and ways of living.

Pupils should examine and explain how and why people express their beliefs in diverse ways.

Are we all refugees?   History

Refugees from the past

There are many stories from the past that tell us of the journeys that people had to make. In the Bible we learn about the Nativity Story.

The Nativity Story from the Bible is summarised here.

- Mary and Joseph travelled from Nazareth to Bethlehem in 5 B.C. before the birth of their son Jesus Christ.
- The family moved to Egypt after Joseph was told in a dream to flee to the now North African country to escape the command of Herod the Great to slaughter baby boys in and around Bethlehem.
- They reached Egypt after a very long journey, where they lived for three years until after the death of Herod in 4 B.C. when Joseph had a dream telling him that it was safe to return to Israel.
- The family travelled to Nazareth, which took days.

Biblical references of the journey to Egypt:

- Matthew 2:13
- Matthew 2:16
- Hosea 11:1
- Matthew 2:22–23
- Luke 2:39–40

Challenge – Now explore the paths other 'refugees' have **travelled**, across different time periods:

· Polish Jew (cf. 'I am David')
· The Israelites (cf. Exodus)
· Cambodia to New Zealand
· Syria to Europe
· Exit from Zimbabwe or South Africa

Do you know of any other refugee stories?

Curriculum connections

Making connections – Evaluating, reflecting on, and connecting the beliefs and practices studied; allowing pupils to challenge ideas studied, and the ideas studied to challenge pupils' thinking; discerning possible connections between these and pupils' own lives and ways of understanding the world.

Should we look after refugee children? Citizenship

Refugee children

Think about what you need, using a set of 'needs' cards. Put them into three piles – 'extremely important', 'fairly important', and 'not important' – according to what is important in your life. Explain to your friends how you have arrived at your decisions.

Need cards

Home	Water	Happiness	Friends	Food
Money	Sweets	Fun	Parents	Pets
Toys	Soap	Seats	Bed	Love
Work	Rest	Swings	Play time	Education

Most important	Fairly important	Least important

Consider Article 22 from the UN Convention on the Rights of the Child

If a child is seeking refuge or has refugee status, governments must provide them with appropriate protection and assistance to help them enjoy all the rights in the Convention. Governments must help refugee children who are separated from their parents to be reunited with them.

Now write a short letter to the government about what a child seeking refuge needs.

Dear government,

Curriculum connections

KS1 PSHE Communities L6 – Pupils learn to recognise the ways they are the same as, and different from, other people.

KS2 PSHE Communities 4 – Pupils learn the importance of having compassion towards others; shared responsibilities we all have for caring for other people and living things; how to show care and concern for others.

Do we need voices to tell a story?   **Art and Design**

Pebble art

Imagine you have nothing to use but natural resources, and you want to leave an image of your journey for others to see afterwards. Like this pebble picture for instance. Create a piece yourself. First think about which of your journeys to select and then what you can use.

After you have created your piece, speak the narrative to go with it.

Curriculum connections

KS1 – Pupils should be taught to use drawing, painting, and sculpture to develop and share their ideas, experiences, and imagination.

KS2 – Pupils should evaluate and analyse creative works using the language of art, craft, and design.

Can you have a health journey?   **Physical education**

A health journey

Discuss ways in which your body goes on a journey. For example, you could have journey towards becoming fitter. Write some ideas here, and take the challenge to make yourself go on a development journey.

Running faster for 50 metres	Balancing on one foot longer			

Curriculum connections

All KSs in the curriculum should provide opportunities for pupils to become physically confident in a way which supports their health and fitness.

Should computers control vehicles?   **Computing**

Smart cars

What kind of journeys will you be going on in 50 years? There are so many new vehicles that are powered by electricity, such as e-bikes, e-cars, and robot lawnmowers. Where you will be travelling to, as space travel will be available for people other than astronauts?

Many designers have created driverless vehicles, which are programmed to be automatic. They do not need a human driver, as they are programmed by a computer.

What do you think will be the advantages and disadvantages of driverless cars? Think about what computers cannot do in particularly.

Advantages	Disadvantages

Curriculum connections

A high-quality computing education equips pupils to use computational thinking and creativity to understand and change the world.

Are we constantly on an emotional journey?   **PSHE**

Emotional journeys

Think about how you feel during the school day. Start by recording what you feel for each lesson, activity, or between lessons. Record your feelings here.

Curriculum connections

KS1 Mental health H15 – Teach pupils to recognise that not everyone feels the same at the same time or feels the same about the same things.

KS2 Mental health H17 – Teach pupils to recognise that feelings can change over time and range in intensity.

Inspirational people

Buzz Aldrin

Buzz is an American former astronaut, engineer, and fighter pilot who made three spacewalks as a pilot of the *Gemini 12* mission and many more on other missions. https://en.wikipedia.org/wiki/Buzz_Aldrin (accessed 19/09/2021)

Amelia Earhart

Earhart was the first female pilot to fly across the Atlantic with Stultz, which she then achieved on her own in 1932. https://airandspace.si.edu/explore-and-learn/topics/women-in-aviation/earhart.cfm (accessed 22/10/2021)

Brendon Price

In 2021 Price was the first person to paddleboard around the UK. Read about his story here.

www.bbc.co.uk/news/uk-england-devon-57860467 (accessed 22/10/2021)

Ann Daniels and Caroline Hamilton

Daniels and Hamilton were the first to reach the North and South Poles as part of all-women teams. https://raisethebar.co.uk/speaker/ann-daniels/ (accessed 25/10/2021)

David Livingstone

Livingstone is best known for his crossing the African continent in 1852–1856. He travelled for years at a time and had no maps to navigate with. https://en.wikipedia.org/wiki/David_Livingstone (accessed 25/10/2021)

Isabella Bird

Bird was a writer, photographer, naturalist, and explorer in the 19th century who travelled the world climbing mountains and riding on horseback along her way. She was the first woman to be elected a fellow of the Royal Geographical Society and only stopped travelling at age 72.

www.theguardian.com/travel/2016/mar/08/top-10-inspiring-female-travel-adventurers (accessed 25/10/2021)

Further resources

Dialogue Works – Issue 22, Journeys

Dialogue Works' Home Talk packs explore concepts in depth with videos, quotes, and helpful age-appropriate activities.

https://dialogueworks.co.uk/wp-content/uploads/2020/10/HomeTalk-week-22-Journeys.pdf

Education through expeditions

Follow an explorer, such as Anthony Jinman, live on their journey.

https://eteschools.com/

Action Aid

There are lots of free resources which cover a range of topics, including refugees. Learn from children in conflict and refugees in their own words.

www.actionaid.org.uk/get-involved/school-resources (accessed 25/10/2021)

Amnesty International

This charity has a wealth of resources for your to explore to do with asylum issues and refugees.

https://www.amnesty.org.uk/education-resources-refugee-asylum-immigration (accessed 22.2.22)

UNICEF

This free teaching pack allows you to explore the refugee and migrant crisis with children. It has 20 activities with a short one-off lesson as a longer project.

www.unicef.org.uk/rights-respecting-schools/resources/teaching-resources/guidance-assemblies-lessons/refugee-crisis-europe/ **(**accessed 25/10/2021)

The British Red Cross

You can sign up to the British Red Cross to receive free resources about refugees and migration.

https://www.redcross.org.uk/get-involved/teaching-resources/refugees-and-migration (accessed 02.02.22)

The Book Corner

Journey by Aaron Becker
This is a picture book which is beautifully illustrated, allowing the reader to create their own interpretation of this story. It is about a lonely girl who escapes from her bedroom and goes on a spectacular journey with a new friend. It is a simple story about kindness and friendship created from the challenges they face along the way. Suitable for KS1.

When Hitler stole pink rabbit by Judith Kerr
Kerr had to flee Germany with her parents as a young girl, and this is a semi-autobiographical memoir of her childhood from her naive perspective as a 9-year-old girl. This is easy to read, and children will relate to her well. Suitable for KS2.

I am David by Mann Holm
David has spent his entire life in a concentration camp, but he escapes and flees across Europe. He must learn about the new world that he has found and fend for himself. Suitable for KS2.

The journey by Francesca Sanna
When a mother and her two children have to flee from a war in their country, they have to seek a new home and leave everything behind. Their journey is filled with fear of the unknown but also great hope. It explores the unimaginable decisions they must make. Suitable for KS2.

The travel book by Lonely Planet Kids
This non-fiction book takes you on a tour of 200 countries with lots of facts about wildlife, how people live, sports, food, festivals, and other quirky insights. As you journey along each river, you will learn so much about culture and the life it brings. Suitable for KS1/2.

NC subject	Activity	Curriculum connections
English	Journeys	All pupils should learn to write effective composition which involves articulating and communicating ideas, and then organising them coherently for a reader. Pupils should give well-structured descriptions, explanations, and narratives for different purposes, including for expressing feelings. Pupils should use spoken language to develop understanding through speculating, hypothesising, imagining, and exploring ideas.
English	The road not taken	Spoken language – Pupils should use spoken language to develop understanding through speculating, hypothesising, imagining, and exploring ideas.
Maths	Mapping journeys with coordinates	Year 1–2 Pupils use the language of position, direction, and motion, including: left and right; top, middle, and bottom; on top of; in front of; above; between; around; near; close and far; up and down; forwards and backwards; inside and outside. Year 3–4 Pupils should be taught to describe positions on a 2D grid as coordinates in the first quadrant.
Science	Journeys inside our bodies	Year 2 Pupils might work scientifically by sorting and classifying things. Year 3–4 Pupils should do this through exploring, talking about, testing, and developing ideas about everyday phenomena and the relationships between living things and familiar environments, and by beginning to develop their ideas about functions, relationships, and interactions. Year 5–6 At upper key stage 2, pupils should encounter more abstract ideas and begin to recognise how these ideas help them to understand and predict how the world operates.
Science	Taking a long trip	Year 1 – Pupils identify and compare the suitability of a variety of everyday materials, including wood, metal, plastic, glass, brick, rock, paper, and cardboard for particular uses. Year 2 – Pupils should ask relevant questions and use different types of scientific enquiries to answer them. Year 5 – Pupils should be taught to compare and group together everyday materials based on their properties, including their hardness, solubility, transparency, conductivity (electrical and thermal), and response to magnets.
History	Refugees from the past	Making connections – Evaluating, reflecting on, and connecting the beliefs and practices studied; allowing pupils to challenge ideas studied, and the ideas studied to challenge pupils' thinking; discerning possible connections between these and pupils' own lives and ways of understanding the world.

NC subject	Activity	Curriculum connections
Geography	Collage of a journey	KS1 – Pupils should be able to name, locate, and identify characteristics of the four countries and capital cities of the United Kingdom and its surrounding seas. KS2 – Pupils should be able to name and locate counties and cities of the United Kingdom, geographical regions and their identifying human and physical characteristics, key topographical features (including hills, mountains, coasts, and rivers), and land-use patterns; and understand how some of these aspects have changed over time. KS2 – Pupils should be able to locate the world's countries, using maps to focus on Europe (including the location of Russia) and North and South America, concentrating on their environmental regions, key physical and human characteristics, countries, and major cities.
Music	Musical journeys	All pupils perform, listen to, review, and evaluate music across a range of historical periods, genres, styles, and traditions, including the works of the great composers and musicians.
Art and Design	Pebble art	KS1 – Pupils should be taught to use drawing, painting, and sculpture to develop and share their ideas, experiences, and imagination. KS2 – Pupils should evaluate and analyse creative works using the language of art, craft, and design.
Design and Technology	Have wheels will travel	Technical knowledge – Pupils should understand and use mechanical systems in their products (for example, gears, pulleys, cams, levers, and linkages).
Computing	Smart cars	A high-quality computing education equips pupils to use computational thinking and creativity to understand and change the world.
Religious education	Journeys people make to show their faith	Devon and Torbay SACRE The principal aim of religious education is to explore what people believe and what difference this makes to how they live, so that pupils can gain the knowledge, understanding, and skills needed to handle questions raised by religion and belief, reflecting on their own ideas and ways of living. Examine and explain how and why people express their beliefs in diverse ways.
Physical education	A health journey	All KSs in the curriculum should provide opportunities for pupils to become physically confident in a way which supports their health and fitness.

NC subject	Activity	Curriculum connections
PSHE	**Convention on the Rights of the Child**	KS1 PSHE Communities L6 – Pupils learn to recognise the ways they are the same as, and different from, other people. KS2 PSHE Communities L4 –- Pupils learn the importance of having compassion towards others; shared responsibilities we all have for caring for other people and living things; how to show care and concern for others.
Citizenship	**Refugee children**	KS1 PSHE Communities L6 – Pupils learn to recognise the ways they are the same as, and different from, other people. KS2 PSHE Communities L4 – Pupils learn the importance of having compassion towards others; shared responsibilities we all have for caring for other people and living things; how to show care and concern for others.

English

What can money buy?

Winning the lottery
You have won the lottery. Your challenge is to spend all the money. Investigate ways that you can donate to a cause that you believe in, such as Greenpeace. Create a presentation to share how you will spend it.

Maths

Should we share our wealth?

Social conscience
Social enterprises are a 'not for profit' company and after they pay all the workers' wages use the profit for good purposes. Decide what you would do if you had to be 'socially responsible' and had a business.

R.E.

Should we be frugal?

The prodigal son
Read and consider the message from the story called The Prodigal Son from The Bible. Discuss the two brothers and how they behaved. Think about the concepts of love, giving, forgiveness and money come together.

Music

Do you need money to be happy?

Tunes about money
Create a simple song. Use a backing track and add spoken lyrics or rap with words that you have written to describe what you think about money.

Money

History

Are riches always money?

British Empire
The British Empire ruled over many other countries and was once very wealthy. Explore the history of how this came to be. Consider if there is a difference between wealth, money and riches.

Computing

Is money real?

Cryptocurrency
Cryptocurrency is becoming more popular. Find out how computing and maths are working together to create money. Create your own code for currency.

Science

> How should we spend money in science?

Clever money
Humans spend money on lots of different things, such as food, clothes, homes, and cars. However consider how we could spend it on scientific research. Make a concept line with important and not so important at each end.

Geography

> Do we need money?

Means of exchange
Rai stones were used as means of exchange for an ancient tribe. They are early examples of how physical objects were used as a means of exchange for food and labour. Locate some countries and investigate the currency they use.

Art and Design

> Does money make the world go round?

Banksy piece
Look a piece of art called 'money makes the world go wrong'. Discuss what the artist has written. Create your own statement about money and draw about an image that conveys it.

Design and Technology

> Do pennies take care of the pounds?

Money bank
It has been traditional for children to have money banks in which they can pop their pocket money into. Design and make a piggybank from jam jars or plastic bottles.

PSHE

> Should money be for needs or wants?

Your money
Think about the things that you can buy and how important they are. Consider what you should buy first. Create a concept line in order of importance and argue for each item's worth.

Citizenship

> What age should children be allowed to work for money?

Children and money
Governments must set a minimum age for children to work and ensure that work conditions are safe and appropriate states the United Nations Convention on the Rights of the Child in Article 32. Explore in depth what work means and what it means to be a child.

P.E.

> Is sport about money?

Money and sport
Many sports clubs now pay their players and athletes huge amounts of money. Some are paid much more than others. Consider if sports people should be paid different amounts.

10 Money

Concept stretchers **SPEC grids**

As part of a P4C enquiry, children brainstorm synonyms, phrases, connections, and examples (SPEC) in a SPEC grid, as in these examples.

Money

Synonyms	Phrases
• Cash • Currency • Change • Coinage/coins/notes • Dosh • Readies • Dough/bread • Lolly	• Money is made of blood, sweat, and tears. • Cash is king • Show me the money • Time is money • I don't have the time or money • Money doesn't grow on trees • Money can't buy you love • Money makes the world go round
Connections	Examples
• Shops/fundraising • Birthdays • Pocket money • Virtual money • Piggy banks • Tooth fairy	• Salary • Pocket money • Coins • Notes • Cheques • Virtual currency

Wealth

Synonyms	Phrases
• Prosperity • Affluence • Means • Capital • Treasure • Fortune • Riches	• Early to bed, early to rise makes a man healthy, wealthy, and wise • Wealth of knowledge • He who pays the piper calls the tune. • Stinking rich • A king's ransom
Connections	Examples
• Famous people/celebrities • Royalty • Entrepreneurs/Influencers • Footballers • Famous singers • Famous actors/actresses • Scrooge (opposite)	• Large houses/mansions • Estates • Enormous gardens • Luxury cars • Designer clothes/trainers • Holidays – skiing/travel • Queen Elizabeth II

DOI: 10.4324/9780429263033-10

Money 115

Curriculum connections

Spoken language – Use spoken language to develop understanding through speculating, hypothesising, imagining, and exploring ideas.

SPEC grids are the work of Roger Sutcliffe, Director and Programme Designer of P4C Plus and Thinking Moves A – Z at Dialogue Works, Philosophical Teaching and Learning. www.dialogueworks.co.uk

Concept stretchers **Concept sorting**

Using a concept line or Venn diagram rings, pupils sort examples into the categories of:

Can buy	Cannot buy

Cut out the examples. Work in pairs or groups to encourage discussion, as appropriate.

Happiness	Love
Friendship	Food
Family	Water
Beauty	Fun
A delicious meal	A partner
A smile	A long life
A happy ending	Health
The best holiday	A happy day
Education	Knowledge
Allegiance	Power
Wisdom	Trust

Curriculum connections

Years 1–6 Spoken language – Pupils should be able to Articulate and justify answers, arguments, and opinions.

116 *Money*

Concept stretchers   **Concept web**

Think about how these concepts can be connected together. Draw a line between and write a sentence along it about how they connect.

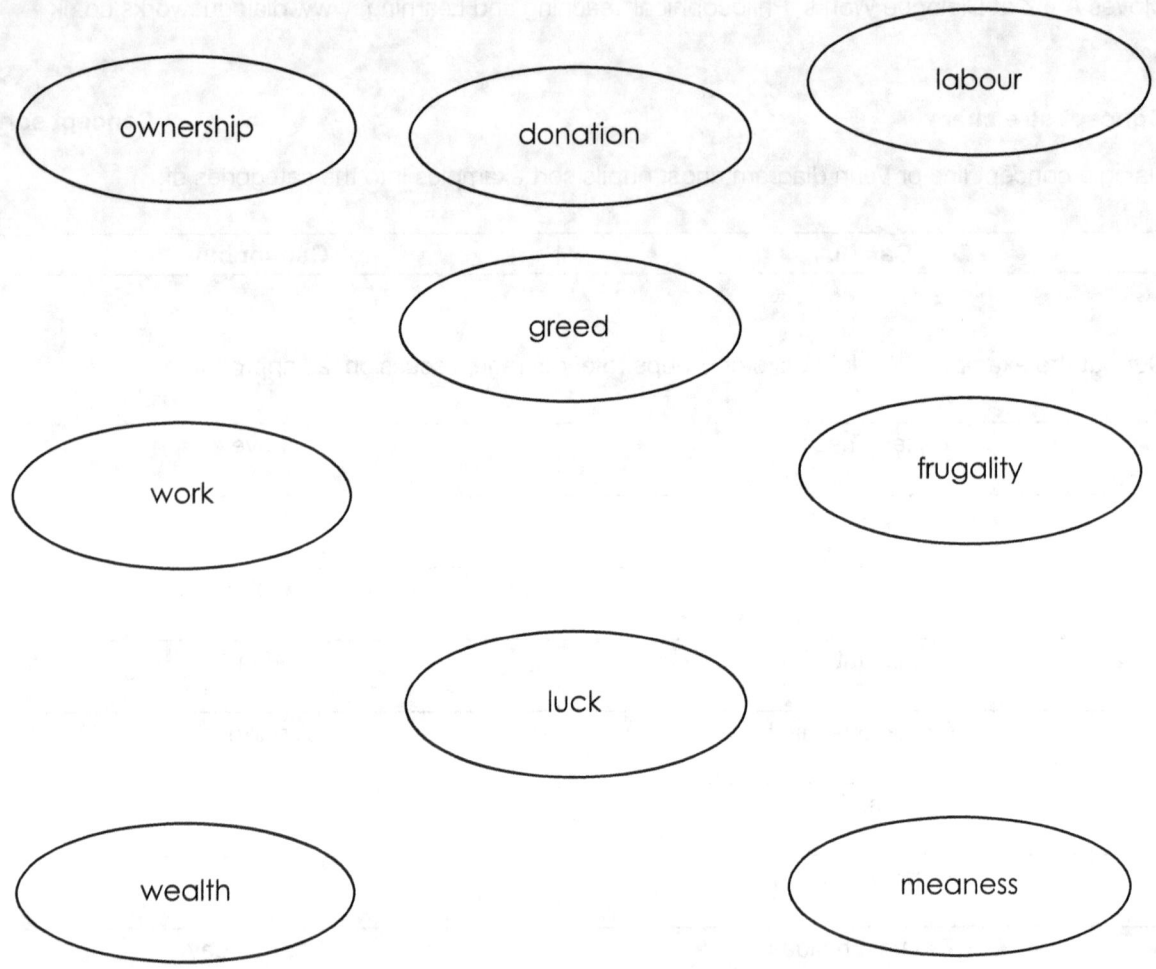

Pick two and write a sentence about how you think that they connect to each other.

1.	2.
Say how they connect.	

Now share your ideas with your group, class, or talk partner.

Curriculum connections

Spoken language – Pupils should learn to consider and evaluate different viewpoints, attending to and building on the contributions of others.

Concept stretchers | **Decision corner**

Would you rather?

Look at these options. Select one from each pair.

Have a huge house with no friends	Have a small house with many friends
Choose one with a tick. Say why.	
Live a short life with lots of money	Live a long life with not much money
Choose one with a tick. Say why.	
Know that you are going to live a healthy life	Know that you are going to live a wealthy life
Choose one with a tick. Say why.	

Once you have thought of your reasons, try to think of a pair of statements yourself that have a dilemma about money. Write them in the boxes.

Curriculum connections

Spoken language – Pupils should learn to participate in discussions, presentations, performances, role play/improvisations, and debates.

Spoken language – Pupils should use spoken language to develop understanding through speculating, hypothesising, imagining, and exploring ideas.

Money

Quote to explore P4C enquiry

Here are some quotes about money

Pick one that interests you to discuss as a P4C enquiry.

Think about the main words in them.

Then share your thoughts about and explore them in more depth within a group.

> "Wealth consists not in having great possessions, but in having few wants."
> – Epictetus

> "Money often costs too much."
> – Ralph Waldo Emerson

> "An investment in knowledge pays the best interest."
> – Benjamin Franklin

> "Money is a terrible master but an excellent servant."
> – P.T. Barnum

Curriculum connections

Spoken language – Pupils should learn to gain and monitor the interest of the listener.

What can money buy?   **English**

Winning the lottery

Congratulations! You have won the lottery. You now have 1 million pounds!

£1,000,000.00

There is a catch! You cannot spend it on anything that benefits you directly.

Your challenge is to spend all the money. Investigate ways that you can donate to a cause that you believe in, such as Greenpeace.

Create a 5-minute presentation explaining who would you give it to and why?

Plan for presentation

Start with an interesting question, such as "What would you spend a million on?"

Main body of presentation – state what you will spend it on and why.

Finish your presentation with a summary – leave a provocative thought with your audience, such as "Why don't you consider giving money to charity as well?"

Curriculum connections

Spoken language – Pupils should be able to participate in discussions, presentations, performances, role play, improvisations, and debates.

In Years 3 and 4, pupils should become more familiar with and confident in using language in a greater variety of situations, for a variety of audiences and purposes, including through drama, formal presentations, and debate.

In Years 5 and 6, pupils' confidence, enjoyment, and mastery of language should be extended through public speaking, performance, and debate.

Should we share our wealth? Mathematics

Social conscience

Many businesses are becoming social enterprises – this means that they are 'not-for-profit' companies. They pay all the workers their wages, and then the profit is used for good purposes.

For example, "Who gives a crap?" makes toilet paper, and they give 50% of their profits to build toilets for people where there are none. Think about other kinds of things that are made and by whom, and what they could do to benefit others.

What would you do if you had to be 'socially responsible'? Write in each box how much money you think that each company should give away and to whom

Café

For example, give local children a breakfast whose parents can't afford it.
Read *Uncle Willie and the Soup Kitchen* by Anne DiSalvo-Ryan.

Paper company

Garden centre

Soft play centre

Curriculum connections

(PSHE Association) L6 – Pupils learn about the different groups that make up their community; what living in a community means.

Year 1 – Pupils should recognise and know the value of different denominations and symbols for pounds and pence.

Year 2 – Pupils should recognise and use symbols for pounds and pence.

How should we spend money in science? Science

Clever money

Humans spend money on lots of different things, such as food, clothes, homes, and cars, but what could we spend it on to do with science?

Make a concept line with "Important" and "Not so important" at each end. Consider some of these together and place them along it. You can add your own ideas as well.

| Space exploration | Virus vaccines | Personalised medicine – gene research | Habitat |
| Food poverty | Improving disability access | Helping animals that are at risk of extinction | Creating wider biodiversity |

Now put them in this table once you have decided where they should sit.

Important	**Not so important**	**Least important**

Finally, select the one that is most important and give one good reason for choosing it.

Curriculum connections

PSHE Association

L19 – Pupils learn that people's spending decisions can affect others and the environment (e.g. fair trade, buying single-use plastics, or giving to charity).

Do we need money?   **Geography**

Means of exchange

Rai stones – Yap Island

Rai stones were used as means of exchange for an ancient tribe. They are early examples of how physical objects were used as a means of exchange for food and labour.

https://en.wikipedia.org/wiki/Rai_stones (accessed 20/09/2020)

Investigate these countries. What money do they use? What is their currency called?

Country	Names of coins/notes	Name of currency
Brazil		
Australia		
South Africa		
India		

Look at a map of the world and identify more countries. Research their currency and fill in the boxes.

Country	Names of coins/notes	Name of currency

Select and draw one of the coins.

Curriculum connections

KS1 Geographical skills and fieldwork – Pupils should learn to use world maps, atlases, and globes to identify the United Kingdom and its countries, as well as the countries, continents, and oceans studied at this key stage.

KS2 – Pupils should extend their knowledge and understanding beyond the local area to include the United Kingdom and Europe, North and South America. They should develop their use of geographical knowledge, understanding, and skills to enhance their locational and place knowledge.

Are riches always money?   **History**

The British Empire

The British Empire ruled over many other countries and was once very wealthy. Explore the history of how this came to be.

Here are some words to help you explore the close associations with money. Find definitions of these words, and write the definitions in the boxes.

Peasantry	Empire	Civilisation	Parliament

KS1 Christopher Columbus

For months, Columbus sailed from island to island in the Caribbean, looking for "pearls, precious stones, gold, silver, spices, and other objects and merchandise whatsoever".

What riches did Columbus find when he went on his voyages?

KS2 Mayans

Research the Mayans and how they lived. What riches did they have?

> What does the word *riches* mean to you?

P4C enquiry

After exploring the words, discuss whether riches are always money.

Curriculum connections

A high-quality history education should inspire pupils' curiosity to know more about the past. Teaching should equip pupils to ask perceptive questions, think critically, weigh evidence, sift arguments, and develop perspective and judgement.

Pupils should gain and deploy a historically grounded understanding of abstract terms, such as *peasantry*, *civilisation*, *empire*, and *parliament*.

KS2 – Pupils should learn about a non-European society that provides contrasts with British history.

Should we be frugal?   **Religious education**

The prodigal son

Read the story from the Bible called The prodigal son

This is the story about a father who has two sons. One of his sons asks for his inheritance and is prodigal (wasteful, reckless, and extravagant) with it. His other son does not. When his prodigal son returns home without anything, the prodigal son is expecting his father to be angry and scornful. However, the father welcomes him with open arms, much to his brother's disgust. The father tells the older son, 'You are ever with me, and all that I have is yours, but thy younger brother was lost and now he is found'.

From the Bible

And when he came to himself, he said, How many hired servants of my father's have bread enough and to spare, and I perish with hunger! I will arise and go to my father, and will say unto him, Father, I have sinned against heaven, and before thee, and am no more worthy to be called thy son: make me as one of thy hired servants. And he arose, and came to his father. But when he was yet a great way off, his father saw him, and had compassion, and ran, and fell on his knees, and kissed him.

– Luke 15:17–20, KJV

> Do you think the father was right to have forgiven his son?

Explore this question with a partner or in a P4C enquiry

Write your notes here.

Curriculum connections

RE lessons should offer structured and safe space during curriculum time for reflection, discussion, dialogue, and debate.

Spoken language pupils should be able to identify, investigate, and respond to questions posed and responses offered.

Should children have to work for money? Citizenship

UNCRC Article 32

The United Nations Convention on the Rights of the Child states in Article 32 that 'Governments must set a minimum age for children to work and ensure that work conditions are safe and appropriate'.

Discuss this statement with a partner. What is interesting to you?

Read this story or a similar one about children working.

The Camel Riders by Elizabeth Laird

This story explores how children were once kidnapped from Pakistan and India and sold to become camel jockeys for rich Arabs. Camel racing is like horse racing, where people bet on which horse is going to win the race.

This story can be compared and contrasted to the cotton industry in the UK, where children were paid to go under the looms. It was dangerous work, but the Children and Young Persons Act 1933 started the change to stop child labour.

> **What can a child lose when they work?**

Here are some connected concept words that you could discuss to start thinking about this question. Can you think of some more?

Freedom	Family	Home
Fun	Familiarity	Education

Curriculum connections

PSHE Association – Shared responsibilities

KS1 L1– Pupils learn about what rules are, why they are needed, and why different rules are needed for different situations.

KS2 L2 – Pupils learn to recognise there are human rights that are there to protect everyone.

Do you need money to be happy?   **Music**

Tunes about money

> Explore the words of these songs.
>
> "Price tag" (feat B.o.B.) by Jessie James
> "Rich man's world" by ABBA
> "Who wants to be a millionaire" by Frank Sinatra

Reflect upon the words to the songs in pairs, or in a group. Write down your thoughts about whether we need money to be happy.

Using the backing track from a simple song like "Best day of my life" by Dido, add simple spoken lyrics that you have written to describe what you think about money. Or, if you prefer, create a rap.

Curriculum connections

Years 3 and 4 – Reading, re-reading, and rehearsing poems and plays for presentation and performance give pupils opportunities to discuss language, including vocabulary, extending their interest in the meaning and origin of words.

Music - As pupils progress, they should develop a critical engagement with music, allowing them to compose, and to listen with discrimination to the best in the musical canon.

Should money be for needs or wants?   **PSHE**

Your money

Think about the following things in order of importance. Which should you pay for first? Put them on a concept line in order of importance.

Tick the wants and circle the needs.

Water bill	Heating bill	Food bill	Transport	Shoes
Drinks	Clothes	School uniform	Pet food	Jewellery
Meals out	Sweets	Pens and books	Furniture	Games

Think about whether they are needs or wants.

In a P4C enquiry, group or in pairs discuss whether money should be for needs or wants.

Write your thoughts here from your discussion.

Curriculum connections

PSHE Association L20 – Pupils are taught to recognise that people make spending decisions based on priorities, needs, and wants.

Does money make the world go round?   **Art and Design**

Banksy piece

People think this piece of artwork was done by Banksy, who keeps anonymous. Anonymous means that we don't know who this person or people are. It says, 'Money makes the world go wrong'. www.dorsetecho.co.uk/news/10822555.banksy-wall-art-wows-weymouth-resident/ (accessed 23/09/2020)

Money makes the world go wrong. Discuss. Is this true?

Explore this statement in a P4C enquiry, group, or in pairs.

Now that you have explored the statement, write your own. Draw an image that would capture the feelings of your new statement.

Research pieces of art that have been sold for lots of money. Write some of the names of the pieces below.

Curriculum connections

Purpose of study – Pupils should also know how art and design both reflect and shape our history and contribute to the culture, creativity, and wealth of our nation. Pupils should know about great artists.

KS2 – Pupils should learn about great artists, architects, and designers in history.

Do pennies take care of the pounds?   **Design and Technology**

Money bank

Some people say that if you look after the pennies then the pounds look after themselves. What do you think this saying means?

It has been traditional for children to have money banks into which they can pop their pocket money. You are going to design a piggybank. What do you want it to be like?

You could make the piggybank from jam jars or plastic bottles. See a website like this one for inspiration, such as https://www.youtube.com/watch?v=o4JgzCD7vy8 (accessed 13/04/2022)

Challenge 1 – Make a piggybank where there is a vortex before it goes in.

Challenge 2 – Make a piggybank with a slot for the coin to travel along.

Curriculum connections

KS1 – Pupils should be taught to design purposeful, functional, appealing products for themselves and other users based on design criteria.

KS2 – Pupils should understand and use mechanical systems in their products (for example, gears, pulleys, cams, levers, and linkages).

Is money real?   **Computing**

Cryptocurrency

> Cryptocurrency is becoming more popular. What is it? Watch this video, or a similar one, to find out how computing and maths are working together to create money.
>
> www.youtube.com/watch?v=s4g1XFU8Gto by The Guardian (accessed 02/07/2021)

Think about how you could create your own numerical code for money. For example, start with how each number would be different, such as 12345678901, 12345678902.

Create some code strings that denote a pound. Create a code for everyone in your class. Swap your codes with a partner so they can check that there are not two codes the same.

Curriculum connections

Mathematics is a creative and highly interconnected discipline that has been developed over centuries, providing the solutions to some of history's most intriguing problems. It is essential to everyday life; critical to science, technology, and engineering; and necessary for financial literacy and most forms of employment.

Computing - The core of computing is computer science, in which pupils are taught the principles of information and computation, how digital systems work, and how to put this knowledge to use through programming.

Is sport about money?   **Physical education**

Money and sport

Many sports clubs now pay their players and athletes huge amounts of money. Some are paid much more than others.

In a P4C enquiry, in groups or in pairs, consider the following questions.

Should this be the case? What aspects of physical exercise are harder than others? Should athletes be rewarded differently?

Try some movements (you can make your own list with your teacher) and rate them in order of difficulty.

1. Kicking a ball in a goal
2. Pole-vaulting over a 60cm bar
3. Cycling for 30 minutes at the same speed
4. Putting a basketball through a net 30 times

What would you say is the hardest sport now you have tried some tricky movements?

Write below.

Curriculum connections

KS1 – Pupils should be able to engage in competitive (both against self and against others) and co-operative physical activities, in a range of increasingly challenging situations.

KS2 – Pupils should be taught to develop flexibility, strength, technique, control, and balance (for example, through athletics and gymnastics).

Inspirational people

Philanthropists

People who give money to other people or to charity are called philanthropists. Here are some famous ones you could research.

Mark Zuckerburg and Priscilla Chan

Mark created Facebook and became very wealthy from it, but in December 2015 he and his wife pledged to give away 99% of the Facebook stake over their lifetimes.

JK Rowling

JK is the famous Harry Potter writer. She has created her own trust called The Volant Charitable Trust, and the royalties from her newest book called *The Ickabog* will be donated there.

Serena Williams

Williams, one of the world's greatest tennis players, has set up her own charity called the Serena Williams Fund, which helps people with a range of issues from racial injustice to inequality. She is a UNICEF Goodwill Ambassador and has also helped immunise children in Ghana.

Oprah Winfrey

Oprah is a famous American TV presenter who donates much of her wealth to other people. In April 2020 she donated $10 million to help Americans in need during the COVID-19 pandemic along with $1 million to the Food Fund. Oprah has donated to her old school and to hurricane relief disaster funds, along with many other donations.

Cristiano Ronaldo

Cristiano is a Portuguese football player. He recently donated $1.08 million to three hospitals in Portugal to help fight COVID-19 in the country and is an ambassador for Save the Children, UNICEF, and World Vision.

Further resources

Charity Home Talk pack
This is a Home Talk pack about charity written by Nick Chandley from Dialogue Works.

The resource pack has lots of stimulating questions and resources to use to support discussions about charity. It is set into age groups so that there is something that is age-appropriate for all children.

https://dialogueworks.co.uk/wp-content/uploads/2021/05/HomeTalk-Charity.pdf (accessed 25/10/2021)

Maths – Nrich
This has many maths activities. The Nrich maths resource website has many money problems to solve.

https://nrich.maths.org/public/topic.php?group_id=15&code=7

Maths Shed

This website also have many maths activities and is a wealth of free resources.

www.mathematicshed.com/maths-money-shed.html

English – *Macbeth*
Macbeth is the Shakespearian story of power, greed, and murder.

Futurelearn.com/courses/explore-english-shakespeare/0/steps/10120 (accessed 20/05/2020)

Moneysense

This a free programme provided by Natwest that has age-appropriate resources that cover all areas about teaching money.

https://natwest.mymoneysense.com/home/ (accessed 10/2/2022)

The Book Corner

Three questions by Jon J. Muth
This book is beautifully illustrated with subtle watercolour images. Young Nikolai has three questions and seeks the answers from the wise old turtle who lives in the mountains. The story has a moral message about priority and the important things in life which are profound and timeless. Suitable for KS1.

Last stop on the market street by Matt De La Pera
CJ takes a journey on a bus with his nana, and the story follows the discussion they have about things he wants. This picture book is about appreciating the riches that money cannot buy, and its message is that caring, thoughtfulness, and community are more important than material wealth. Suitable for KS1.

Mr. Mean by Roger Hargreaves
Mr. Mean lives up to his name and is mean by name and mean by nature. A wizard comes along to teach him a lesson. The story's message is that we should share wealth. Suitable for KS1.

The camel riders by Elizabeth Laird
This story, based on truth, explores how children were once kidnapped from Pakistan and India, and sold to become camel jockeys for rich Arabs. It explores the concept of child labour and abduction. Suitable for KS2.

The billionaire boy by David Walliams
Joe has everything he wants except true friends, so to remedy this he enrols at the local comprehensive school. He keeps it hidden that he is a billionaire's son and soon learns that you can't buy friendship. This is a popular story with very modern language. Suitable for KS2.

NC subject	Activity	Curriculum connections
English	Winning the lottery	Spoken language – Pupils should participate in discussions, presentations, performances, role play/improvisations, and debates. In Years 3 and 4, pupils should become more familiar with and confident in using language in a greater variety of situations, for a variety of audiences and purposes, including through drama, formal presentations, and debate. In Years 5 and 6, pupils' confidence, enjoyment, and mastery of language should be extended through public speaking, performance, and debate.
Maths	Social conscience	(PSHE Association) L6 – Pupils learn about the different groups that make up their community; what living in a community means. Year 1 – Pupils should recognise and know the value of different denominations and symbols for pounds and pence. Year 2 – Pupils should recognise and use symbols for pounds and pence.
Science	Clever money	PSHE Association L19 – Pupils learn that people's spending decisions can affect others and the environment (e.g. fair trade, buying single-use plastics, or giving to charity).
History	The British Empire	A high-quality history education should inspire pupils' curiosity to know more about the past. Teaching should equip pupils to ask perceptive questions, think critically, weigh evidence, sift arguments, and develop perspective, and judgement. Pupils should gain and deploy a historically grounded understanding of abstract terms, such as *peasantry*, *civilisation*, *empire*, and *parliament*. KS2 – Pupils should learn about a non-European society that provides contrasts with British history.
Geography	Means of exchange	KS1 Geographical skills and fieldwork – Pupils should learn to use world maps, atlases, and globes to identify the United Kingdom and its countries, as well as the countries, continents, and oceans studied at this key stage. KS2 – Pupils should extend their knowledge and understanding beyond the local area to include the United Kingdom and Europe, North and South America. They should develop their use of geographical knowledge, understanding, and skills to enhance their locational and place knowledge.
Music	Tunes about money	Year 3 and 4 – Reading, re-reading, and rehearsing poems and plays for presentation and performance give pupils opportunities to discuss language, including vocabulary, extending their interest in the meaning and origin of words. As pupils progress, they should develop a critical engagement with music, allowing them to compose, and to listen with discrimination to the best in the musical canon.

NC subject	Activity	Curriculum connections
Art and Design	Banksy piece	Purpose of study – Pupils should also know how art and design both reflect and shape our history, and contribute to the culture, creativity, and wealth of our nation. Pupils should know about great artists. KS2 – Pupils should learn about great artists, architects, and designers in history.
Design and Technology	Money bank	KS1 – Pupils should be taught to design purposeful, functional, appealing products for themselves and other users based on design criteria. KS2 – Pupils should understand and use mechanical systems in their products (for example, gears, pulleys, cams, levers, and linkages).
Computing	Cryptocurrency	Mathematics is a creative and highly interconnected discipline that has been developed over centuries, providing the solution to some of history's most intriguing problems. It is essential to everyday life; critical to science, technology, and engineering; and necessary for financial literacy and most forms of employment. The core of computing is computer science, in which pupils are taught the principles of information and computation, how digital systems work, and how to put this knowledge to use through programming.
Religious education	The prodigal son	NATRE (National Association of Teaching Religious Education) RE lessons should offer a structured and safe space during curriculum time for reflection, discussion, dialogue, and debate. Pupils should be taught to identify, investigate, and respond to questions posed and responses offered.
Physical education	Money and sport	KS1 – Pupils should be able to engage in competitive (both against self and against others) and co-operative physical activities, in a range of increasingly challenging situations. KS2 – Pupils should be taught to develop flexibility, strength, technique, control, and balance (for example, through athletics and gymnastics).
PSHE	Your money	PSHE Association curriculum L20 – Pupils are taught to recognise that people make spending decisions based on priorities, needs, and wants.
Citizenship	Children and money	Spoken language – Pupils should participate in discussions, presentations, performances, role play/improvisations, and debates.

English

Is anything impossible?

Impossible = I'm possible
Read a biography of a resilient person and study its features. Research a well-known person or interview family member who is inspirational to you and write their biography. Focus on how they have been resilient.

Is anything possible?

It couldn't be done
The famous poem 'It couldn't be done' By Edgar Albert Guest explores attitudes to new ideas or things. Explore the words in depth and re-write the poem using the words and phrases that you like from the poem with some of your own.

R.E.

Can inspirational people affect the lives of others?

The resilience of others
Consider an inspirational person, such as Jesus. Think about why this person is inspirational and the impact it can have on other people's lives and beliefs. Discuss who inspires you.

Music

Can music make us feel more resilient?

Songs about resilience
Select a song about resilience and think about the lyrics that you like. Create a poem with some of the phrases from them and add others that you have gathered from your previous work.

History

What kind of resilience have we seen in the past?

Resilience people in the past
Humans have shown resilience in many ways over the course of history. Sometimes it was purely about survival and, at other times, it was about fighting other people who invade your land. Explore an example of human resilience from the past.

Geography

Is the landscape resilient?

The Earth's resilience
In geography resilience is the ability of a community to cope with a natural hazard. Learn about natural disasters, such as a storm, and how the Earth can be resilient.

Citizenship

Is there anything that can't be done?

Be part of the solution
Boyan Slat says that "you can be part of the problem or part of the solution." People overcome problems with solutions when it is against all the odds. Find out what he did and then consider big problems that people think cannot be resolved.

Resilience

Computing

What is digital resilience?

Being safe online
Think about the words share, read, think, believe and agree. Consider whether these concepts follow each other. Discuss how we are safe online.

Science

Do all scientists need to be resilient?

Inventors and their inventions
Select an innovative person and research what they created. Think about how they were resilient. Explain what challenges they faced and overcame.

Maths

Do you need resilience to solve problems?

Pascal's triangle
Pascal's Triangle is a well-known fascinating exploration of numbers and sequences. It takes a curious and playful mind to explore it. Work through the activities to find patterns.

What makes people less resilient?

Tricky triangles
These triangles are lots of fun to solve.
Your challenge is to make each individual triangle make 13 by putting the digits 0 to 9 in each triangle. Keep going until you find the answer.

Art and design

Is there a relationship between art and resilience?

The dot
In the story called The Dot Vashti creates artwork with only dots. Read the story together and think about how Vashti does not give up and demonstrates resilience. Create your own piece of art with just dots as well.

Design and Technology

Should the things we make be resilient?

The book of changes
Choose a process of nature, such as the land being worn away, and make a flip paper book. Think about whether things we make should be permanent or not whilst creating your book.

P.E.

Can you be good at sport without being resilient?

Character analysis of sports person
Think about accomplished sports people in the news or someone you know from your own hobbies. Research and write about their character and how they have shown resilience. You could interview a person in your life about their sporting achievements.

PSHE

What does resilience look like in The Learning Pit?

The learning pit
Discuss The Learning Pit by James Nottingham. Think about the concept words - doubt, reflection and yielding. Explore what you could say to yourself to get you out of the pit. Design your own Learning Pit poster with speech bubbles.

11 Resilience

Concept stretchers **SPEC grid**

As part of a P4C enquiry, children brainstorm synonyms, phrases, connections, and examples (SPEC) in a SPEC grid, as in this example.

Synonyms	Phrases
• Determination • Persistence • Keeping going • Willpower • Strength • Backbone • Fortitude • Adaptability • Bounce-back-ability • Toughness • Hardiness • Grit • Self-confidence • Sense of purpose • Stubbornness	• Exeter City FC showed great resilience in fighting back from a losing position to win the game • He'll get over it – young people are amazingly resilient • Bindweed is incredibly resilient – I dig out the roots in my garden every year, and it just keeps on coming back! • Rubber is a resilient material – it can be pressed, bent, or stretched, and it still bounces back • She has a resilient attitude towards learning • This may take some time and effort • 'I can always improve!' (Instead of: 'This is too hard' or 'I can't make this any better'.)
Connections	Examples
• Growth mind-set • Success, reward • Failure, giving up • Belief, self-belief • Courage • Possible/impossible • Learning • Competition (winning/losing) • Passion	• The tortoise (from 'The hare and the tortoise') • Thomas Edison, inventor • Dyson, inventor • Sparsh Shah, music artist • Spencer Silver, chemist • A persistent puppy! (as in 'The new puppy' animation)

Curriculum connections

Spoken language – Pupils should be able to consider and evaluate different viewpoints, attending to and building on the contributions of others.

SPEC grids are the work of Roger Sutcliffe, Director and Programme Designer of P4C Plus and Thinking Moves A – Z at Dialogue Works, Philosophical Teaching and Learning. www.dialogueworks.co.uk

DOI: 10.4324/9780429263033-11

Concept stretchers   **Concept sorting**

Success

Using a concept line, sort these examples to show which ones would make you feel 'most' or 'least' successful.

Feel least successful	Feel most successful

1. Cut out and sort the examples below. Work in pairs or groups to encourage discussion, as appropriate.

Winning a 'lucky-dip' prize	Achieving 'expected' in your KS2 SATS Mathematics test
Receiving your netball team's most improved player award	Winning a competition
Working really hard to try to understand	Being the most popular
Learning certificate for making connections	Falling over
Having extra support in a separate group to understand fractions	Coming last at an inter-school cross-country running event
Giving up and throwing your pencil case on the floor when you didn't understand	Getting a trophy for coach's player of the year
Laughing when your mum burnt the family dinner	Knowing you were lazy
Having the goalkeeper save your attempt during a football penalty shoot-out	Refusing to forgive an older boy who was deliberately hurtful to your little sister
Not retaliating after your classmate said you pushed them in the playground (even though it was an accident) and you had to explain and miss your break	Making it halfway up a mountain
Learning to ride a bike	Losing your cool
Finding yourself in 'the Learning Pit'	Responding very badly to a negative comment
Misbehaving in a public place	Moving up a level in a computer game

2. As a group, once all examples have been assigned a position, decide whether you all agree.
   Is it possible to argue that any of these could be placed on the opposite side?
   Would it be possible to argue that <u>all</u> of these could be placed on the opposite side?

3. Ask each pair/group to think of one other great example of their own success and failure to add to the concept line discussion. (Teacher or pupils could scribe, depending on age.)

Curriculum connections

Spoken language - Pupils should be taught to understand and use the conventions for discussion and debate.

Concept stretchers   **Concept line**

Success or failure

Find or create some opposing examples, such as:

Success	Failure
You worked really hard.	You were lazy.
You had your favourite dinner.	Someone burnt the family dinner.
You won a competition.	You came second in a competition.
You scored the winning penalty in a shoot-out.	You played every match for your sports team this year but didn't win any of the trophies.
You are really popular with friends.	You did some great work – but your teacher didn't commend you.

Can you spot any assumptions?

For example:

1. Is burnt always bad? Are there different grades of burnt?
   Do 'caramelised' onions or 'chargrilled' burgers still taste good?
   Would you be more positive if it was your little brother's first attempt at cooking dinner for your family?
2. Is 'coming second' always negative or positive? Can you think of any examples?
3. Is winning more important than taking part (reliably showing up every week)?

> Is success simply a matter of opinion?

Curriculum connections

Spoken language - Pupils should be taught to understand and use the conventions for discussion and debate.

Concept stretchers Quotes to explore

Resilience quotes

Here are some quotes about resilience. Pick one that interests you to discuss as a P4C enquiry.

'It always seems impossible until it's done.' (Nelson Mandela)	'Every morning we are born again. It is what we do today that matters most.' (Buddha)
'Sometimes the smallest step in the right direction ends up being the biggest step of your life. Tiptoe if you must, but take the step.' (Naeem Callaway)	'Many of life's failures are people who did not realise how close they were to success when they gave up!' (Thomas Edison)
'It's hard to beat a person who never gives up.' (Babe Ruth)	'Keep on failing – it works!' (Dyson)
'Success is not final, failure is not fatal: It is the courage to continue that counts.' (Winston Churchill)	'I've failed over and over and over again in my life. And that is why I succeed.' (Michael Jordan)

Think about the main concept words from the quote and write them here.

When you air the quote, say why it interests you. Make notes for your discussion.

Curriculum connections

Spoken language – Pupils should be able to consider and evaluate different viewpoints, attending to and building on the contributions of others.

Concept stretchers **Question chain**

Success and resilience

Explore the relationship between success and resilience with your class. Stand up if you think 'yes'; sit down if you think 'no'.

Can you explain why or give an example to the group?

- Is hard work the same as resilience?

- Does hard work always achieve success?

- Can single events tell us whether someone is a successful or resilient person?

- Are successful people more resilient?

- Can luck help in making people resilient?

- Do you think other factors play a part in resilience?

- Can we measure resilience?

- What does resilience mean to you?

- In pairs, discuss what resilience means to you. Then write a definition.

Curriculum connections

Spoken language – Pupils should be able to consider and evaluate different viewpoints, attending to and building on the contributions of others.

Is anything impossible? **English**

Impossible = I'm possible

Study the features of a biography. Use an example model biography of someone who has shown inspirational resilience at some point in their life.

Pupils could either research well-known people or do background research at home, interviewing an inspirational family member or friend if they prefer.

Examples

Sparsh Shah — https://tedxgateway.com/portfolio/sparsh-shah/
Serena Williams — https://en.wikipedia.org/wiki/Serena_Williams
Alex Honnold — www.alexhonnold.com/

Write a biography for your chosen inspiring person in the writing style of a biography.

Name
Born (where, when, parents, etc.)
Early life
Career/life highlights
What they are doing now

Curriculum connections

The National Curriculum for England aims to write clearly, accurately, and coherently, adapting their language and style in and for a range of contexts, purposes, and audiences.

Year 2 – Pupils should be taught to develop positive attitudes towards and stamina for writing by writing narratives about personal experiences and those of others (real and fictional).

Year 5–6 Pupils should plan their writing by identifying the audience for and purpose of the writing, selecting the appropriate form and using other similar writing as models for their own.

Is anything possible? English

'It couldn't be done'

The famous poem 'It couldn't be done' by Edgar Albert Guest explores attitudes towards new ideas or things. Use these links to listen to it and read it.

Car advertisement   https://vimeo.com/77284378 (accessed 23.1.22)
Words to the poem   www.poetryfoundation.org/poems/44314/it-couldnt-be-done (accessed 23.1.22)

Re-write the poem using your own words or phrases that you like from the poem.

Practise and learn the poem by heart.

Now explore the following question in a P4C enquiry, group, or partner.

> **Are there any things that cannot be done?**

Curriculum connections

Year 3–4 Pupils should be developing their understanding and enjoyment of stories, poetry, plays and non-fiction, and learning to read silently.

Year 5–6 Pupils should maintain positive attitudes to reading and an understanding of what they read by continuing to read and discuss an increasingly wide range of fiction, poetry, plays, non-fiction, and reference books or textbooks.

Do you need resilience to solve problems?   **Mathematics**

Pascal's Triangle

Pascal's Triangle is a well-known fascinating exploration of numbers and sequences. It takes a curious and playful mind to explore it. You can find the Fibonacci sequence in it and many recurring patterns.

Keep adding the two numbers together to create a new number. Complete another ten rows.

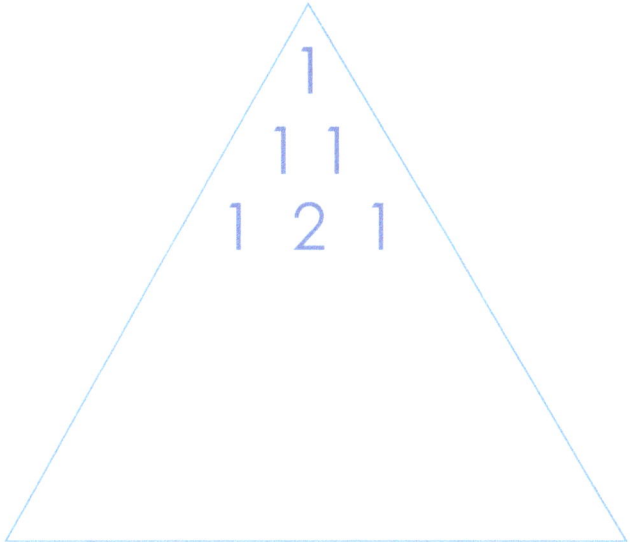

Now try adding the numbers vertically, diagonally, and horizontally.

What do you notice? Write your observations here.

For more research into its history see: www.britannica.com/science/Pascals-triangle (accessed 24/21/2021)

Curriculum connections

All pupils can solve problems by applying their mathematics to a variety of routine and non-routine problems with increasing sophistication, including breaking down problems into a series of simpler steps and persevering in seeking solutions.

What makes people less resilient? **Mathematics**

Tricky triangles

Here's a challenge for you. Solve this problem. Don't give up! Keep trying until you find the solution.

Put the digits 0 to 9 in each triangle. Your challenge is to make the numbers in each triangle add up to 13. Keep going and try and try again.

If you manage to solve that puzzle, now try it so the numbers add up to 14. Write the solution below.

Curriculum connections

All pupils can solve problems by applying their mathematics to a variety of routine and non-routine problems with increasing sophistication, including breaking down problems into a series of simpler steps and persevering in seeking solutions.

Do all scientists need to be resilient?   **Science**

Inventors and their inventions

In groups select one of the people or innovations from the list and research them. Write a couple of sentences about how they were resilient.

The Post-It Note
Research the life and work of Spencer Silver, inventor of the Post-It Note. www.post-it.com/3M/en_US/post-it/contact-us/about-us/
Stephanie Kwolek
Stephanie Kwolek invented Teflon. Kwolek was awarded the National Medal of Technology for her research on synthetic fibres. www.biography.com/news/famous-women-inventors-biography (accessed 22/01/2021)
Wonka-Vite
Read Roald Dahl's *Charlie and the Great Glass Elevator* chapter 18, where Willa Wonka's Wonka-Vite is created to make a human lose 20 years.
Charles Macintosh
Charles' invention of waterproof material led to the raincoat as we know it today. www.bbc.co.uk/bitesize/topics/zxwxvcw/articles/z763nrd
WD40
Three scientists decided to make a product that stopped rust by 'water displacement'. It took them 40 attempts to get it right, and this is where its name came from. www.wd40.com/history/

Curriculum connections

The quality and variety of language that pupils hear and speak are key factors in developing their scientific vocabulary and articulating scientific concepts clearly and precisely. Pupils might find out about people who have developed useful new materials.

KS1 – Identify and compare the suitability of a variety of everyday materials, including wood, metal, plastic, glass, brick, rock, paper, and cardboard for particular uses.

KS2 – Pupils should be taught to compare and group together everyday materials on the basis of their properties, including their hardness, solubility, transparency, conductivity (electrical and thermal), and response to magnets.

What kind of resilience have we seen in the past?   **History**

Resilient people in the past

Humans have shown resilience in many ways over the course of history. Sometimes it was purely about survival and getting through one day to the next. At other times, it was about fighting other people.

Here are several examples of human resilience. Select one and think about how they have shown the characteristics of not giving up. Think about their lifestyles.

Roman Army   www.bbc.co.uk/bitesize/topics/zwmpfg8/articles/zqbnfg8
Ancient Mayas   www.bbc.co.uk/bitesize/topics/zq6svcw/articles/zg2htv4
Ancient Greeks   www.bbc.co.uk/bitesize/topics/z87tn39
Shang Dynasty   www.bbc.co.uk/bitesize/topics/z39j2hv
Indus Civilisation   www.bbc.co.uk/bitesize/topics/zxn3r82

After you have researched one of these, write five ways they showed resilience. For example, 'They walked a long way to get water every day.'

1.
2.
3.
4.
5.

Curriculum connections

A high-quality history education will help pupils gain a coherent knowledge and understanding of Britain's past and that of the wider world. It should inspire pupils' curiosity to know more about the past. Teaching should equip pupils to ask perceptive questions.

Is the landscape resilient? Geography

The Earth's resilience

In geography resilience is the ability of a community to cope with a hazard; some communities are better prepared than others, so a hazard is less likely to become a disaster.

Can you think of natural disasters that can occur? For example, a storm. Discuss with a partner.

Coastal erosion

Think of the cliffs at the sea. The waves beat against the cliffs. What is the process of this over time? Are the cliffs resilient?

What do humans do to make the coastline resilient? Should we make the coastline more resilient? Discuss in a P4C enquiry, group or with a partner.

Curriculum connections

Ensure that pupils understand the processes that give rise to key physical and human geographical features of the world, how these are interdependent, and how they bring about spatial variation and change over time.

Should the things we make be resilient?   **Design and Technology**

The book of changes

In your design and technology lessons you design, make, and create things. Think about whether things we make should be permanent or whether, like some natural features of the natural world, things should be fallible (not permanent).

Flip book

Make a flip paper book showing the resilience and pattern of coastal erosion.

See how to make a book here:

www.youtube.com/watch?v=Un-BdBSOGKY (accessed 20/10/2021)

1. Cliffs and the waves hitting
2. Water retracting to the sea
3. Land being worn away
4. Pebbles being created

KS2 Challenge

This time, make a static book with a lever, pulley or sliding system which can show a moving part of the coastal erosion pattern – maybe the waves or the pebbles.

Draw your design below.

Curriculum connections

KS2 – Pupils should explore and use mechanisms (for example, levers, sliders, wheels, and axles), in their products.

Is there a relationship between art and resilience? Art and Design

The dot

"What can you create with just a dot?" asks author of The Dot Peter Reynolds. www.youtube.com/watch?v=CIpw7PG7m1Q (accessed 01/07/2021)

Read the story together and think about how Vashti demonstrates resilience.

What kind of art activities need a lot of resilience?

Painting		

What concept words can you think of to describe what qualities Vashti had to "keep going"? Write them here.

Self-belief			

Use pencil, charcoal, watercolours, pastels, scratched black pastel over colour, or 3D materials in different ways of making your own circle artwork. Keep on going until you achieve your favourite. Use the story as a stimulus and focus point.

Explore examples of work from different artists inspired by circles, such as Sir Terry Frost.

Some examples are:

- Wassily Kandinsky – *Circles in a Circle* (1923), *Several Circles* (1926)
- Damien Hirst – Spot painting, Quisqualic Acid, Cinchonidine (Unique), Spin paintings
- David Charles Williams – *Centred Painting: 'Skin Deep'* 2017
- Sumit Mehndiratta – *Nailed it Series No. 140, Composition No. 214*

Curriculum connections

All pupils should produce creative work, exploring their ideas and recording their experiences.

Can inspirational people affect the lives of others? Religious education

The resilience of others

What qualities do inspirational people have in common? Write some of them here.

Brave	Determined			

What impact can inspirational people have on the lives of others?

Consider one of the following people and write some notes – Nelson Mandela, Florence Nightingale, Jesus, Mother Theresa, Buddha, Thomas Edison, Winston Churchill, Anne Frank, Martin Luther King Jr., Lord Sugar, Michael Jordan, Mohammed Ali.

Who inspires you? Explain why.

Say how they impact upon you. Think about the following concepts. Can you add your own?

Behaviour	Goodness			

Curriculum connections

KS1 – Pupils learn to recognise that beliefs are expressed in a variety of ways and begin to use specialist vocabulary.

KS2 – Pupils consider the beliefs, teachings, practices, and ways of life central to religion.

Is there anything that can't be done?   **Citizenship**

The Great Pacific Garbage Patch

> "You can be part of the problem or part of the solution."
> Boyan Slat

Boyan Slat designed and founded The Ocean CleanUp when he was 18 years old. It is a machine that sits on water and sucks the plastic waste that is floating in The Great Pacific Garbage Patch down into a weir-type hole. He created it against all odds when everyone said it could not be done.

www.youtube.com/watch?v=hdZxYQmu8kE

- Which of your own goals seems impossible to achieve?

- Which really big problems in the world need solutions?

- What wonders of the world exist that seemed impossible? (Golden Gate Bridge, The Eurotunnel)

Curriculum connections

KS2 – The pupils learn about the wider world and the interdependence of communities within it. They develop their sense of social justice and moral responsibility and begin to understand that their own choices and behaviour can affect local, national, or global issues and political and social institutions.

What does resilience look like in the Learning Pit? PSHE

The Learning Pit

Present and discuss a model of the Learning Pit (James Nottingham) as the opening stimulus to your enquiry. If you haven't used the Learning Pit before, learn about it here: www.challenginglearning.com/learning-pit/

Design your own Learning Pit poster. First try with self-doubt. For example, you could try drawing a line for the pit and then do some speech bubbles with things that you say in your head.

Self-doubt

Now add speech bubbles of what you can say to pull yourself out of the pit. Try pairing up and asking your partner what else you can say to pull yourself out.

Curriculum connections

KS1 H24 – Pupils learn how to manage when finding things difficult.

KS2 H27 – Pupils learn to recognise their individuality and personal qualities.

What is digital resilience? **Computing**

Being safe online

We read opinions, statements, stories and many other things online.

Think about the words shown in the circles. Do these concepts follow each other?

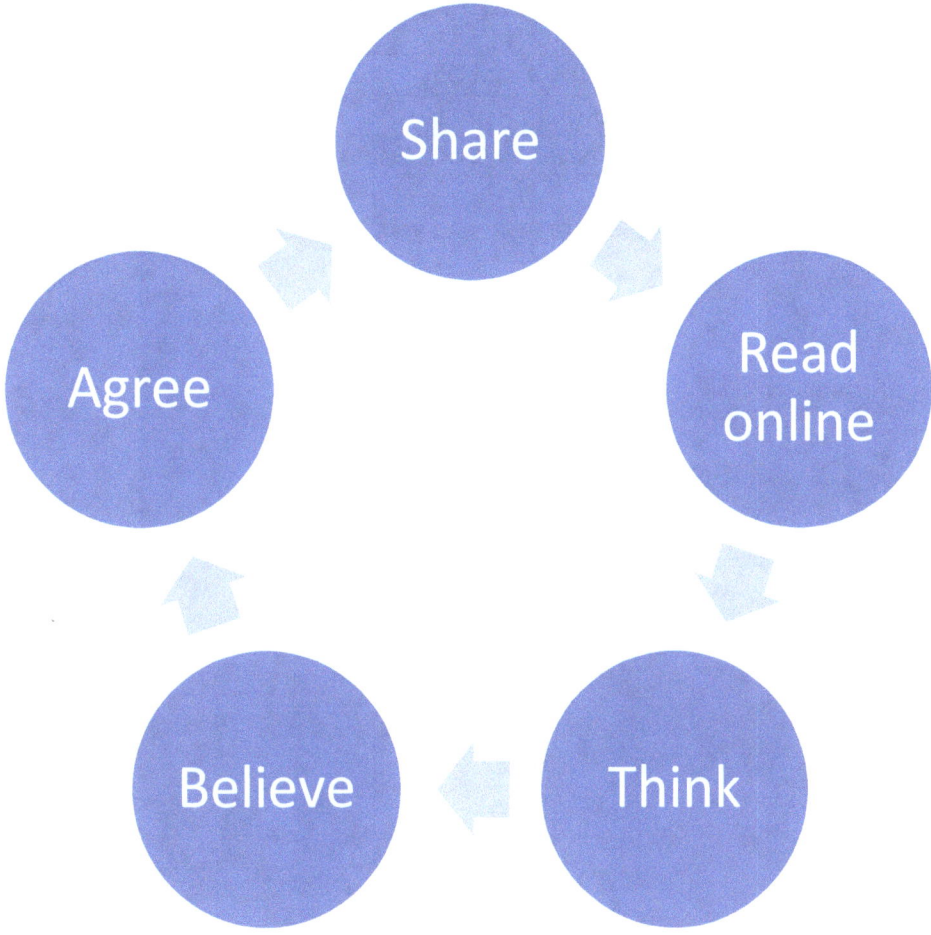

Would you change anything about the circles?

Discuss in a P4C enquiry, group or with a partner. Create your own circles and words.

Curriculum connections

KS1 L9 – Pupils know that not all information seen online is true.

KS2 L11 – Pupils can recognise ways in which the internet and social media can be used both positively and negatively.

KS2 L12 – Pupils know how to assess the reliability of sources of information online and how to make safe, reliable choices from search results.

Can music be motivational and make us feel more resilient? **Music**

Songs about resilience

Select and think about one of the following songs. What lyrics do you like?

"The only way is up" by Jazz
"Fight song" by Rachel Platten
"Tubthumping" by Chumbawumba
"Rise up" by Andra Day
"Roar" by Katy Perry
"I will survive" by Gloria Gainer

Create a poem with some of the phrases from them and your recent work.

Curriculum connections

A high-quality music education should engage and inspire pupils to develop a love of music and their talent as musicians, and so increase their self-confidence, creativity, and sense of achievement.

Can you be good at sport without being resilient? Physical education

Character analysis of a sports person

Think about good sports people in the news or someone you know from your own hobbies. Research and write about their character and how they have shown resilience. You could interview a person in your life about their sporting life. For example, you may know someone who has run a marathon.

What sayings do they use to show that they have had to be resilient?

This is a link to how to be prepared for a marathon. Have a read and select the advice that you think is really helpful. www.greatrun.org/training/marathon-advice-the-dos-and-donts/

Think about whether you need to be resilient to be a good at sport. Discuss in P4C enquiry, group, or with a partner.

Curriculum connections

A high-quality physical education curriculum inspires all pupils to succeed and excel in competitive sport and other physically demanding activities.

Inspirational people

Greta Thunberg

Thunberg is a climate change activist, and from a young age has encouraged other young people to demonstrate about change needed to stop climate change. She has been the subject of derision from world leaders, but she continues to be determined.

www.childrenandnature.org/resources/earth-day-young-leaders-advocate-for-change/ (accessed 25/10/2021)

Nelson Mandela

Mandela was an anti-apartheid revolutionary who became South Africa's first black president in 1994. He was imprisoned for 27 years, as he had planned to overthrow the government which continued apartheid.

https://en.wikipedia.org/wiki/Nelson_Mandela (accessed 25/10/2021)

Women in WWII

During WWII many women took on jobs which were new to them, such as producing munitions or building ships and aeroplanes. They had to overcome the attitude at the time that they were not capable of doing men's work. Read about their stories here:

www.striking-women.org/module/women-and-work/world-war-ii-1939-1945 (accessed 25/10/2021)

Queen Elizabeth II

Her majesty Queen Elizabeth has reigned longer than any other monarch in British history. She has remained composed and resilient in trying times, such as war, financial recessions, and pandemics. She has many public engagements to fulfil and is under scrutiny each time.

www.royal.uk/her-majesty-the-queen (accessed 25/10/2021)

Further resources

"What is resilience?" video
This video explains what resilience is and how it is linked to our emotions. It explains how to recognise and master emotions when we are dealing with challenges, such as loss, bullying, schoolwork.

www.youtube.com/watch?v=zeu9X88g8DE (accessed 25/10/2021)

Mathematical Resilience Day 2018
Use the following link to find resources that were used during the Developing Mathematical Resilience Day held at the Centre for Mathematical Sciences.

https://nrich.maths.org/resilience2018

Anna Freud resources for resilience
The National Centre for Children and Families has produced a Coronavirus toolkit, including resources for building resilience. There are lots of worksheets with guidance about how to build resilience for children.

www.mentallyhealthyschools.org.uk/media/2047/coronavirus-toolkit-6-resilience.pdf

Oxfam Education Resources
Learn about climate resilience and how climate change is affecting people.

https://oxfamilibrary.openrepository.com/handle/10546/620557/browse?type=keyword&value=climate+resilience

Resilience activities
Here are some good worksheets and examples to use.

www.justonenorfolk.nhs.uk/emotional-health/children-young-peoples-emotional-health/emotional-health-activities/resilience-activities (accessed 25/10/2021)

The Book Corner

The proudest blue by Ibtihaj Muhammad
This story follows the experience of a young girl who on her first day of school finds that not everyone sees her hijab as beautiful. She finds new ways to be strong when she faces hurtful words and confusing behaviour. This is a story of universal emotions and powerful bonds with siblings. Suitable for KS2.

The hare and the tortoise
This is a well-known traditional British story. A hare brags to the tortoise that he will win a race as he is faster, but as he is so confident takes time for a nap. This allows the steady and slow tortoise to win. Suitable for KS1.

Wonder by R. J. Palacio
August is born with facial disfigurements and wants to hide his face from the world. He learns that he must embrace how he looks and realise that his talents and character are not defined by his looks. August overcomes bullying and learns how to manage new friendships. Suitable for KS2.

The children carried on by Tannagh Pfotenhauer
This book is an ode to children and written about children for children about what they have faced during the pandemic. Suitable for KS1.

NC subject	Activity	Curriculum connections
English	Impossible = I'm possible	Year 2 – Pupils should be taught to develop positive attitudes towards and stamina for writing by writing narratives about personal experiences and those of others (real and fictional). Year 5–6 Pupils should plan their writing by identifying the audience for and purpose of the writing, selecting the appropriate form and using other similar writing as models for their own.
English	'It couldn't be done'	Year 3–4 Pupils should be developing their understanding and enjoyment of stories, poetry, plays, and non-fiction and learning to read silently. Year 5–6 Pupils should maintain positive attitudes toward reading and an understanding of what they read by continuing to read and discuss an increasingly wide range of fiction, poetry, plays, non-fiction, and reference books or textbooks.
Maths	Pascal's Triangle	All pupils can solve problems by applying their mathematics to a variety of routine and non-routine problems with increasing sophistication, including breaking down problems into a series of simpler steps and persevering in seeking solutions.
Maths	Tricky triangles	All pupils can solve problems by applying their mathematics to a variety of routine and non-routine problems with increasing sophistication, including breaking down problems into a series of simpler steps and persevering in seeking solutions.
Science	Inventors and their inventions	Pupils might find out about people who have developed useful new materials. KS1 – Identify and compare the suitability of a variety of everyday materials, including wood, metal, plastic, glass, brick, rock, paper, and cardboard for particular uses. KS2 – Pupils should be taught to compare and group together everyday materials on the basis of their properties, including their hardness, solubility, transparency, conductivity (electrical and thermal), and response to magnets.
History	Resilient people in the past	A high-quality history education will help pupils gain a coherent knowledge and understanding of Britain's past and that of the wider world. It should inspire pupils' curiosity to know more about the past. Teaching should equip pupils to ask perceptive questions.
Geography	The Earth's resilience	Ensure that pupils understand the processes that give rise to key physical and human geographical features of the world, how these are interdependent and how they bring about spatial variation and change over time are competent in the geographical.
Music	Songs about resilience	A high-quality music education should engage and inspire pupils to develop a love of music and their talent as musicians, and so increase their self-confidence, creativity, and sense of achievement.
Art and Design	The dot	All pupils should produce creative work, exploring their ideas and recording their experiences.

NC subject	Activity	Curriculum connections
Design and Technology	The book of changes	KS2 – Pupils should explore and use mechanisms (for example, levers, sliders, wheels, and axles), in their products.
Computing	Being safe online	PSHE Association curriculum KS1 L9 – Pupils know that not all information seen online is true. KS2 L11 – Pupils can recognise ways in which the internet and social media can be used both positively and negatively. KS2 L12 – Pupils know how to assess the reliability of sources of information online; and how to make safe, reliable choices from search results.
Religious education	The resilience of others	KS1 – Pupils learn to recognise that beliefs are expressed in a variety of ways and begin to use specialist vocabulary. KS2 – Pupils consider the beliefs, teachings, practices, and ways of life central to religion.
Physical education	Character analysis of sports person	A high-quality physical education curriculum inspires all pupils to succeed and excel in competitive sport and other physically demanding activities.
PSHE	The Learning Pit	KS1 H24 – Pupils learn how to manage when finding things difficult. KS2 H27 – Pupils learn to recognise their individuality and personal qualities.
Citizenship	Be part of the solution	Citizenship KS2 – The pupils learn about the wider world and the interdependence of communities within it. They develop their sense of social justice and moral responsibility and begin to understand that their own choices and behaviour can affect local, national, or global issues and political and social institutions.

English

> Do we experience time the same?

Time is a..
Bloom's poem has several metaphors to describe what time is like. Think about what time is like for you. Create your own poem which uses other things to compare time to.

Maths

> Should we measure time?

The measure of time
The Mondawa tribe do not have a word for time or its measure. Imagine what it would be like if we did not have a measure of time in our society. Consider the pros and cons of this.

R.E.

> Does infinity exist?

God is truly infinite
In the Christian sacred book, The Bible, it says that 'God truly is infinite' (1 Psalms 139:7-10). The idea of infinity is hard to hold in the mind. Explore what is infinite and what is finite.

Music

> Does time have a beginning?

Singing about time
Consider the lyrics to the songs about time and select some phrases. Create your own backing track and with your chosen phrases rap over the music to make a song about time.

History

> How do we experience time?

Important events in time
Think about other ways to measure time, such as using important events. Consider the most important events in your life and put on a time line. Argue why they should be there.

Computing

> Will time always stay the same?

Create your own timer
Using Scratch, a free visual programming language, create your own timer. Plan what you will use it for.

Time

Science

Does time only exist in the mind?

Time before clocks
Humans have been measuring time for thousands of years. Find out what we used before mechanical watches. Discuss the things that stay constant in our lives to use as a measure. Think about where time exists.

Geography

Does anything stay the same in time?

How Earth has changed over time
Select two features of The Earth and say how they are different and how they are the same. Then choose some geographical features and think about how they are changed over time.

Art

Is your memory linked to time?

Salvador Dali's time
Explore Salvador Dali's image called The Persistence of Memory. Think about how he is presenting time and memory. Create an image that portrays your thoughts about time.

Design and Technology

Does time go on forever?

A time-measurer
Explore how a sand timer, a sundial or the hour glass works. Find out who created them and try making your own.

PSHE

Can you plan your future?

Children are the future
Discuss the selected paragraph from Korczak. Think about the key concept words here that need some more understanding. Make some goals for yourself that are achievable soon.

Citizenship

How should we spend our time?

Leisure time
The UN Convention on the right of a Child says in Article 31 that every child has the right to relax, play and take part in a wide range of cultural and artistic activities. Explore this statement together. Make a list in a Charter of Time of how you want to spend your time.

P.E.

Could you always win if you had more time?

Using a timer
Time yourself doing an activity then try and beat your time. Or, as a school you may want to check out your fitness with a beep test. Think about how using a timer can make you fitter.

12 Time

Concept stretchers   **SPEC grids**

As part of a P4C enquiry, children brainstorm synonyms, phrases, connections, and examples (SPEC) in a SPEC grid, as in these examples.

Time

Synonyms	Phrases
• While • Period • Spell • Stretch • Stage • Interval • Stint • Timescale	• Waste your time wisely • You need to make time • A stitch in time saves nine • Time is money • You need to invest time in it • You did the crime; you do the time • Time and tide wait for no man • Just in the nick of time
Connections	**Example**
• Watches/clocks • Late for school/early • Pastimes/hobbies • Digital/analogue • Being told to wait • Boredom • Turn-taking	• Age • DOB • Dates • Seconds, minutes, hours • Months, weeks, days • Chinese zodiac year • Celebration days

Infinity

Synonyms	Phrases
• Forever/Ever • Everlasting/Always • Continuously/Continually • Endless/Limitless • Eternity/Limitlessness • Persistently • Googol	• I could go on forever • I will love you forever • Time waits for no man • To infinity and beyond • God's wisdom exceeds infinity • Hold infinity in the palm of your hand • I know there is infinity beyond ourselves
Connections	**Examples**
• Love • Spirit • Life • Evolution • Space-time continuum • Big Bang theory • Russian dolls	• Love for family members • Role model relationships • Feelings for friends • Mirror reflection • Theory of Relativity/Butterfly Effect theory • Ever-decreasing circles

DOI: 10.4324/9780429263033-12

Curriculum connections

Years 1–6 Spoken language – Pupils should be able to articulate and justify answers, arguments, and opinions.

SPEC grids are the work of Roger Sutcliffe, Director and Programme Designer of P4C Plus and Thinking Moves A – Z at Dialogue Works, Philosophical Teaching and Learning. www.dialogueworks.co.uk

Concept stretchers   **Concept sorting**

Using a concept line or Venn diagram rings, pupils sort examples into the categories of:

Endless	Ends

Cut out the examples. Work in pairs or groups to encourage discussion, as appropriate.

Love	Human Spirit
Life	School holidays
Doing a cross country	Christmas Day
Birthday party	Having fun
Weather	Tides
Moon cycles	The earth turning
Night and day	Hope
Waiting	Sadness
Friendship	Sorrow
Regret	Bad
Pain	Loss

Curriculum connections

Spoken language - Pupils should be taught to understand and use the conventions for discussion and debate.

168 *Time*

Concept stretchers **Concept web**

In pairs link the concepts. Give your reasons as you draw the lines.

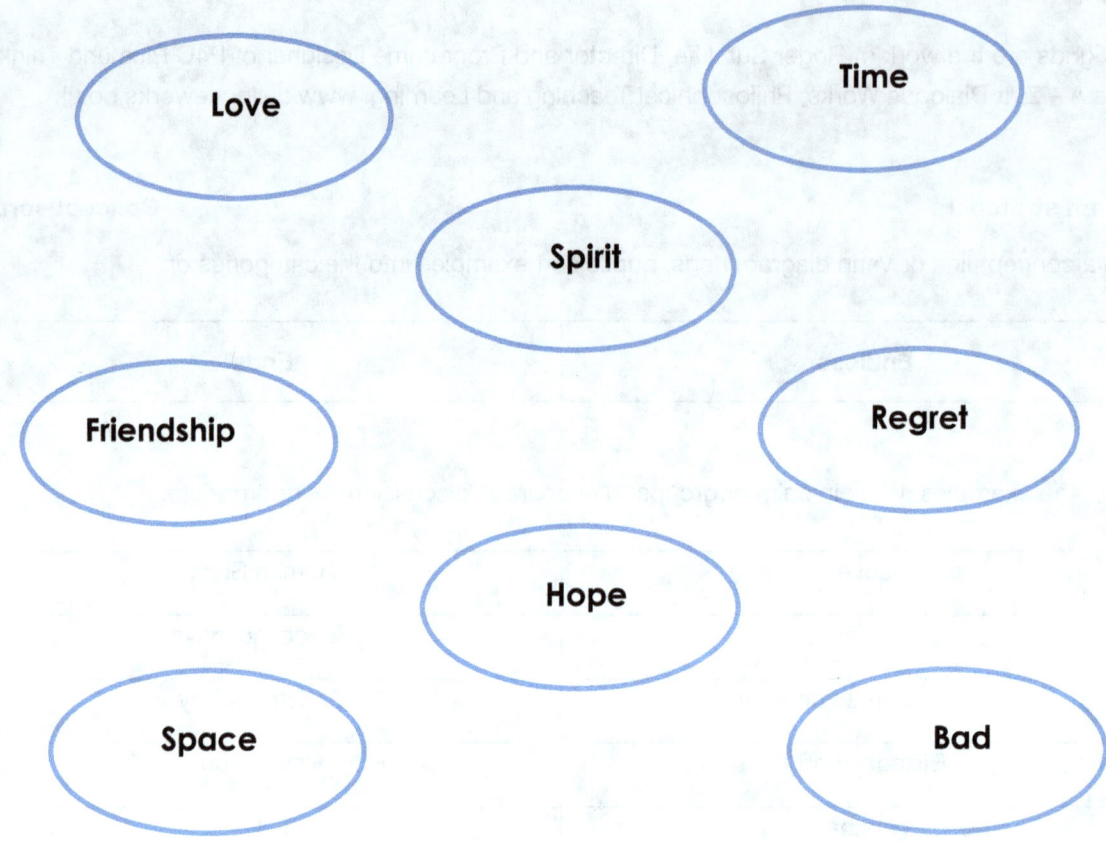

Select two that interest you. Explain the links that you have made and why.

Curriculum connections

Spoken language – Pupils should be taught to consider and evaluate different viewpoints, attending to and building on the contributions of others.

Quotes to explore   **P4C enquiry**

In pairs, select one of these quotes.

> 'Lost time is never found again.' – Anonymous

> 'If you love life, don't waste time,
> for time is what life is made up of.' – Bruce Lee

> 'Time waits for no man.' – Folklore

> 'We will be friends forever, won't we, Pooh?'
> asked Piglet.
> 'Even longer', Pooh answered.

Give your thoughts about why you have selected it. Try to gain the interest of the listener by giving some interesting thoughts about concept words. For example, for the first quote you could talk about the concept of "lost" time. Where does it go? Is *lost* the same for physical objects as a something we cannot touch, like time?

Select one of the quotes with a class vote and use in a P4C enquiry.

Curriculum connections

Spoken language – Pupils should be able to gain and monitor the interest of the listener.

Do we experience time the same? English

Time is a . . .

Read the poem by Valeria Bloom here:

https://childrens.poetryarchive.org/poem/time/.

Bloom uses several metaphors to describe what time is like, such as 'Time's a bird, which leaves its footprints'.

Think about what time is like for you. Here are some concepts that you might want to use, but write your own as well. Write a note next to the circle to say why each concept is like time. Discuss your reasons with a partner.

Create your own poem which compares time to other things.

Time's a busy bee that never stops,
Time's a flea that is impossible to catch and hold . . .

Curriculum connections

Year 2 – Pupils consider what they are going to write before beginning by planning or saying out loud what they are going to write about.

Year 3 – Pupils should be able to consider what they are going to write before discussing and recording ideas.

KS2 – Pupils learn to evaluate and edit by assessing the effectiveness of their own and others' writing.

Should we measure time? **Mathematics**

The measure of time

The Mondawa tribe don't have a word for time or its measure, such as *month* or *year*. Read this BBC article about them.

www.bbc.co.uk/news/science-environment-13452711 (accessed 19/05/2020)

Explore the words that we use to measure time and write below.

Imagine what it would be like if we didn't have a measure of time in our society. Write a list of all the good things about this and all the bad things.

Good	Bad

Select one side of the argument and present your ideas to your friends.

Curriculum connections

Year 1 – Pupils can sequence events in chronological order using language (for example, *before* and *after*, *next*, *first*, *today*, *yesterday*, *tomorrow*, *morning*, *afternoon*, and *evening*).

Year 2 – Pupils can compare and sequence intervals of time.

Does time only exist in the mind? Science

Time before clocks

Humans have been measuring time for thousands of years, but the modern watch has only been in existence since the 1570s, at a rough guess. The Babylonians and Egyptians created the 24-hour clock. Learn more about this here:

www.bbc.co.uk/bitesize/clips/zwj2hyc (accessed 29/07/2021)

Think about the things that stay constant in our lives, such as the rotation of the earth, to use as a measure. Write them here. Think about where time exists.

Sunrise			

Curriculum connections

Pupils should develop understanding of the nature, processes, and methods of science through different types of scientific enquiries that help them to answer scientific questions about the world around them.

Does time go on forever?   **Design and Technology**

A time-measurer

Explore how people measured time before clocks were invented

The sand timer (or the hourglass) was invented by a monk. Explore how this works. Here's how to make your own:

www.craftcorners.com/how-to-make-your-own-sand-timer/ (accessed 29/07/2021)

See how long it takes for the sand to travel between the two bottles. How can you make it last longer or shorter?

The Egyptians used a sundial. Think about how sundials work and make one.

How to make a sundial:

www.bbc.co.uk/bitesize/clips/z6fnvcw (accessed 29/07/2021)

Will this work forever?

> Write here what went well and what you need to change to make it better.

Curriculum connections

Through a variety of creative and practical activities, pupils should be taught the knowledge, understanding, and skills needed to engage in an iterative process of designing and making.

How do we experience time?　　　　　　　　　　　　　　　　　　　　　　　　　　　　**History**

Important events in time

A philosopher called Immanuel Kant argued that we do not experience time itself, but through other things, such as a clock.

If we used important events to measure time, which ones would you argue are the most important to be used on a timeline? Think of some of your own.

Invention of a calculator	First phone call
Extinction of dinosaurs	Death of a glacier
Family members' birthdays	Loss of loved ones
Famous people doing things	Death of Jesus
Death of an important person	

Can you remember any significant events in your local area? Place them on a line from least to most important.

Say which event was the most important to you and why.

Curriculum connections

KS1 – Pupils should be taught significant historical events, people, and places in their own locality.

KS2 – Pupils should continue to develop a chronologically secure knowledge and understanding of British, local, and world history, establishing clear narratives within and across the periods they study.

Does anything stay the same in time?   **Geography**

How the Earth has changed over time

Here are some features of the earth. Select two and say how they are different and how they are the same. For example, oceans and rivers both contain water, but one is fresh water, and the other is salt water.

Mountain	Ocean	River	Crater	Forest
Moor	Valley	Seabed	Lake	Desert

Place the two you have selected into the circles. Think about how they overlap.

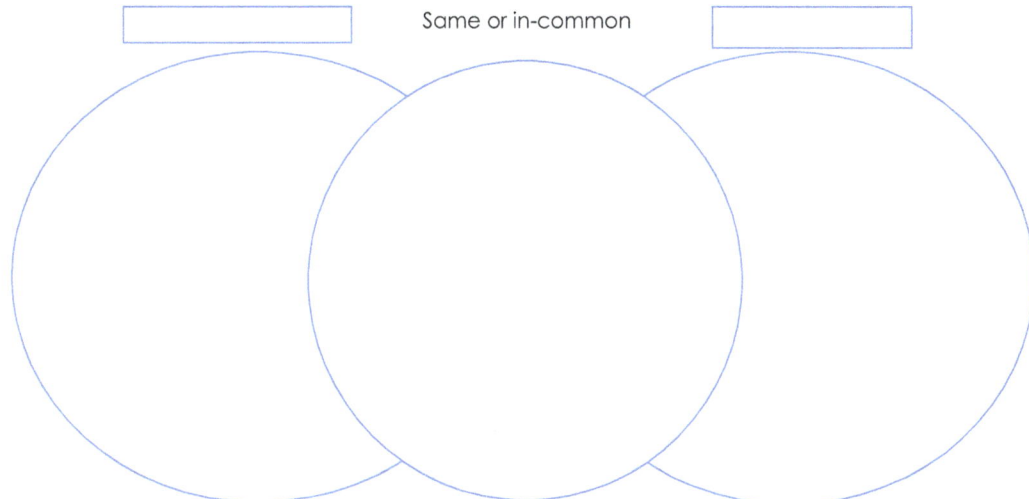

Now select one of these geographical features and think about how it changes over time. Think about what questions you need to ask, such as: Does it get taller? or Does it get deeper?

These words may help with some of the questions you need to ask.

Erosion	Rain	Usage	Global warming	Human acts

Write any questions you have here. You do not need to know the answers to these questions.

Once you have thought of some questions, research the answers with a good, reliable resource.

Curriculum connections

Geographical knowledge, understanding, and skills provide the frameworks and approaches that explain how the earth's features at different scales are shaped, interconnected, and change over time.

Does time have a beginning?   **Music**

Singing about time

Explore the words to these songs and think about how they explore time.

- "Yesterday" by The Beatles
- "Time" (2011 remastered) by Pink Floyd
- "Step back in time" by Kylie Minogue
- "If I could turn back time" by Cher
- "When I'm sixty-four" by The Beetles
- "In the year 2525" by Zager and Evans

These songs explore the future, like "In the year 2525", or the past, like "Yesterday". If you could choose between going forward in time or back in time, which would you choose?

Write a few sentences about going forward in time or back in time.

_____

_____

_____

_____

Now listen to the sound of clocks ticking. Can you make a piece of music that creates and uses tick-tock sounds? If not, create your own backing track that has the sense of clocks ticking, for example voice sounds or blocks.

Now say, sing, or rap the sentences you've written over the music and record.

Curriculum connections

Music – The national curriculum for music aims to ensure that all pupils perform, listen to, review, and evaluate music across a range of historical periods, genres, styles, and traditions, including the works of the great composers and musicians.

Is your memory linked to time? Art

Salvador Dali's time

Explore Salvador Dali's *The Persistence of Memory*.

https://en.wikipedia.org/wiki/The_Persistence_of_Memory (accessed 23/07/2021)

> Talk to a partner. What do you think this picture is about? Write some thoughts here.

P4C enquiry

Using your own question or "Is you memory linked to time?" explore the idea that your memory and time are linked in some way. Make notes below.

Curriculum connections

Pupils should know about great artists, craft makers and designers, and should understand the historical and cultural development of their art forms.

How should we spend our time? **Citizenship**

Leisure time

The UN Convention on the Right of a Child says in Article 31 that every child has the right to relax, play, and take part in a wide range of cultural and artistic activities. Explore this statement together.

www.unicef.org.uk/what-we-do/un-convention-child-rights/ (accessed 16/09/2020)

Your charter of time

Make a charter of time, listing all the activities you would like to do with your time.

How do you want to spend it? Think about playing, learning, thinking, talking, etc.

<u>Charter of time</u>

Work in pairs or groups to gather ideas.
Now think about which one is the most important to you. Number them, with "1" being the most important.

Curriculum connections

KS1 H17 – Pupils learn about things that help people feel good (e.g. playing outside, doing things they enjoy, spending time with family, getting enough sleep).

KS2 L2 – Pupils learn to recognise there are human rights that are there to protect everyone.

KS2 H16 – Pupils learn about strategies and behaviours that support mental health – including how good quality sleep, physical exercise/time outdoors, being involved in community groups, doing things for others, clubs, and activities, hobbies, and spending time with family and friends can support mental health and wellbeing.

Does infinity exist? RE

God is truly infinite

In the Christian sacred book, the Bible, it says that 'God truly is infinite' (Psalm 139:7–10).

The idea of "infinity" is hard to hold in the mind. Let's start by thinking about things that are **finite** – this means that they have a beginning and an ending. See if you can think of some things, and list them here.

A fish				

Now look at these words and think about whether or not they are **infinite** – this means they go on forever. Pick one and say why you think it may be infinite.

Money	Time	Love	Friendship	Stone
Sunrise	Galaxy	Starlight	Sunlight	Stream

> Write a sentence about one and say why you think that it is infinite.

There is an idea in philosophy called Infinite Regress that means something must come from something. However, what reasons are we given that tell us God is infinite?

Talk together in a pair/group/philosophy circle and see what you can think of. Write some here.

Curriculum connections

Religious education contributes dynamically to children and young people's education in schools by provoking challenging questions about meaning and purpose in life, beliefs about God, ultimate reality, issues of right and wrong, and what it means to be human.

Will time always stay the same?   **Computing**

Create your own timer

Using Scratch, a free visual programming language, create your own timer.

First, think about which game you would like to create a timer for. For example, if you like playing draughts and don't like how long a partner can take, you could create a timer for a 60-second timer for only taking this long to do your move as your own new rule.

Game	Timer (indicate seconds or minutes)

https://junilearning.com/blog/coding-projects/how-to-make-scratch-timer/ (accessed 27/09/2021)

Curriculum connections

The core of computing is computer science, in which pupils are taught the principles of information and computation, how digital systems work, and how to put this knowledge to use through programming.

Could you always win if you had more time? **Physical education**

Using a timer

Think of a way to time yourself doing an activity. Choose one of your favourite movements, such as bouncing a basketball.

See how many you can do whilst timed. Then try and beat your time to become quicker.

Activity	Time	Number of movements

Or, as a school, you may want to check out your fitness with a beep test:

www.youtube.com/watch?v=IroAhVO83iI (accessed 27/9/2021)

Curriculum connections

KS1 – Pupils should be able to engage in competitive (both against self and against others) and co-operative physical activities, in a range of increasingly challenging situations.

KS2 – Pupils should be taught to compare their performances with previous ones and demonstrate improvement to achieve their personal best.

Can you plan your future? PSHE

Children are the future

Children, let your dreams and aspirations
Be proud
Set your sights high
Try to win glory
Something will always come out of it
A Voice for the Child by NSPCC, words of Janusz Korczak

Discuss these words from Korczak. Think about the key concept words here that need more understanding.

| Glory | High | Aspirations | Win |

In time, you are going to decide your future and what you would like to do with all the time that you have, be it work or leisure (play) time.

What do you think you would like to do?

> Think about what you like doing now. It can be many things.

> Select one thing from the list.
>
> Write down one achievement you would like to do by the end of the week.
>
> Now write one you'd like to do in a month's time.
>
> Try one for a year's time.

It is good to make plans and set goals. You can take small steps towards a goal, and it is easier when you take small steps and don't think of it as a big thing.

Curriculum connections

KS1 L14 – Pupils learn that everyone has different strengths.

KS2 L25 – Pupils learn to recognise positive things about themselves and their achievements; set goals to help achieve personal outcomes.

Inspirational people

Professor Brian Cox

Professor Brian Cox is an English physicist who had been awarded the Kelvin Prize (2010), Michael Faraday Prize (2012) and the University Research Fellow (2005).

Cox explains how time can only go in a line in some really interesting videos:

www.bbc.co.uk/programmes/p00wv834v (accessed 08/08/2021)

Timothy Berners-Lee

Timothy Berners-Lee is a British computer scientist, knighted by the Queen Elizabeth II for his pioneering work. He is especially famous for his proposal to share information by using the technology of *hypertext*, the cornerstone of the World Wide Web, which has sped up the time taken to exchange information and knowledge. Berners-Lee also made the world's first website in 1991.

Alan Guth

An American theoretical physicist and cosmologist, Guth developed the theory of *cosmic inflation*. Winner of the Fundamental Physics Prize and the Kavli Prize, Guth came up with ground-breaking ideas in inflationary theory, discovering why the cosmos is as large as it is.

Stephen Hawking

Stephen William Hawking CH CBE FRS FRSA was an English theoretical physicist, cosmologist, and author. He wrote A brief History of Time.

Further resources

Easy read time teacher
This website has lots of resources that are free to help you teach children to read the time.

www.easyreadtimeteacher.com/free-resources/ (accessed 04/11/2021)

Teaching ideas
There are plenty of downloadable sheets for teaching time to children.

www.teachingideas.co.uk/subjects/time (accessed 04/11/2021)

Teaching packs
This website has some videos about time with some book recommendations.

www.teachingpacks.co.uk/guides/time/ (accessed 04/11/2021)

The Complete Philosophy Files by Stephen Law
This book is full of questions about life and has imaginative ways of exploring them. File 13 - Is time travel possible? investigates a conversation between Kobir and Carol after watching a TV show called The Time Commandos.

ISBN 978-4440-0334-5

The Book Corner

How to live forever by Colin Thompson
This story dives deep into the concept of living forever and explores the problems with living forever. Suitable for KS1/2.

Tom's midnight garden by Philippa Pearce
Tom can travel through time using a mistiming grandfather clock. He travels back in time to be in the same garden of his house to meet a girl called Hatty. Suitable for upper KS2.

The Gruffalo by Julia Donaldson
This book is good for time exploration with younger children. The reader gets taken on a wild rumpus to meet the Gruffalo. Suitable for KS1.

The 1,000-year-old boy by Ross Welford
Alfie is 1,000 years old and can remember the last Viking invasion. Unlike other people who want to learn to live forever, he wants to stop but must learn to live a modern life. Suitable for upper KS2.

NC subject	Activity	Curriculum connections
English	Time is a …	Year 2 – Pupils consider what they are going to write before beginning by planning or saying out loud what they are going to write about. Year 3 – Pupils should be able to consider what they are going to write before by discussing and recording ideas. KS2 – Pupils learn to evaluate and edit by assessing the effectiveness of their own and others' writing.
Maths	The measure of time	Year 1 – Pupils can sequence events in chronological order using language (for example, *before* and *after*, *next*, *first*, *today*, *yesterday*, *tomorrow*, *morning*, *afternoon*, and *evening*). Year 2 – Pupils can compare and sequence intervals of time.
Science	Time before clocks	Pupils should develop understanding of the nature, processes, and methods of science through different types of scientific enquiries that help them to answer scientific questions about the world around them.
History	Important events in time	KS1 – Pupils should be taught significant historical events, people, and places in their own locality. KS2 – Pupils should continue to develop a chronologically secure knowledge and understanding of British, local, and world history, establishing clear narratives within and across the periods they study.
Geography	How the Earth has changed over time	Geographical knowledge, understanding, and skills provide the frameworks and approaches that explain how the earth's features at different scales are shaped, interconnected, and change over time.
Music	Singing about time	Music – The national curriculum for music aims to ensure that all pupils perform, listen to, review, and evaluate music across a range of historical periods, genres, styles, and traditions, including the works of the great composers and musicians.
Art and Design	Salvador Dali's time	Pupils should know about great artists, craft makers, and designers and understand the historical and cultural development of their art forms.
Design and Technology	A time-measurer	Through a variety of creative and practical activities, pupils should be taught the knowledge, understanding, and skills needed to engage in an iterative process of designing and making.
Computing	Create your own timer	The core of computing is computer science, in which pupils are taught the principles of information and computation, how digital systems work, and how to put this knowledge to use through programming.
Religious education	God is truly infinite.	Religious education contributes dynamically to children and young people's education in schools by provoking challenging questions about meaning and purpose in life, beliefs about God, ultimate reality, issues of right and wrong, and what it means to be human. Devon and Torbay Agreed Syllabus 2019
Physical education	Using a timer	KS1 – Pupils should be able to engage in competitive (both against self and against others) and co-operative physical activities, in a range of increasingly challenging situations. KS2 – Pupils should be taught to compare their performances with previous ones and demonstrate improvement to achieve their personal best.

NC subject	Activity	Curriculum connections
PSHE	**Children are the future**	KS1 L14 – Pupils learn that everyone has different strengths. KS2 L25 – Pupils learn to recognise positive things about themselves and their achievements; set goals to help achieve personal outcomes. PSHE Association Curriculum
Citizenship	**Leisure time**	KS1 H17 – Pupils learn about things that help people feel good (e.g. playing outside, doing things they enjoy, spending time with family, getting enough sleep). KS2 L2 – Pupils learn to recognise there are human rights that are there to protect everyone. KS2 H16 – Pupils learn about strategies and behaviours that support mental health – including how good quality sleep, physical exercise/time outdoors, being involved in community groups, doing things for others, clubs, and activities, hobbies, and spending time with family and friends can support mental health and wellbeing. PSHE Association Curriculum

War and peace

English

Should age matter in war?

Impossible decisions
Read Erika's Story by Ruth Vander Zee and Roberto Innocenti. Reflect upon the story and your thoughts using The Four Sharings by Aidan Chambers. Think about the Who makes a war? situation of war and how people have to make difficult decisions.

Can we achieve peace one day?

Shaping peace together
The United Nations theme for 2020 was Shaping Peace Together. Think about what you would call the next theme for the UN International Day of Peace. Justify why you have chosen it.

R.E.

Is it better to be peaceful than start conflict?

Thou shalt not kill
This is one of the Ten Commands from The Book of Exodus in The Bible. Consider if there are any scenarios where you believe that it is okay. Think of some examples and discuss with others.

Music

What is war good for?

Songs of peace
Think about the words in the songs about war. Capture some of the phrases and words that are meaningful to you. Write and discuss questions that the lyrics create in your mind.

History

Who makes a war?

Leaders and tyrants
Create a Venn diagram and explore whether characteristics of love and peace have commonalities. Explore some well-known people from history and think about where you would place them.

Maths

Can conflict be good?

Co-ordinates
Play battleships to explore how coordinates help you understand position. Whilst playing the game think about the words or phrases that come into your mind.

Computing

Should secret codes be decoded by others?

Codebreakers
During wars people need to communicate with secret codes so that the enemy does not listen to what they are planning. Find out about the mathematicians and computer scientists who were cracking the enemy's secret code during WWII.

Science

Is human behaviour always predictable?

Military science
Learn about military science and how projectiles are used in war. The science of projectiles is very important in sport and war. Create your own projectile and plan a science experiment to see which one travels the furthest.

P.E.

Is war all about fighting?

Projectiles and yoga
Some people want to disagree peacefully and do not think war is the only way to achieve what you want. Yoga promotes peace and patience, and in contrast many sports create conflict to win with a projectile. Explore both ways to keep fit.

Citizenship

Do we have to make impossible decisions in war?

Children in war
The UN Convention on the Rights of the Child says in Article 38 that governments must not allow children under the age of fifteen to take part in war or join the armed forces. Explore this article in depth.

Geography

Is war about geography?

Where wars have happened
World War II was the largest war and in which the most people died. Find out which countries were involved and affected by it. Investigate some other significant wars that changed the geography of a country.

Art and design

Should we always forgive?

Emoji story
We use emojis and pictograms to express ourselves in text messages. Write a story of about war using them.

Design and Technology

Can all codes be decoded?

The Caesar cipher
Learn about how to decipher a code and how to encipher a code. Create a wheel to help you create a displacement code. Decode some of your friend's codes.

PSHE

Is peace always possible?

The Nobel Peace Prize 2019
Learn about The Nobel Peace Prize 2019 and some people who have been awarded this prize. Find the people who have been awarded it for creating peace.

13 War and peace

Concept stretchers   **SPEC grids**

As part of a P4C enquiry, children brainstorm synonyms, phrases, connections, and examples (SPEC) in a SPEC grid, as in these examples.

War

Synonyms	Phrases
• Conflict • Fight • Battle • Combat • Warfare • Confrontation • Hostilities	• One for all and all for one! • United we stand, divided we fall. • Fight the good fight. • At loggerheads • All's fair in love and war. • Make love, not war. • War of words
Connections	**Examples**
• Remembrance Sunday • VE Day • VJ Day • Family stories • Playground fights	• World War II • Partition of India • World War I • Iraq War • Korean War • Refugees

Peace

Synonyms	Phrases
• Calm/Tranquil • Concord • Peacetime • Armistice • Harmony/Freedom • Reconciliation • Ceasefire • Love	• Give peace a chance. • Peace and quiet • Anything for a quiet life • Rest in peace • Keep the peace • Inner peace • Peace of mind • Peace be with you.
Connections	**Examples**
• Nobel Peace Prize • Making up • Quiet/Countryside • Reflection time in assembly • Feelings	• International Day of Peace (UN) • Iraq War ending • Afghanistan War ending • Place of worship • Taking comfort with trusted adults

Curriculum connections

Years 1–6 Spoken language – Pupils should learn how to articulate and justify answers, arguments, and opinions.

SPEC grids are the work of Roger Sutcliffe, Director and Programme Designer of P4C Plus and Thinking Moves A – Z at Dialogue Works, Philosophical Teaching and Learning. www.dialogueworks.co.uk

Concept stretchers   **Concept sorting**

Using a concept line or Venn diagram rings, pupils sort examples into the categories of:

Causes war	Doesn't cause war

Cut out the following examples. Work in pairs or groups to encourage discussion, as appropriate.

Morals	Opinions
Culture	Women
Kings	Men
Queens	Children
Land	Money
Ownership	Oil
Prime Minister	Ignorance
Politicians	Ignorance
Arrogance	Pride
Power	Money
Kindness	Stubbornness

Curriculum connections

Spoken language – Pupils should also be taught to understand and use the conventions for discussion and debate.

192 *War and peace*

Concept stretchers   **Concept web**

Think of how these concept words might be connected.

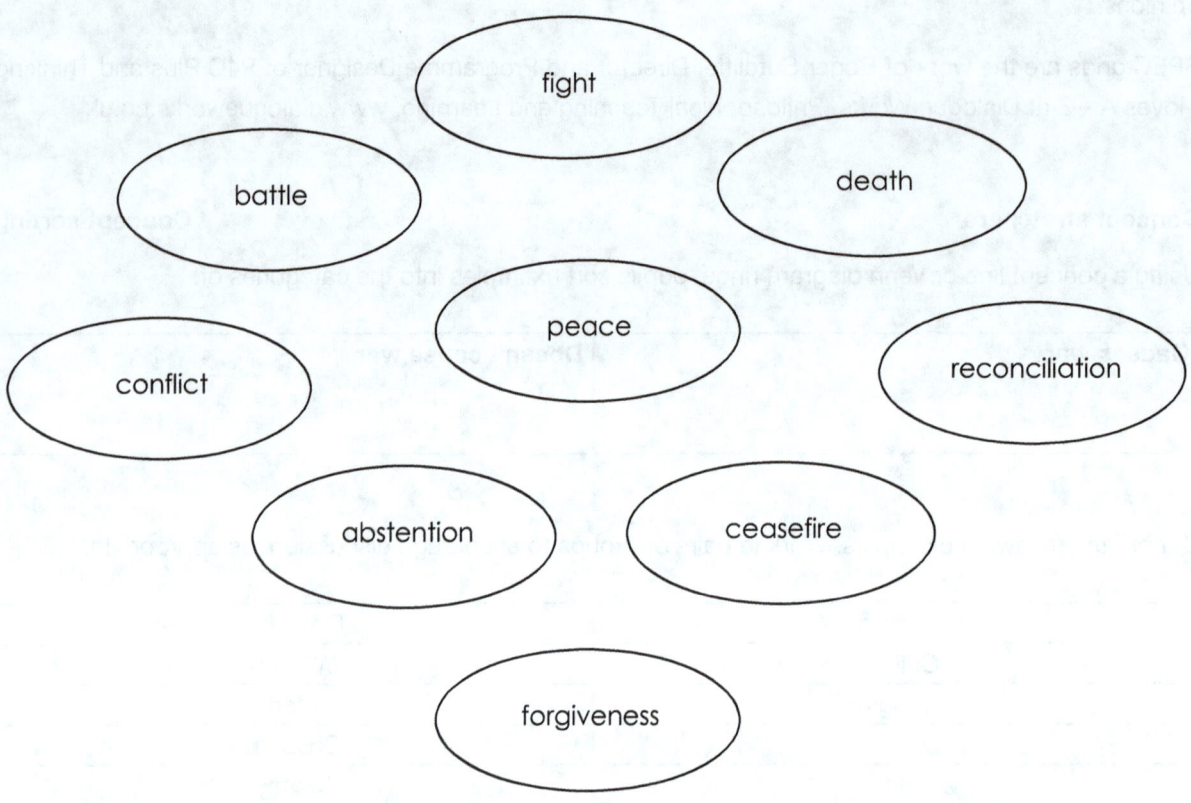

Select two concept words and say how you think they are connected.

Curriculum connections

Spoken language - Pupils should also be taught to understand and use the conventions for discussion and debate.

Concept stretchers **Decision pairs**

Would you rather?

Read these statements and choose one out of each pair. Discuss it with a partner or in a group. Say why you have chosen it. Take questions from your audience about your reasons.

Say nothing when someone hurts your feelings	Tell them and risk losing a friend
Choose one of the statements and state your reason why.	
Tell a teacher when your friend has been unkind to someone else and be known as a tell-tale	Not tell a teacher when your friend has been unkind to someone else and keep your friendship
Choose one of the statements and state your reason why.	
Live in a peaceful place, but you all get paid the same for your work	Live in a country with people fighting, with high pay for many people
Choose one of the statements and state your reason why.	
Fight for what you believe in but risk losing your safety	Let things that you disagree with happen and know that you are going to be safe
Choose one of the statements and state your reason why.	

Curriculum connections

Spoken language - Pupils can maintain attention and participate actively in collaborative conversations, staying on topic and initiating and responding to comments.

Spoken language - Pupils can participate in discussions, presentations, performances, role play/improvisations, and debates.

War and peace

Quotes to explore   **P4C**

Here are some quotes for you to use to start a philosophical enquiry. Which one do you like? Discuss with a partner.

Share your thoughts about the concept words in the quotes, such as right, with your group or class. Maybe you would like to change a word or two before you decide to offer it as a question to be explored in a P4C enquiry.

> "War does not determine who is right but who is left." – Bertrand Russell

> "All's fair in love and war." - Francis Edward Smedley

> "Is yelling for silence like fighting for war?" - Anonymous

> "The greatest victory is that which requires no battle." - Unknown

Curriculum connections

Spoken language – Pupils consider and evaluate different viewpoints, attending to and building on the contributions of others.

Concept stretchers   **Creative thinking**

Compare and contrast – Love and hate

Create a Venn diagram and see what characteristics of love and peace overlap. Here are a few words and phrases to get you thinking. Add some more of your own.

One person	Many people	Long lasting	Short-lived
One-sided	Reciprocated	Family	Stranger

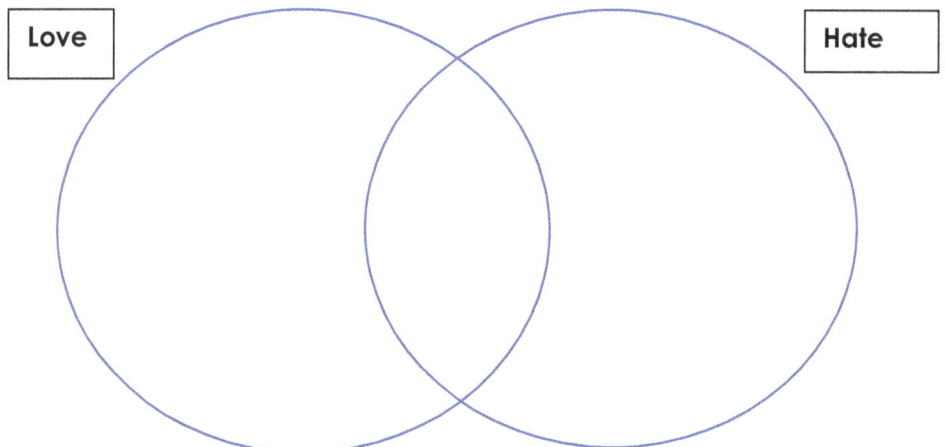

Love	Hate

Curriculum connections

Spoken language – Pupils can consider and evaluate different viewpoints, attending to and building on the contributions of others.

Do we have to make impossible decisions in war? **English**

Impossible decisions

Read Erika's Story by Ruth Vander Zee and Roberto Innocenti. This story tells of a mother who is in the Second World War and knows that she is going to the concentration camp. She makes an extremely heart-breaking and difficult decision about her child.

Reflect upon your thoughts using *The Three Sharings* by Aidan Chambers, Tell Me: Children, Reading & Talk. Primary English Teaching Association. 1994

LIKES	DISLIKES
What do you like about the story?	What do you dislike about the story?
CONNECTIONS	**PUZZLES**
What connections do you make in the story?	What did you find puzzling?

CONCEPTS – WORDS
Which concept word for you best reflects the message of the story?
Love, adoption, sacrifice, impossibilities, mother, surrogate, or think of your own.
Create a question around that concept word.
How far does a mother's love go?

Curriculum connections

Spoken language - Teaching should equip pupils to ask perceptive questions, think critically, weigh evidence, sift arguments, and develop perspective and judgement.

Spoken language - Pupils can maintain attention and participate actively in collaborative conversations, staying on topic and initiating and responding to comments.

Can we achieve peace one day? English

Shaping peace together

The United Nations theme for 2020 was Shaping Peace Together, and at the time of writing this, COVID-19 had killed thousands of people across the world.
www.un.org/sustainabledevelopment/

www.un.org/en/observances/international-day-peace

Reflect upon the following questions:

Did we come together as a world during the COVID-19 pandemic?? Can we achieve the same for peace?

Think about what theme you would choose for the next UN International Day of Peace. Justify why you have chosen it.

Discussion

What it the greatest threat to world peace? Ask each pupil to choose and write it down. Present these cards into the enquiry. Share each word or phrase. The group must decide whether it is a threat or not a threat. Use the boxes shown. Write them in after each person has shared their response.

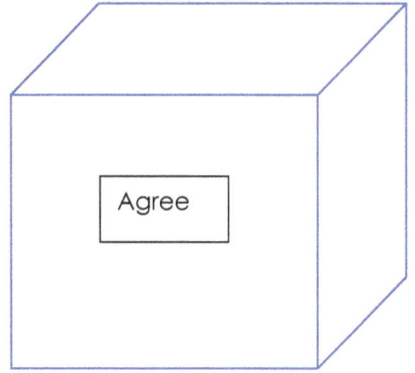
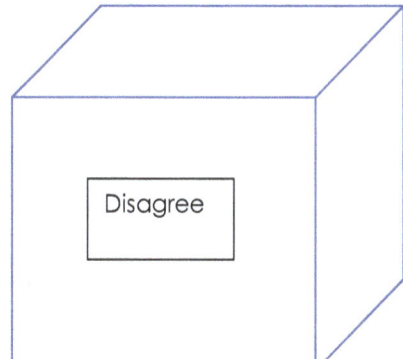

Curriculum connections

Spoken language – Pupils can participate in discussions, presentations, performances, role play/improvisations, and debates.

198 *War and peace*

Can conflict be good? **Mathematics**

Coordinates

Play Battleships to explore how coordinates help you understand position, or use the "War" card game: https://bicyclecards.com/how-to-play/war/

My ship   Opponent's ship

	1	2	3	4	5	6	7	8	9			1	2	3	4	5	6	7	8	9
A											A									
B											B									
C											C									
D											D									
E											E									
F											F									
G											G									
H											H									
I											I									
J											J									

Whilst playing the game, think about the words or phrases that come into your mind and write them here (for example, *leading into battle* and *dominating*).

These words will be useful in finding a question for a P4C enquiry.

Curriculum connections

Year 4 – Pupils should be taught to describe positions on a 2D grid as coordinates in the first quadrant.

Is human behaviour always predictable? Science

Military science

Military science studies war tactics. This includes learning about how to move large numbers of people, the study of warfare, weapons, equipment, and many other things including projectiles. You can read more about this here:

https://en.wikipedia.org/wiki/Military_science (accessed 24/07/2021)

Projectiles

Think about projectiles. A projectile is any object moved by projection of force. Any object in movement through space (the air) can be called a projectile, such as a tennis ball, cricket ball, a stone released from a catapult, or a rocket in space. The science of projectiles is very important in sport and war.

Marketplace game

> Think of more objects that are projectiles. Write them here.

Now, in a group, walk around and find a partner. Share one of your projectiles and take an idea from your partner that you haven't thought of yourself. When you both have a new idea, go to a new partner.

Create your own projectile

You are going to create your own projectile with the following items:

1. Paper
2. Cardboard
3. Tin foil

Plan a science experiment to see which one travels the furthest. Think about how you are going to make it a fair test. Write what you need to keep the same.

1.	Shape of projectile
2.	
3.	
4.	
5.	

Which projectile went the furthest? What have you learnt? What would you like to know now?

200　*War and peace*

Curriculum connections

The principal focus of science teaching in lower key stage 2 is to enable pupils to broaden their scientific view of the world around them. They should do this through exploring, talking about, testing, and developing ideas about everyday phenomena.

Can anyone be a leader? History

Leaders and tyrants

Create a Venn diagram and see what characteristics of a leader and a tyrant overlap. Here are a few words to get you thinking.

Force	Making laws	Obedience	Wealth	Consent
Ruling	Leading	Powerful	Royalty	Army
Government	People	Fear	Agreement	Fairness
Justice	Fairness	Voting	Powerful	Prisons

Place these words into the Venn diagram. Discuss with your partner or group about where you have placed them.

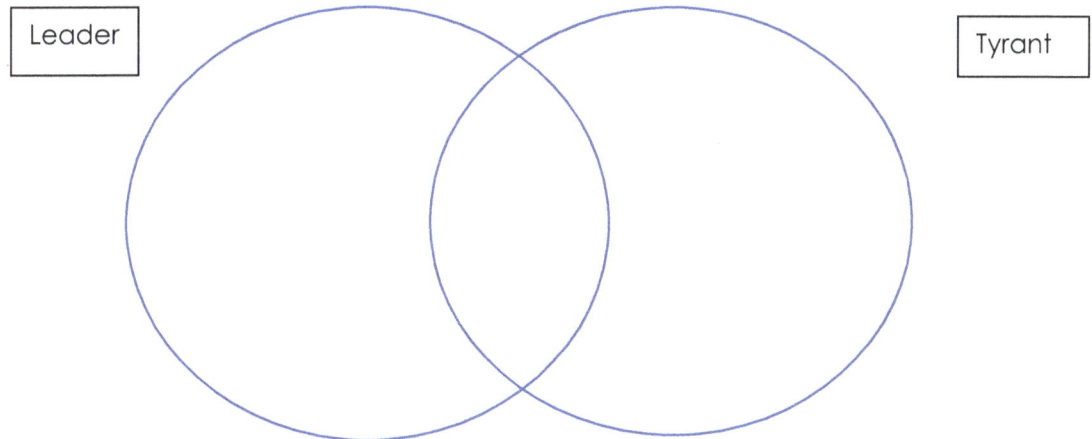

Explore some well-known people from history and think about where you would place them on the Venn diagram. Here are some suggestions, but you can use your own.

| Margaret Thatcher | Winston Churchill | Mother Theresa | Angela Merkel |
| Barrack Obama | Mahatma Gandhi | Dalai Lama | Queen Elizabeth II |

Curriculum connections

Spoken language – Pupils consider and evaluate different viewpoints, attending to and building on the contributions of others.

KS1/2 History – Pupils should inspire pupils' curiosity to know more about the past. Teaching should equip pupils to ask perceptive questions, think critically, weigh evidence, sift arguments, and develop perspective and judgement.

Is war about geography? Geography

Where wars have happened

World War II

This was the largest war and the one in which the most people died. This short film shows which countries were involved in WWII and where they are in the world:

www.bbc.co.uk/teach/class-clips-video/history-ks2-geography-of-world-war-two/zv99rj6 (accessed 02/09/2021)

On a map, look at where the countries involved in this war are. Think about why they might have decided to become an ally (a support) to the UK when they decided to go to war with Germany and its leader, Adolf Hitler.

Investigate some other significant wars that changed the geography of a country.

The partition of India

When the British stopped the rule of India, it left the country in a state of disarray as there was growing tension between the Hindus and Muslims. Many thousands of people moved from their homes and became refugees, but the main result is that East Pakistan and Pakistan were created for the Muslims to live in. Find out more about the geography after this war here:

www.bbc.co.uk/newsround/46428985 (accessed 02/09/2021)

The breakup of Czechoslovakia – The Velvet Revolution

It has been nearly 30 years since the split of Czechoslovakia into two countries. It is a bit complicated, but this video shows you how it happened: Did it change the geography of the country?

www.youtube.com/watch?v=h4KbZIRgSkg (accessed 02/09/2021)

Battles of the world

This aminated time-lapse video shows you where battles of the world have taken place:

https://www.youtube.com/watch?v=HK5OsDWYJmQ

Curriculum connections

History – Teaching should ensure that pupils know and understand significant aspects of the history of the wider world: the nature of ancient civilisations, the expansion and dissolution of empires, characteristic features of past non-European societies, achievements and follies of mankind.

Is war all about fighting? **Physical education**

Projectiles and yoga

Play dodgeball

Split the class in half and put benches in between. Find a soft ball to play dodgeball. Now try to hit one of the other team's legs below the knee to eliminate them from the game until only one person is left.

Create your own game

Most competitive games use a projectile. This is usually a ball, but can you think of other sports that don't use a ball? Write them here.

Now create your own game. It must be based on a projectile. Think about:

1. The rules
2. Team numbers
3. How to get points
4. How to win
5. How to make it fun

My new game

Once you have played the new game with your class, think about ways to improve it!

Yoga

Some people want to disagree peacefully and don't think war is the only way to achieve what you want. This takes a lot of patience and determination.

Try some yoga positions to create peace and balance in your body. Use breathing techniques. You could watch a video to help you, like the one included here.

www.youtube.com/watch?v=X655B4ISakg (accessed 24/07/2021)

Curriculum connections

The curriculum should provide opportunities for pupils to become physically confident in a way which supports their health and fitness.

Should we always forgive? Art and design

Emoji story

We use emojis and pictograms to express ourselves in text messages. Can you think of a way to write a story of how you think "the story of war" goes using them?

Challenge

Can you create an alternation story where you show how conflict can be avoided? You could use funny or creative ways to do this.

Curriculum connections

Art – The curriculum should teach pupils to produce creative work, exploring their ideas.

What is war good for? Music

Songs for peace

Think about the words in the song "War, what is it good for?" by Edwin Starr. Capture some of the phrases and words here.

```

```

Think of some questions that the lyrics create in your mind.

> Write your questions here.

Here are some examples.

> **Possible questions for P4C enquiry**
>
> Will there ever be world peace?
> Is war ever right?
> Can we win with non-violence?

Other songs that talk about war and peace

"Pipes of peace" by Paul McCartney
"What the world needs now is love" by Dionne Warwick

Curriculum connections

All pupils should perform, listen to, review, and evaluate music across a range of historical periods, genres, styles, and traditions, including the works of the great composers and musicians.

KS1 – Pupils should listen with concentration and understanding to a range of high-quality live and recorded music.

KS2 – Pupils should develop an understanding of the history of music.

Is it better to be peaceful than start conflict? **Religious education**

Thou shalt not kill

Do you believe in this command from one of the Ten Commandments? Are there any scenarios where you believe that killing is okay? Think of some examples and write below. Share them with others.

[ ]

One could argue that mercy killing (killing someone when they are going to die but are in a lot of pain and are suffering) is okay. Talk about the reasons for and against this with a partner or in a group.

Mercy killing (or euthanasia)

FOR	AGAINST

Curriculum connections

Spoken language – Pupils participate in discussions, presentations, performances, role play/improvisations, and debates.

Spoken language – Pupils consider and evaluate different viewpoints, attending to and building on the contributions of others.

PSHE R34 – Pupils know how to discuss and debate topical issues, respect other people's point of view, and constructively challenge those they disagree with.

Should age matter in war?   **Citizenship**

Children in war

The UN Convention on the Rights of the Child says in Article 38 that governments must not allow children under the age of 15 to take part in war or join the armed forces. Governments must do everything they can to protect and care for children affected by war and armed conflicts.

> What do you think is the right age for a person to decide that they can take part in war?
> Discuss in a P4C enquiry, group or with a partner. Write your thoughts here.

Curriculum connections

Spoken language – Pupils can maintain attention and participate actively in collaborative conversations, staying on topic and initiating and responding to comments.

Should secret codes be decoded by others?   **Computing**

Codebreakers

During wars people need to communicate with secret codes so that the enemy does not listen to what they are planning. However, there are usually mathematicians and computer scientists trying to "crack" – or work out – the secret code.

https://bletchleypark.org.uk/ (accessed 24/07/2021)

Curriculum connections

A high-quality computing education equips pupils to use computational thinking and creativity to understand and change the world.

Can all codes be decoded?   **Design and Technology**

The Caesar cipher

The Roman ruler Julius Caesar was using a "displacement code" sometimes called a "skip" code. This is when you replace a letter from the alphabet with a number. Caesar used three letters ahead.

Read about it here: www.secretcodebreaker.com/history2.html (accessed 24/07/2021)

To crack a code is to decipher, and to create a code it to encipher. Create a wheel to help you create a displacement code. Write the alphabet on the inner and outer wheel. Put a split pin in the middle.

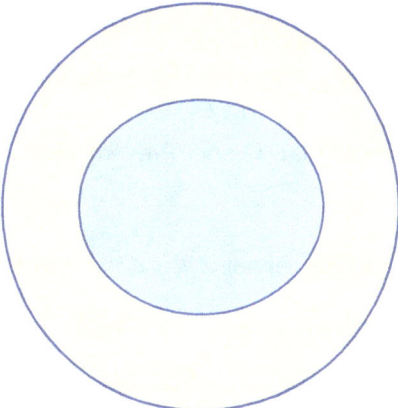

Write your new code here. Give it to a friend to decode.

Curriculum connections

Using creativity and imagination, pupils design and make products that solve real and relevant problems.

Is peace always possible? PSHE

The Nobel Peace Prize 2019

The Nobel Peace Prize 2019 was awarded to Abiy Ahmed Ali for his efforts to achieve peace and international cooperation, particularly for his decisive initiative to resolve the border conflict with neighbouring Eritrea. He lives in the Federal Democratic Republic of Ethiopia and is currently the 4th Prime Minister.

https://en.wikipedia.org/wiki/Abiy_Ahmed (accessed 21/08/2021)

Activity 1

Research who has won the prize in the past ten years.

Activity 2
Choose one person and find out about that person. Present what you find to your peers.

Activity 3
Whom would you nominate from your life, either a friend, family member, or famous person? Give three reasons why.

I nominate_____

1._____

2._____

3._____

With a partner think about the following question:
Is peace always possible?

Curriculum connections

Spoken language – Pupils can participate in discussions, presentations, performances, role play/improvisations, and debates.

Inspirational people

Mahatma Gandhi

Gandhi was a law student born and raised in India. He believed in peaceful ways to make change happen and believed in non-violence. He promoted non-cooperation and was imprisoned for this.

https://en.wikipedia.org/wiki/Mahatma_Gandhi (accessed 22/10/2021)

Mother Theresa

Mother Theresa was born in Kosovo and later became an Albania-Indian Roman Catholic nun. Teresa received several honours, including the 1962 Ramon Magsaysay Peace Prize and the 1979 Nobel Peace Prize.

https://en.wikipedia.org/wiki/Mother_Teresa (accessed 22/10/2021)

Aung San Suu Kyi

Kyi is a Burmese politician, diplomat, author, and a 1991 Nobel Peace Prize laureate. Influenced by both Mahatma Gandhi's philosophy of non-violence and more specifically by Buddhist concepts, she has been put under house arrest many times for her political behaviour.

https://en.wikipedia.org/wiki/Aung_San_Suu_Kyi (accessed 20.01.22)

Ala Ali – Iraq peacebuilder

Ala Ali has over 17 years of experience working in the field of civil society in Iraq, including the Kurdistan Region, working as a peacemaker.

www.peaceinsight.org/en/authors/ala-ali/

Further resources

The complete philosophy files by Stephen Law
This book is a rich resource which explores the philosophical arguments to difficult questions. File 10 – Killing people uses conversations, scenarios, and stories to investigate whether it is wrong to kill. It will stretch your philosophical enquiry to think of scenarios that will challenge one's beliefs.

The Oxfam Library
Syria: A Children's Crisis? Learn about the crisis and think critically about who is affected. https://oxfamilibrary.openrepository.com/handle/10546/620661

National Geographic Kids downloadable resources
www.natgeokids.com/uk/primary-resource/second-world-war-primary-resource/ (accessed 17/09/2020)

TES resources
https://www.tes.com/teaching-resource/world-war-2-timeline-6077001 (accessed 01/02/22)

The Book Trust
The Book Trust has lots of advice about books of a particular interest and is good go-to place to find new stories for a topic.

www.booktrust.org.uk/news-and-features/features/2018/november/10-kids-books-about-war-a-journey-and-a-sense-of-hope/

The Book Corner

Goodnight, Mr. Tom by Michelle Mogorian
Willie Beech is evacuated to the English countryside on the brink of the outbreak of the Second World War and taken in by Mr. Tom. Willie is frightened of everything but slowly learns to live his new life. However, he must return to London to his mother, and his life changes again. Suitable for KS2.

The war horse by Michael Murpurgo
This a fascinating story about being in the Second World War from the perspective of a horse called Joey. Amazingly he sees the war from all sides after he is sold to the British Army and then is owned by many different people during the war. Suitable for KS2.

Where the poppies now grow by Hilary Robinson and Martin Impey
Childhood friends grow up together and then sign up for war to find it is not what they thought. This simple rhyming story shows the changing landscape of their innocence, war, and then peace. Suitable for KS1/2.

A little piece of ground by Elizabeth Laird
Ramallah dreams of being a champion footballer, but his life is severely hampered by Israeli troops and tanks in Palestine. The book shows what is like for children who live under the watch of troops and are repressed by unresolved political issues. This is a touching story which navigates difficult subject matter. Suitable for KS2.

Once by Morris Gleitzman
Felix, a young Jewish boy, has been living in a convent orphanage in Nazi-occupied Poland for three years and believes that his parents will come back for him. He decides that he must go and find his book-selling parents as he has seen Nazis burning books. Suitable for KS2.

NC subject	Activity	Curriculum connections
English	Erika's story	History KS1/2 – Pupils should inspire pupils' curiosity to know more about the past. Teaching should equip pupils to ask perceptive questions, think critically, weigh evidence, sift arguments, and develop perspective and judgement. History KS1/2 Pupils should be taught to understand historical concepts such as continuity and change, cause and consequence, similarity, difference, and significance,
English	Shaping peace together	Spoken language – Pupils can participate in discussions, presentations, performances, role play/improvisations, and debates.
Maths	Coordinates	Year 4 – Pupils should be taught to describe positions on a 2D grid as coordinates in the first quadrant.
Science	Military science	The principal focus of science teaching in lower key stage 2 is to enable pupils to broaden their scientific view of the world around them. They should do this through exploring, talking about, testing, and developing ideas about everyday phenomena.
History	Leaders and tyrants	History KS1/2 – Pupils should inspire pupils' curiosity to know more about the past. Teaching should equip pupils to ask perceptive questions, think critically, weigh evidence, sift arguments, and develop perspective and judgement. Spoken language – Pupils consider and evaluate different viewpoints, attending to and building on the contributions of others.
Geography	Where wars have happened	History – Teaching should ensure that pupils know and understand significant aspects of the history of the wider world: the nature of ancient civilisations, the expansion and dissolution of empires, characteristic features of past non-European societies, achievements and follies of mankind.
Music	War	All pupils should perform, listen to, review, and evaluate music across a range of historical periods, genres, styles, and traditions, including the works of the great composers and musicians. KS1 – Pupils should listen with concentration and understanding to a range of high-quality live and recorded music. KS2 – Pupils should develop an understanding of the history of music.
Art and Design	Emoji story	Art – The curriculum should teach pupils to produce creative work, exploring their ideas.
Design and Technology	The Caesar cipher	Using creativity and imagination, pupils design and make products that solve real and relevant problems.
Computing	Codebreakers	A high-quality computing education equips pupils to use computational thinking and creativity to understand and change the world.

NC subject	Activity	Curriculum connections
Religious education	**Thou shalt not kill**	Spoken language – Pupils participate in discussions, presentations, performances, role play/improvisations, and debates. Spoken language – Pupils consider and evaluate different viewpoints, attending to and building on the contributions of others. PSHE R34 – Pupils know how to discuss and debate topical issues, respect other people's point of view, and constructively challenge those they disagree with.
Physical education	**Projectiles and yoga**	The curriculum should provide opportunities for pupils to become physically confident in a way which supports their health and fitness.
Citizenship	**Children in war**	Spoken language – Pupils can maintain attention and participate actively in collaborative conversations, staying on topic and initiating and responding to comments. Spoken language – Pupils can participate in discussions, presentations, performances, role play/improvisations, and debates.
PSHE	**The Nobel Peace Prize 2019**	Spoken language – Pupils can participate in discussions, presentations, performances, role play/improvisations, and debates.

Waste

English

> Who is responsible for waste?

One plastic bag
Read "one plastic bag" by Miranda Paul. Write a story about a piece of rubbish using the repetitive style from the story. Think about places you have seen litter, especially plastic.

> Is less plastic or better plastic the solution?

The packaging problem
Learn about how we wrap up food is having a huge impact on our world. Write to a food manufacturer or supermarket to request a change to their packaging. Explain your reasons and cite factual evidence.

R.E.

> Can we teach people to waste less?

Wastefulness
In the religions across the world, the notion of waste or wastefulness is addressed in their sacred writings. Write a proverb that conveys what you think about wastefulness.

Music

> Can we waste what we cannot see?

Unseen waste
Think about what we waste but cannot touch, such as money, friendship, time, love, and music. Explore some music from the past that people keep alive.

History

> Do you exist if you don't produce waste?

Human waste
Find out about how waste has been managed in the past. Research what the Victorians, Ancient Egyptians, and Ancient Greeks did with the things they no longer needed.

Geography

> Is plastic drastic or fantastic?

Clean-up
Think about how to preserve local beauty spots and features of the landscape. Use local maps to find out where they are. Organise a clean-up where one is needed.

Citizenship

> Is there good waste and bad waste?

Cities that recycle
UNESCO Sustainable Development Goal 11 promotes sustainable cities and Goal 12 promotes responsible consumption. Find out about some cities that are working hard to manage waste and other resources, and think about how your school can reduce consumption of plastic items.

Maths

> What counts as waste?

Multiplication and waste
Learn about how much waste we create. Calculate how much waste you create of particular items. Create number sentences and stories that capture how much you are using for long periods of time.

Science

> Do materials ever disappear?

Materials and their properties
It is important to know how waste materials behave once they are no longer needed. Think about if they degrade. Explore what would happen if the material got into the sea and whether they change in water. Research the impact on wildlife.

Art and design

> Is waste a problem or a resource?

Beautiful waste
Explore how artists have used waste to create art. Find images to inspire you to create a piece of art from waste.

PSHE

> Is cleanliness for us or for others?

Pandemics and health
We have all lived through the Covid-19 pandemic and it highlighted to society that we all need to have good hygiene. Think about the ways we prevent infection.

Computing

> Can robots be zero-waste advocators?

A helpful robot for recycling
Learn how to program a robot to say something helpful, such as giving a reminder about recycling waste. Think about how it may help change human's behaviour.

Design and Technology

> Can we build using waste?

3D waste structure
Learn how to use waste items to create structures. Build a tower with lolly sticks and experiment with the ways to make the structure stronger as you get higher.

P.E.

> Can waste always be repurposed?

Assault courses
Make an assault course with repurposed waste items, such as plastic bottles, plastic tubs, and cardboard boxes, using items from around your school and home.

14 Waste

Concept stretcher **SPEC grids**

As part of a P4C enquiry, children brainstorm synonyms, phrases, connections, and examples (SPEC) in a SPEC grid, as in these examples.

Synonyms	Phrases
• Rubbish • Unused • Excess • Surplus • Unwanted • Discarded • Remaining • Leftover	• Throw away • Another person's rubbish is another person's treasure • A load of rubbish • Waste not, want not • Waste of time • Waste of space • Youth is wasted on the young
Connections	**Examples**
• School recycling • Community recycling areas • Home recycling and bins	• House bin • Waste pipe in kitchen • Recycling bins • Public bin • Dog bin

Curriculum connections

Spoken language – Pupils should be taught to use spoken language to develop understanding through speculating, hypothesising, imagining, and exploring ideas.

SPEC grids are the work of Roger Sutcliffe, Director and Programme Designer of P4C Plus and Thinking Moves A – Z at Dialogue Works, Philosophical Teaching and Learning. www.dialogueworks.co.uk

Quotes to explore P4C enquiry

Waste quotes

In a group or with a partner, think about the following quotes about waster.

> 'There is no such thing as away.
> When we throw anything away it must go somewhere.'
> – Annie Leonard

> 'Waste is only waste if we waste it.'
> – Will.I.am

> "It is just one straw, said 8 billion people."
> – Anonymous

Write some of your thoughts below.

Curriculum connections

Spoken language – Pupils consider and evaluate different viewpoints, attending to and building on the contributions of others.

Concept stretcher   **Concept web**

Think about how these concepts can be connected. As you gather your thoughts, draw a line between the two and write a sentence along it about how they connect.

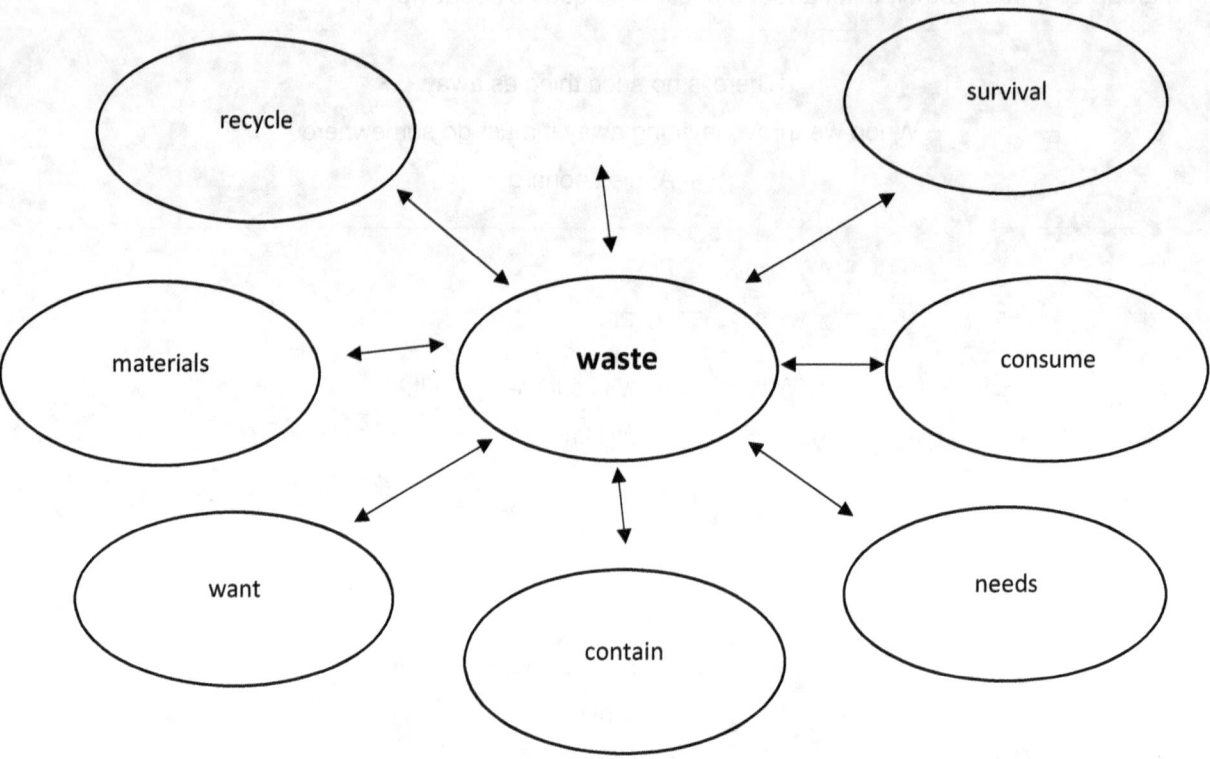

Pick two concepts

1.	2.
Write a sentence about how you think they connect.	

Now share your ideas with your group, class, or talk partner.

Curriculum connections

Spoken language – Pupils consider and evaluate different viewpoints, attending to and building on the contributions of others.

Concept stretchers   **Decision pairs**

Would you rather?

Look at these statements. Select one from each pair and give your reasons as to why you chose it.

Would you rather?

Have a mountain of plastic bottles	Have a mountain of rubber tyres
Choose one with a tick. Say why.	
Have every toy that you want and one friend	Have one toy and lots of friends
Choose one with a tick. Say why.	
Be a plastic bottle	Be a teacup made of china
Choose one with a tick. Say why.	

Now discuss your answers with a talk partner, group, or class discussion.

See if you can think of your own pair of statements about waste that pose a dilemma. Write them here.

Curriculum connections

Spoken language – Pupils participate in discussions, presentations, performances, role play/improvisations, and debates.

Spoken language – Pupils use spoken language to develop understanding through speculating, hypothesising, imagining, and exploring ideas.

Who is responsible for waste? English

One plastic bag

Think about places you have seen litter, especially plastic. Write three places here.

Read *One plastic bag* by Miranda Paul. www.youtube.com/watch?v=7JHesyiYfeE (accessed 22/06/2021)

> Using a repeated phrase in the text, write a story about a piece of rubbish. Here are some examples:
>
> *I tried once, I tried twice, and I tried three times but . . .*
>
> *One said you can't do it, three said you can't do it, ten people said you can't do it.*

Challenge: In your writing can you use:

metaphors adjectives similes

WORK BANK – Use a thesaurus to broaden your language.

Find other words for these and others of your own.

Rubbish	Mess	Care	Environment

Curriculum connections

Year 2 – Pupils should be taught to develop positive attitudes towards and stamina for writing by writing narratives about personal experiences and those of others (real and fictional).

Year 3–4 Pupils should be taught discussing writing similar to that which they are planning to write in order to understand and learn from its structure, vocabulary, and grammar.

Year 5–6 Pupils should be taught to draft and write by selecting appropriate grammar and vocabulary, understanding how such choices can change and enhance meaning.

Is less plastic or better plastic a solution? English

The packaging problem

Learn about why the way we wrap up food is having a huge impact on our world. Organisations, such as "Wrap" and "Iceland", are addressing the food wrapping problem.

https://wrap.org.uk/taking-action/plastic-packaging# (accessed 22/06/2021)

Choose a food manufacturer or supermarket to write request a change to packaging. Explain your reasons and cite factual evidence.

> The "Iceland" supermarket has become the first food shop in the UK to announce that they are going to be plastic free by 2023. Watch the Managing Director, Richard Walker, talk about why the shop has taken this decision. You can use it to make points in your own letter.
>
> https://about.iceland.co.uk/plastic-free-by-2023/ (accessed 22/06/2021)

> Explore the Unilever organisation's slogan to address the plastic problem – 'Less Plastic, Better Plastic, No Plastic'. Also make some notes on the plastic facts that they quote on their website.
>
> www.unilever.com/planet-and-society/waste-free-world/rethinking-plastic-packaging/ (accessed 22/06/2021)

Points to make in your letter:
1.
2.
3.
4.
5.
6.

Curriculum connections

Year 3 and 4 – Pupils should continue to have opportunities to write for a range of real purposes and audiences as part of their work across the curriculum.

Year 5 and 6 – Pupils should be taught to plan their writing by identifying the audience for and purpose of the writing, selecting the appropriate form and using other similar writing as models for their own noting and developing initial ideas, drawing on reading and research where necessary.

What counts as waste? Mathematics

Multiplication and waste

What is classed as waste? Watch BBC Bitesize. www.bbc.co.uk/bitesize/topics/zp22pv4/articles/z2rhcj6 (accessed 15/06/2021)

Now use the waste calculator to see how calculations can work out how much waste we create.

www.biffa.co.uk/education (accessed 15/06/2021).

Now try . . .

If you drank one plastic bottle of water per day for five years and threw away each bottle, how many plastic bottles would you use?

Now calculate the same for your whole class for five years.

Now think of your own calculation about things that we use (water, cups, straws, plastic forks, etc.).

Challenge – Can you create a number sentence that substitutes a letter for an unknown number (this number could change per person)? For example, 365 days x m where m means the number of plastic bottles you use a day.

Can you create some more?

Curriculum connections

Year 2 – Pupils can solve problems involving multiplication and division, using materials, arrays, repeated addition, mental methods, and multiplication and division facts, including problems in contexts.

Year 3 – Pupils can solve problems, including missing number problems, involving multiplication and division, including positive integer scaling problems and correspondence problems in which *n* objects are connected to *m* objects.

Year 6 – Pupils can express missing number problems algebraically.

226 *Waste*

Do materials ever disappear? **Science**

Materials and their properties

It is important to know how waste materials behave once they are no longer needed. For example, if they get into the sea they may not change, and this can impact wildlife.

Think of these materials. Sort them into characteristics.

Watch a video about how waste is separated, like this one: www.wm.com/us/en/inside-wm/social-impact/education-resources (accessed 15/06/2021)

Discuss "One species' waste is another species' food".

Paper		Flexible
Steel		Magnetism
Cotton		Absorbent
Cardboard		Transparent
Plastic sheet		Hard
Glass		Rigid

Watch a video about the natural world's cycle and how important it is. Some processes are linear and only go in direction. They can be described as "take, make, and dispose". The others are a cycle.

www.ellenmacarthurfoundation.org/our-work/activities/schools-colleges (accessed 22/06/2021)

Curriculum connections

Year 1 – Pupils can identify and name a variety of everyday materials, including wood, plastic, glass, metal, water, and rock.

Year 2 – Pupils can find out how the shapes of solid objects made from some materials can be changed by squashing, bending, twisting, and stretching.

Year 6 – Properties and change of materials – Compare and group together everyday materials based on their properties.

Do you exist if you don't produce waste?   History

Human waste

How has waste been a challenge in the past? Set up expert groups A – D, and ask them to research one of the questions below. Then reconvene with one person from each expert group joining in a new group (there should be an A, B, C, D person in this new group) and share what they learnt.

Who/When	Waste	Question to research
Victorians **1837–1901**	Horse manure and human waste on the streets	What did the Victorians do about human waste? www.youtube.com/watch?v=Au_Ut95-Mlo (accessed 16/06/2021)
Ancient Egyptians	A huge rubbish pile of mostly paper found in Oxyrthynchus	What can you find in ancient waste? https://en.wikipedia.org/wiki/Oxyrhynchus www.youtube.com/watch?v=sy7q3a87Lfc
Ancient Greeks **500 BCE**	Municipal (household) waste pile created in Athens	Were the Ancient Greeks the first to create a waste pile? www.wasterecyclingworkersweek.org/history-of-the-garbage-man/ (accessed 16/06/21)
Georgians	Horse manure, human excrement, market meat waste	Where the Georgians the best recyclers? https://janeaustenslondon.com/2014/02/18/recycling-georgian-style/ (accessed 16/06/21)

How might these concepts be linked? Discuss with your peers.

Treasure	Remains	Market	Cleanliness
Excess	Education	Need	Surplus

Select two concepts that you find interesting and say how they connect.

P4C enquiry – Explore in a P4C enquiry what historians mean when they say that 'if you don't produce waste, you don't exist'.

Curriculum connections

KS1 and KS2 – All pupils should know and understand significant aspects of the history of the wider world: the nature of ancient civilisations, the expansion and dissolution of empires, characteristic features of past non-European societies, achievements and follies of mankind.

History skills – Pupils should use primary sources of evidence.

Is plastic drastic or fantastic?   **Geography**

Clean-up

Let's imagine you are in charge of your local environment and that you have to preserve local beauty spots and features of your landscape. Using local maps, think about where you would like to focus your attention. You are going to carry out a bin audit and organise a clean-up in that place or area. (It could be on-site at your school if you can't go off-site.)

Places of focus:	When you will visit:
Bin audit: What did you find? List here.	**Local environment litter inspection:** What did you find? List here.
What can you do to help recycle the rubbish? Do you need a tin can bin as well, for example?	**How does the litter get there?**

Write an inspection report here – use full sentences.

Curriculum connections

A high-quality geography education should inspire in pupils a curiosity and fascination about the world and its people that will remain with them for the rest of their lives. Teaching should equip pupils with knowledge about diverse places, people, resources, and natural and human environments, together with a deep understanding of the earth's key physical and human processes. As pupils progress, their growing knowledge about the world should help them to deepen their understanding of the interaction between physical and human processes and of the formation and use of landscapes and environments.

Is waste a problem or a resource? | Art and Design

Beautiful waste

Explore how artists have used waste to create art. Find images, such as in the following links, to inspire you to create a piece of art from waste.

> https://blog.artsper.com/en/get-inspired/top-10-of-recycled-art/ (accessed 09/06/21)
>
> Mount Recyclemore at G7 created in Cornwall – ITV News (10/06/2021) www.bbc.co.uk/news/uk-england-cornwall-57406136

Select one type of waste and one topic, for example – flowers and landscape – to create a piece of art.

Paper (newspaper)	Wood	Flowers	Plastic
E-waste	Tin foil (milk tops)	Wrapping paper	Cardboard

Landscape	Vase of flowers	Seascape	Water
Car	Tractor	House	Wood

Curriculum connections

Art and design aim to ensure that all pupils should produce creative work.

Can we build using waste?   **Design and Technology**

3D waste structure

Lolly stick tower

Lolly sticks are made of wood and often not used after you have eaten. Collect these sticks and bring them to school (after they have been quarantined) so that you can use them.

In groups, think about how you can join the sticks together to make a tower. Sketch your idea first.

How can you make the tower strong?

Will you need to think about a special way to join the sticks?

Do you need another waste product to make the tower more stable?

Curriculum connections

KS2 Design – Pupils can communicate their ideas through discussion and annotated sketches.

Make – Pupils perform practical tasks, such as joining and shaping.

Evaluate – Pupils can evaluate their design against the criteria.

Technical knowledge – Pupils apply their understanding of how to strengthen, stiffen, and reinforce structures.

Can we waste what we cannot see? **Music**

Unseen waste

Can we waste the following things? Discuss.

Music

Love

Time

Money

Friendship

"Fisherman's friends"

Watch and listen to a song by the Cornish Sea Shanty singers called "Fisherman's friends". www.youtube.com/watch?v=FkNwhbyiA4Y (accessed 16/06/2021)

What could happen to traditional songs and ways of singing if people don't practise them? Should we keep old music traditions?

Curriculum connections

All key stages appreciate and understand a wide range of high-quality live and recorded music drawn from different traditions and from great composers and musicians.

Can robots be zero-waste advocators? **Computing**

A helpful robot for recycling

We can program robots to do so many things! How about deciding what a robot can say to help with the recycling and waste problem?

> Select Chatbot – You can make the robot say something. Think about and write here what your robot can say to remind people to recycle.
>
> https://projects.raspberrypi.org/en/codeclub/scratch-module-1 (accessed 09/6/2021)

Decide:

1. Where the robot should be? (For example, beside a sweet shop)
2. What the robot should say? (For example, "Please remember to put your rubbish in the bin".)

Curriculum connections

All pupils can evaluate and apply information technology, including new or unfamiliar technologies, analytically to solve problems.

Is there good waste and bad waste? **Citizenship**

Cities that recycle

Watch this film about UNESCO Sustainable Development Goal #11.

www.youtube.com/watch?v=RPoDircL5zc (accessed 15/06/2021)

Now watch this film about some cities that are working hard to manage waste and other resources. Capture in the boxes one thing that you find interesting from each city.

www.youtube.com/watch?v=fsWr0LfM_uQ (accessed 15/06/2021)

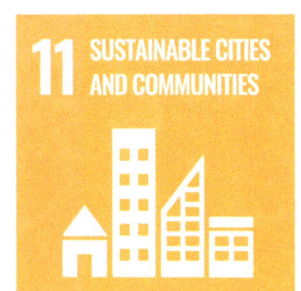

Copenhagen	Singapore	Reykjavik	Berlin

Watch this film about UNESCO Sustainable Development Goal #12.

www.youtube.com/watch?v=2MxKrGXAyH8 (accessed 15/06/2021)

The video talks about making just enough of what we need to eat and use. This is called consumption. Can you think of a way in which you or your school could cut down consumption of something made from plastic?

Concept discussion – concept line

Place the words along the line from very important to not very important for human consumption. Do this on your own after the group discussion.

Crisps	Beef	Water	Ice lollies	Butter	Milk
Lettuce	Bread	Oranges	Wheat	Apples	Plums
Carrots	Lamb	Sweets	Broccoli	Juice	Chocolate

Curriculum connections

PSHE Association Curriculum – Living in the wider world

KS1 L3 – Pupils learn about things they can do to help look after their environment.

KS2 L5 – Pupils learn ways of carrying out shared responsibilities for protecting the environment in school and at home; how everyday choices can affect the environment (e.g. reducing, reusing, recycling; food choices).

Is cleanliness for us or for others? PSHE

Pandemics and health

We have all lived through the COVID-19 pandemic, and it highlighted to society that we all need to have good hygiene.

Basically, our waste (spit, faeces, urine, breath) from our bodies can affect other people with our germs. We try to stop spreading germs to prevent the spread of infection.

Think about the ways we were preventing infection during the COVID-19 pandemic". Write them here.

Here are some good videos by WaterAid that explain hygiene:

www.wateraid.org/uk/get-involved/teaching/hygiene-activities-for-kids

P4C Enquiry

Discuss the following question - Is hygiene for us or other people?

Write your thoughts here.

Curriculum connections

KS1 H5 – Pupils learn simple hygiene routines that can stop germs from spreading.

KS2 H9 – Pupils learn that bacteria and viruses can affect health; how everyday hygiene routines can limit the spread of infection; the wider importance of personal hygiene and how to maintain it.

Can we teach people to waste less?   **Religious education**

Wastefulness

In the religions across the world, the notion of waste or wastefulness is addressed in their sacred writings.

The Quran – *Fataawa al-Lajnah al-Daa'imah* (22/341)

Leftover food must be saved for the next time, or it should be given to the needy; if there are no needy people, then it should be given to animals, even after it has dried out, for the one who is able to do that.

The Bible – John 6:12

And when they had eaten their fill, he told his disciples, "Gather up the leftover fragments, that nothing may be lost."

> Write some principles of your own about wastefulness.

Curriculum connections

KS1 – At key stage 1 pupils should study Christianity, one other religion, and consider other worldviews.

KS2 – Pupils consider the beliefs, teachings, practices, and ways of life central to religion. They learn about sacred texts and other sources and consider their meanings.

Can waste always be repurposed?   **Physical education**

Assault courses

Your challenge is to make an assault course with repurposed waste items, such as plastic bottles, plastic tubs, and cardboard boxes.

Collect waste items from around your school and home. In pairs or groups design an assault course that is going to be fun and give you lots of exercise!

Select four types of activity and design your assault course so that it uses those skills.

Running	Throwing	Jumping	Catching	Hopping
Shuttle runs	Passing a baton	Balancing	Dribbling a ball	Bouncing a ball

Curriculum connections

Pupils are physically active for sustained periods of time. Pupils should be taught to master basic movements including running, jumping, throwing, and catching, as well as developing balance, agility, and coordination, and begin to apply these in a range of activities.

Inspirational people

Boyan Slat – The great ocean cleanup

Slat was so motivated to clean up the ocean that he has dedicated his life and work to designing and financing cleaning up the Great Pacific Garbage Patch.
(www.nationalgeographic.org/encyclopedia/great-pacific-garbage-patch/)

Ina Budde – Circular.fashion

Budde and her business partner have found a way to stop clothes going on a one-way path to landfill and created a way for them to be reused or recycled.

https://circular.fashion/vision/ (accessed 15/06/2021)

Lush Cosmetics – The choice to have no packaging

Lush Cosmetics has been aiming to reduce as much packaging as possible, and you can ask to have no packaging for over half of their products.

www.lush.com/uk/en/a/our-environmental-policy (accessed 15/06/2021)

James Longcroft – Choose packaging

Longcroft has dedicated his work to finding a solution to the plastic water bottle and has created a bottle that is completely biodegradable.
www.choosepackaging.co.uk/about-us (accessed 15/06/2021)

Packaging made from mushrooms

There have been many innovations to find solutions to degradable packaging and one new way is from the tiny threads that are below the ground called Mycelium. This is the main part of the mushroom plant. Find out how this plant is going to help the waste problem.
https://mushroompackaging.com/ (accessed 24/06/2021)

Further resources

Biffa Education
This website has lots of great activities – such as the Waste Clock, to find out how much waste you have created since you were born, and the Fact Generator.
www.biffa.co.uk/education (accessed 15/06/2021)

Changeworks
This company offers interactive waste workshops and CPD training for schoolteachers.
www.changeworks.org.uk/what-we-do/waste/waste-education-for-schools (accessed 15/06/2021)

Wm.com
This has some good videos, one in particularly explains how waste is separated after it gets taken from the home waste bins.
www.wm.com/us/en/inside-wm/social-impact/education-resources (accessed 15/06/2021)

BBC Bitesize
What should we do with our rubbish?

www.bbc.co.uk/bitesize/topics/zrssgk7/articles/z9w26sg

Why do we waste food?

www.bbc.co.uk/bitesize/topics/zfmpb9q/articles/zxhkbqt (accessed 15/06/2021)

Recycling – what is the best way to sort rubbish? Machine or people?

www.bbc.co.uk/bitesize/clips/z7x2tfr (accessed 15/06/2021)

Waste Wise Kids
This is a not-for-profit company, and you can join their school programme for a registration fee.

www.wastewisekids.org/schools/ (accessed 15/06/2021)

Carymoor Environmental Trust – KS2 education pack
www.carymoor.org.uk/userfiles/page/5aa7cd731adf2-food-waste-education-pack.pdf

This is a 54-page downloadable pack with worksheets and activities ready to go.

The Book Corner

The adventures of a plastic bottle: a story about recycling by Alison Inches
Follow the journey of a plastic bottle as it goes from the refinery plant to the store shelf to its new life as a fleece jacket. Humorous with an ecological stance. Suitable for KS1.

One plastic bag: Isatou Ceesay and the recycling women of Gambia by Miranda Paul
This inspiring story tells the true story of how one African woman began a campaign to recycle plastic bags that were dropped on the floor and left as rubbish. Ceesay found a way to recycle these bags and make a difference in her community. Suitable for KS1.

One world by Michael Foreman
A brother and a sister create their own tiny marine world in a bucket whilst playing at the beach by a rock pool. It makes clear the underlying concern about pollution within the environment and the seashore. Suitable for KS1.

Charlie and Lola: look after your planet by Lauren Child
Lola is throwing out lots of things from her bedroom, as she doesn't want it to be messy, and Charlie persuades her to recycle them instead. Lola learns about recycling and how it is important to look after our planet. Suitable for KS1.

World without fish, 2014 by Mark Kurlansky
This is a nonfiction account for children about what is happening to the world's oceans and what they can do about it. It describes how lots of the fish we eat could go extinct and the domino effect that would create. It has beautiful images which complement the text well. Suitable for KS1/2.

NC subject	Activity	Curriculum Connections
English	One plastic bag	Year 2 Pupils should be taught to develop positive attitudes towards and stamina for writing by writing narratives about personal experiences and those of others (real and fictional). Year 3–4 Pupils should be taught discussing writing similar to that which they are planning to write in order to understand and learn from its structure, vocabulary, and grammar. Year 5–6 Pupils should be taught to draft and write by selecting appropriate grammar and vocabulary, understanding how such choices can change and enhance meaning.
English	The packaging problem	Year 3–4 Pupils should continue to have opportunities to write for a range of real purposes and audiences as part of their work across the curriculum. Year 5–6 Pupils should be taught to plan their writing by identifying the audience for and purpose of the writing, selecting the appropriate form, and using other similar writing as models for their own noting and developing initial ideas, drawing on reading and research where necessary.
Maths	Multiplication and problem solving about waste	Year 2 – Pupils can solve problems involving multiplication and division, using materials, arrays, repeated addition, mental methods, and multiplication and division facts, including problems in contexts. Year 3 – Pupils can solve problems, including missing number problems, involving multiplication and division, including positive integer scaling problems and correspondence problems in which *n* objects are connected to *m* objects. Year 6 – Pupils can express missing number problems algebraically.
Science	Materials and their properties	Year 1 – Pupils can identify and name a variety of everyday materials, including wood, plastic, glass, metal, water, and rock. Year 2 – Pupils can find out how the shapes of solid objects made from some materials can be changed by squashing, bending, twisting, and stretching. Year 6 – Properties and change of materials – Pupils can compare and group together everyday materials based on their properties, including their hardness and solubility.
History	Human waste	KS1 and KS2 – All pupils should know and understand significant aspects of the history of the wider world: the nature of ancient civilisations, the expansion and dissolution of empires, characteristic features of past non-European societies, achievements and follies of mankind. History skills – Pupils should use primary sources of evidence.

NC subject	Activity	Curriculum Connections
Geography	Clean-up	A high-quality geography education should inspire in pupils a curiosity and fascination about the world and its people that will remain with them for the rest of their lives. Teaching should equip pupils with knowledge about diverse places, people, resources, and natural and human environments, together with a deep understanding of the earth's key physical and human processes. As pupils progress, their growing knowledge about the world should help them to deepen their understanding of the interaction between physical and human processes, and of the formation and use of landscapes and environments.
Music	Unseen waste	All key stages appreciate and understand a wide range of high-quality live and recorded music drawn from different traditions and from great composers and musicians.
Art and Design	Beautiful waste	Art and design aim to ensure that all pupils should produce creative work.
Design and Technology	3D waste structure	KS2 Design – Pupils can communicate their ideas through discussion and annotated sketches. Make – Pupils perform practical tasks, such as joining and shaping. Evaluate – Pupils can evaluate their design against the criteria. Technical knowledge – Pupils apply their understanding of how to strengthen, stiffen, and reinforce structures.
Computing	A helpful robot for recycling	All pupils can evaluate and apply information technology, including new or unfamiliar technologies, analytically to solve problems.
Religious education	Wastefulness	KS1 – At key stage 1 pupils should study Christianity, one other religion, and consider other worldviews. KS2 – Pupils consider the beliefs, teachings, practices, and ways of life central to religion. They learn about sacred texts and other sources and consider their meanings.
Physical education	Assault courses	Pupils are physically active for sustained periods of time. Pupils should be taught to master basic movements including running, jumping, throwing, and catching, as well as developing balance, agility, and coordination, and begin to apply these in a range of activities.
PSHE	UNESCO sustainable development goals	PSHE Association Curriculum – Living in the wider world KS1 L3 – Pupils learn about things they can do to help look after their environment. KS2 L5 – Pupils learn ways of carrying out shared responsibilities for protecting the environment in school and at home; how everyday choices can affect the environment (e.g. reducing, reusing, recycling; food choices).

NC subject	Activity	Curriculum Connections
Citizenship	**Cities that recycle**	PSHE Association Curriculum – Living in the wider world KS1 L3 – Pupils learn about things they can do to help look after their environment. KS2 L5 – Pupils learn ways of carrying out shared responsibilities for protecting the environment in school and at home; how everyday choices can affect the environment (e.g. reducing, reusing, recycling; food choices).

Water

English

What can water be?
Water can be
Read the story water can be written by Laura Purdie Salas. It is a kenning which creates new words to entertain the reader. Think together about the characteristics of water to gather some ideas to write your own kenning.

What is it like to be water?
A day in the life of a raindrop
Write a piece about the day in the life of a raindrop. Start with it falling from the sky out of a cloud. Think about what happens to it before it reaches the sea.

R.E.

Is water an essential part of spirituality?
Water and religion
Research how people use water in religious worship for the major religions – Hinduism, Christianity, Islam, Buddhism, Judaism, and Sikhism. Recall what you have learnt in your expert groups.

Music

Does water create music?
Creating tunes with water
Recreate a scale of notes using water in glass jars or glasses. Compare to other musical scales.

History

Are waterways the greatest way to travel?
Canal systems
Research and learn about the waterways of Great Britain. Discuss what the benefits and disadvantages are of moving by water. Find out about the places where canals are still the main form of travel.

Do past human achievements help us learn for the future?
Harnessing water for survival
Humans have harnessed (stored) water to survive. Think about all the ways we use water today. Explore one important event in past times when water has successfully been harnessed.

Maths

Does the maths of water exist?
Water facts
Research some water facts using reliable websites, books, and encyclopaedias. Choose the statistic that you find most interesting and represent it in three ways – pie chart, percentage and a fraction. Think about which way gives the most impact.

Computing

Can technology help inform the future?
Green screen fun
Create a video to educate young children about water preservation. Think about what we can learn from the past to inform the future.

Can we ever debug ourselves?
Bug in the water cycle
Find out what debugging is and how to do it for perfect coding. Concentrate on how to spot mistakes.

Science

Should we explore life below water?

Ocean literacy
UNESCO has created The 7 Principles of Ocean Literacy. Spend some time exploring these. Discuss the one of the principles in depth with a partner and whether you agree. Work together to find reasons for both sides of the argument.

Geography

What is water?

The water cycle
Observe an indoor water cycle to learn how water can be a gas, liquid, or solid. Draw the water cycle with notations to explain each stage of the process.

Water had a beginning. Will it have an end?

The oceanmaker
Watch The Oceanmaker film and discuss it using "The Four Sharings" by Aidan Chambers. Use the puzzles section to formulate philosophical questions. Think about whether water could have an end and how it may happen.

Art and Design

Is water beautiful?

Water from above
Look at photographs of rivers, seas and oceans from above and write down any thoughts you have while looking at them. Try photographing your own shots of water.

Design and Technology

Can we create access to running water for all?

A tippy tap
Not all communities around the world have access to taps so people make tippy-taps to create running water for handwashing. Make your own tippy-tap.

Citizenship

Are we the guardians of water?

Guardians of water
We have to use water in our lives in many ways and especially need it to drink. Our life depends on it. UNESCO Sustainable Development Goals Goal 6 is to have clean water and sanitation for the whole world. Think about how we can be better guardians of it.

P.E.

What relationships do humans have with water?

Water and our health
Think about the relationships we have with water. Find out how it keep us healthy when we exercise and how much water is in our body.

PSHE

Is having clean water a human right?

Enough to drink
Consider the statement that you have the right to eat and drink enough so you can grow up healthy. Learn about how the right to water entitles everyone to a sufficient amount of reasonably affordable and accessible water necessary for survival.

15 Water

Concept stretcher   **SPEC grid**

As part of a P4C enquiry, children brainstorm synonyms, phrases, connections, and examples (SPEC) in a SPEC grid, as in this example.

Synonyms	Phrases
• Liquid/H_2O • Sea/River/Stream • Ocean • Ice/Frozen • Sea water • Rainwater • Aquatic/Marine • Reservoirs/Dams	• Water of life • You're in hot water. • Don't make waves. • She was wet between behind her ears. • To be in bad waters • To throw water on the fire • Come hell or high water
Connections	**Examples**
• Bath/Rainwater/Tap water • Well • Tears	• Pacific Ocean • Atlantic Ocean • The water cycle • Weather – rain • El Niño and La Niña

Curriculum connections

Spoken language – Pupils use spoken language to develop understanding through speculating, hypothesising, imagining, and exploring ideas.
SPEC grids are the work of Roger Sutcliffe, Director and Programme Designer of P4C Plus and Thinking Moves A – Z at Dialogue Works, Philosophical Teaching and Learning. www.dialogueworks.co.uk

Quotes to explore P4C enquiry

Water quotes

> 'If there is magic on this planet, it is contained in water'.
>
> – Loren Eiseley

> 'No man ever steps in the same river twice, for it's not the same river and he's not the same man'.
>
> – Heraclitus

> 'Many a calm river begins as a turbulent waterfall, yet none hurtles and foams all the way to the sea'.
>
> – Mikhail Lermontov

Write notes here on your discussion about one of the quotes.

Curriculum connections

Spoken language – Pupils use spoken language to develop understanding through speculating, hypothesising, imagining, and exploring ideas.

248 *Water*

Concept stretcher **Concept web**

Think about how these concepts can be connected. Draw a line between the two and write a sentence along it about how they connect.

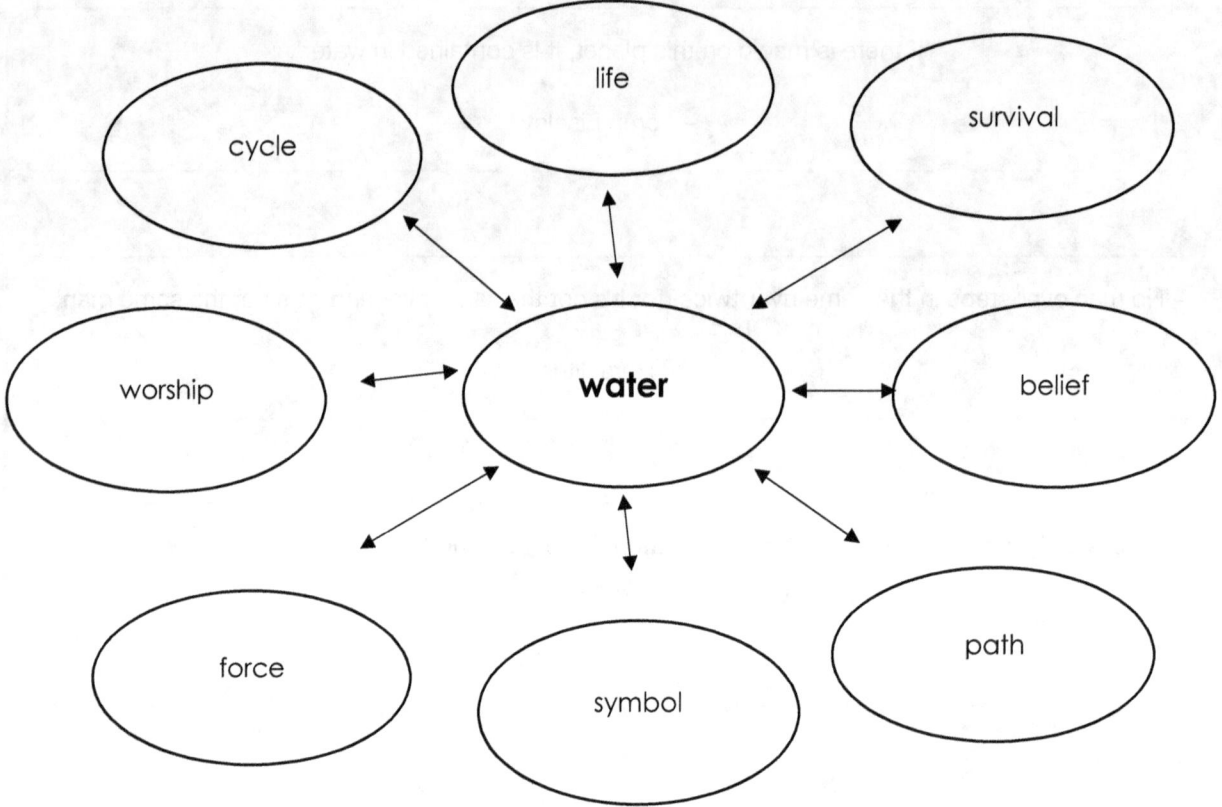

Pick two concepts and write a sentence about how you think they connect to each other.

1.	2.
How they connect	

Now share your ideas with your group, class, or talk partner.

Curriculum connections

Spoken language – Pupils should be able to consider and evaluate different viewpoints, attending to and building on the contributions of others.

Concept stretchers   **Decision pairs**

Would you rather?

Look at these choices. Select one from each pair and give your reasons as to why you chose it.

Have really cold water on a hot day	Have really warm water on a cold day
Choose one with a tick. Say why.	
Have all you need to drink but no cup	Have a cup but need to walk one mile for water
Choose one with a tick. Say why.	
Have a home surrounded by ice	Have a home surrounded by water
Choose one with a tick. Say why.	

Once you have thought of your reasons, see if you can think of a pair of statements yourself that have a dilemma about water. Write them here.

Curriculum connections

Spoken language – Pupils should learn to participate in discussions, presentations, performances, role play/improvisations, and debates.

What can water be? English

Water can be . . .

Read the story *Water can be . . .* by Laura Purdie Salas and illustrated by Violeta Dabija. www.youtube.com/watch?v=8e24xU2TrRM (accessed 21/05/2021)

It is a kenning which uses compound nouns by placing nouns alongside each other to create new words to entertain the reader.

> "A life-giver" as we need it to survive

> "A hope-bringer" as we need it to clean things

Discuss with a partner/group/circle what water is, is like, and does to gather ideas for this poem.

Can you use these words together?

Thirst	Drought	Stream	Make	Roar	Flow	Wave
Flow	Friend	Ripple	Drop	River	Trickle	Wet

Now write some of your own.

Select your favourite ones and write your own kenning.

Water can be . . .

Curriculum connections

KS1/2 – Comprehension skills develop through pupils' experience of high-quality discussion with the teacher, as well as from reading and discussing a range of stories, poems, and non-fiction.

What is it like to be water? English

A day in the life of a raindrop

After thinking about water, write a piece about the life of a drop of water. Start with a raindrop falling from the sky out of a cloud.

Choose a style to write it in.

Look at a video as a stimulus. Some examples are below:

Micro-storm time-lapse video: www.youtube.com/watch?v=ObYRYF3d38Y (accessed 18/05/2021)

Slow-motion raindrop falling video: www.youtube.com/watch?v=tIJQkR-ofFo (accessed 18/05/2021)

A day in the life of a drop of water

Curriculum connections

KS2 – Pupils should also learn the conventions of different types of writing, for example, a diary written in the first person.

Does the maths of water exist? Mathematics

Water facts

Research some water facts using reliable websites, books, and encyclopaedias.

www.oxfam.org.uk/oxfam-in-action/water-for-all (accessed 25/05/2021)

www.unwater.org/water-facts/scarcity/ (accessed 28/06/2021)

Write them here.

Now choose the statistic that you find most interesting. Represent it in three ways – pie chart, percentage, and fraction. Think about which way gives the most impact.

Show the three ways here.

Did you know that Florence Nightingale was the first person to use pie charts? Research why she did this. Find one fact and write it here.

One fact about Florence Nightingale and the pie chart:

Curriculum connections

KS1 – Pupils should be taught to interpret and construct simple pictograms, tally charts, block diagrams, and tables.

KS2 – Pupils should be taught to solve comparison, sum, and difference problems using information presented in a line graph.

Should we explore life below water?   **Science**

Ocean Literacy

UNESCO have created the 7 Principles of Ocean Literacy. Spend some time exploring these. https://oceanliteracy.unesco.org/about/ (accessed 25/05/2021)

> **The 7 Principles of Ocean Literacy**
>
> 1. Earth has one big ocean with many features.
> 2. The ocean and life in the ocean shape features of Earth.
> 3. The ocean is a major influence on weather and climate.
> 4. The ocean makes Earth habitable.
> 5. The ocean supports a great diversity of life and ecosystems.
> 6. The oceans and humans are inextricably interconnected.
> 7. The ocean is largely unexplored.

Discuss the philosophical question with a partner. Work together to find reasons for both sides of the argument.

Why we should explore life below water – Advantages	Why we should not explore life below water – Disadvantages

Curriculum connections

Spoken language in science – The national curriculum for science reflects the importance of spoken language in pupils' development across the whole curriculum – cognitively, socially, and linguistically.

What is water? **Geography**

The water cycle

Observe an indoor water cycle. You might make one in your lesson or watch a video.

Here are some videos to get you started.

KS1 BBC Teach – www.youtube.com/watch?v=d2o9SvBlOns (accessed 24/05/2021)

KS2 BBC Teach – www.youtube.com/watch?v=1fkWLbZFbJM (accessed 24/05/2021)

When is water a . . .

Gas?	Liquid?	Solid?
Write a sentence here.		

Now share with a talk partner what you understand about the water cycle.

Draw the cycle of water here.

Think in a P4C enquiry, group or with a partner about what is water.

Curriculum connections

Year 4 – Pupils should identify the part played by evaporation and condensation in the water cycle and associate the rate of evaporation with temperature.

Water had a beginning. Will it have an end?   Geography

"The Oceanmaker" by Lucas Martell

Watch The Oceanmaker by Martell and conside the following things below.
www.youtube.com/watch?v=0uml5yPcHFY (accessed 05/02/2021)

LIKES	DISLIKES
What do you like about the story?	What do you dislike about the story?
CONNECTIONS	**PUZZLES**
What connections do you make in the story?	What did you find puzzling?

Grid based on "The Four Sharings" by Aidan Chambers ("Tell Me")

Discuss some of your thoughts with a partner or group. Try to formulate philosophical questions about what you have explored in your discussion.

Write your questions here.

Curriculum connections

A high-quality geography education should inspire in pupils a curiosity and fascination about the world and its people that will remain with them for the rest of their lives. Teaching should equip pupils with knowledge about diverse places, people, resources, and natural and human environments, together with a deep understanding of the earth's key physical and human processes.

Is water travel the greatest way to travel?   **History**

Canal systems

Research and learn about the waterways of Great Britain. Here are some good videos to start your research.

KS1 BBC Teach – www.youtube.com/watch?v=xx3RRqbymP8 (accessed 24/05/2021)

KS2 BBC Teach – www.youtube.com/watch?v=NBmQkS8NtJI (accessed 24/05/2021)

What are the benefits and disadvantages of moving by water?

ADVANTAGES	DISADVANTAGES

Today there are still some places where canals are the main form of travel, such as Giethoorn, in the Netherlands.

www.youtube.com/watch?v=R3t1cg2ZOxc (accessed 24/05/2021)

Now discuss in your philosophy circle whether you think water is the greatest way to travel.

> Make some notes here.

Curriculum connections

KS2 – Pupils should Learn about a significant turning point in British history, for example the first railways.

Do past human achievements help us learn for the future?   **History**

Harnessing water for survival

Humans have harnessed (stored) water to survive. Can you think of all the ways we use water today? Write your ideas here.

Cleaning dishes			

Water as a resource

Explore one important event in past times when water has successfully or unsuccessfully been harnessed. Select one of the times and research it with a group.

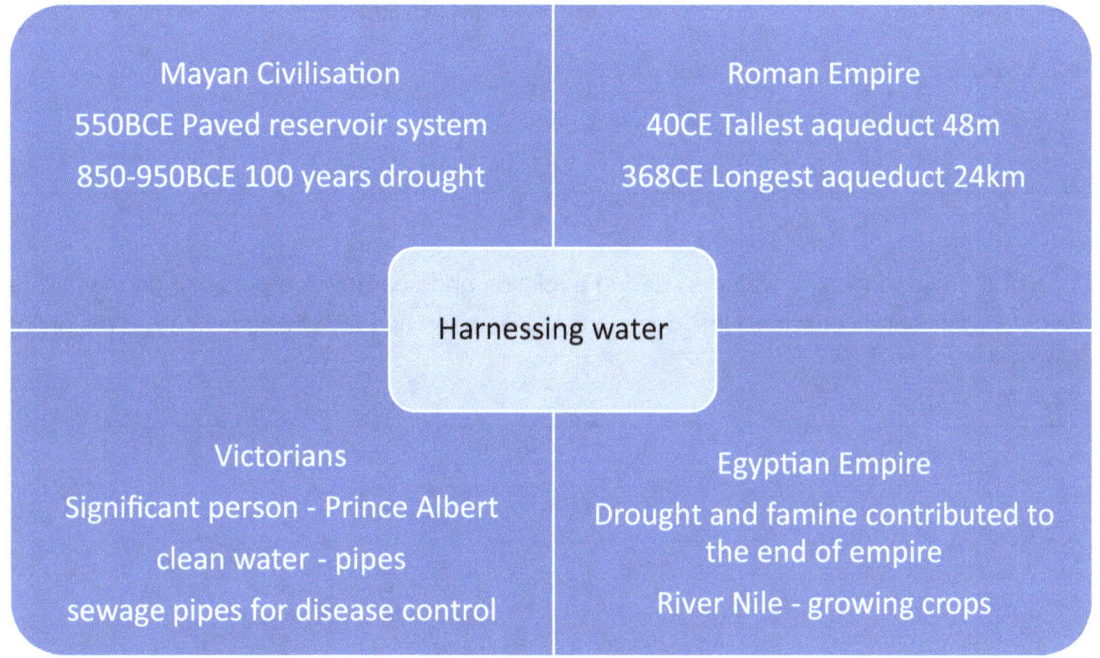

Make notes here. What clever things did they do with the water?

Curriculum connections

Pupils should learn the lives of significant individuals in the past who have contributed to national and international achievements. Some should be used to compare aspects of life in different periods (for example, Elizabeth I, and Queen Victoria).

258 *Water*

Is water an essential part of spirituality? RE

Water and religion

Research how people use water in religious worship.

Hinduism (a Hindu)	Christianity (a Christian)
Islam (a Muslim)	Buddhism (a Buddhist)
Judaism (a Jew)	Sikhism (a Sikh)

Select one of the ways in which water is used in a religion and share with a group or partner. Write your thoughts here from your discussion. Note questions to take to an enquiry which focuses on the philosophical question.

P4C enquiry

Consider the question - Is water an essential part of spirituality?

Curriculum connections

RE lessons should offer structured and safe space during curriculum time for reflection, discussion, dialogue, and debate.

Pupils should be able to identify, investigate, and respond to questions posed and responses offered.

Is having clean water a human right? PSHE

Enough to drink

Read *I have the right to be a child* by Alain Serres, Aurelia Fronty, and Sarah Ardizzone. (www.phoenixyardbooks.com ISBN 9781907912115)

This book shares some of the United Nations Convention on the Rights of a Child. Article 24 states that you have the right to eat and drink enough so you can grow up healthy.

The UN considers that the right to water entitles everyone to a sufficient amount of reasonably affordable and accessible water necessary for survival, i.e. drinking, cooking, and personal hygiene.

Many people die each year without access to clean water. Explore what Oxfam are doing to help them: www.oxfam.org.uk/oxfam-in-action/water-for-all

Do we have a responsibility to achieve this for other countries who are less fortunate than us? Reflect on this question on you own and write down a couple of reasons for each side of the argument.

Yes	No

Concepts to explore from this question:

Responsibility	Fortune	Country	We	Hygiene

Use your thoughts to create some reasons and further questions to take to a P4C enquiry.

Curriculum connections

KS1 H1 – Pupils should learn about what keeping healthy means; different ways to keep healthy.

KS2 H1 – Pupils should know how to make informed decisions about health.

Is water beautiful? Art and Design

Water from above

Edward Burtynsky is a photographer who takes amazing and unusual shots of water from above. Have a look at some of them here: www.edwardburtynsky.com/projects/photographs/water (accessed 24/05/2021)

Write down any thoughts, observations, or questions that come into your mind while looking at the photographs.

In a P4C enquiry/pair/group discuss why you may or may not agree that water is beautiful.

Can you think of when water may be ugly?

> **Art exploration**
>
> Using a camera, take unusual shots of water. They could be taken at school, at home, or in the garden.

Curriculum connections

Pupils should be taught about a range of artists.

KS2 – Pupils should be taught to develop their techniques, including their control and their use of materials, with creativity, experimentation, and an increasing awareness of different kinds of art, craft and design.

Does water create music? Music

Creating tunes with water

Recreating scale of notes using water in glass jars or glasses.

Compare to other musical scales.

Think about whether the water is creating music? Can water create music?

Curriculum connections

KS2 – Pupils should learn to improvise and compose music for a range of purposes using the interrelated dimensions of music.

Can technology help inform the future about water? Computing

Green screen fun

Use the LEGO Movie Maker, along with LEGO figure characters, to create a story that informs people about what happens when foul water and sewage go into fresh water supplies. Aim to educate children who are younger than you, using language that they will understand.

Think about what we can learn from the past to inform the future about water and how to look after it. Share what you have learnt about water from your exploration of this topic.

Curriculum connections

Pupils should be taught to use technology purposefully to create, organise, store, manipulate, and retrieve digital content.

Can we create access to running water for all?   **Design and technology**

Making a tippy tap

Design criteria – make something that will allow water to run as a tap

Not all communities around the world have running water. They use clever ways to make sure that they can create water than runs so everyone can use soap to wash their hands.

Watch this WaterAid video on their website.

https://www.youtube.com/watch?v=C4d1nLpqx0M (accessed 02.02.22)

Use this WaterAid worksheet to help you.

https://www.wateraid.org/uk/sites/g/files/jkxoof211/files/schools-challenge-ks1-tippy-tap-instructions.pdf (accessed 12.0.22)

Curriculum connections

Evaluate – Pupils can evaluate their design against the criteria.

Technical knowledge – Pupils understand and use mechanical systems in their products (such as pulleys, cams, levers, and linkages).

Can we ever debug ourselves?   **Computing**

Bug in the water cycle

Learning to debug a program for perfect coding

Find out what debugging is and how to do it. Watch a video to learn more. Here's one you could watch:

www.youtube.com/watch?v=CGPjraqX_ac (accessed 05/08/2021)

Find opportunities to debug. For example, Barefoot Computing has some great activities. www.barefoot-computing.org/resources/bug-in-the-water-cycle (accessed 02/07/2021)

Curriculum connections

Pupils should learn how to debug simple programs.

What relationship do humans have with water? Physical education

Swimming

Where have you swum? Write the places in the space provided.

What types of swimming strokes are there?

When have you been swimming with the school? Think about how far you can swim on your own.

Think about the relationships we have with water. How does water keep us healthy when we exercise?

How much water is in our body?

Find out how much water we need to replace when exercising for these different activities.

Running	Walking	Dancing	Swimming

In your school swimming lessons, think about what the water feels like, looks like, sounds like, and is it different from underneath as you learn to swim 25 metres.

Curriculum connections

In either KS1 or KS2 pupils should be taught to swim competently, confidently, and proficiently over a distance of at least 25 metres.

Are we the guardians of water? Citizenship

Guardians of water

We use water in our lives in many ways, and we especially need it to drink. Our lives depend on it.

UNESCO sustainable development goals

UNESCO has created Sustainable Development Goals with the aim to achieve them by 2030. Goal 6 is to have clean water and sanitation for the whole world.

Discuss whether the following things depend upon water:

A tree	A river	The sun	A mouse
An ant	A car	A house	The moon
A table	A train	A glass	A chair

How can we be better guardians of our water?

What do you think we must to do to help protect water?

Is it our job to look after water? Are we its guardians?

Curriculum connections

H1 – Pupils should learn about what keeping healthy means; different ways to keep healthy.

H3 – Pupils should learn about choices that support a healthy lifestyle and recognise what might influence these.

Inspirational people

Anna Luísa Beserra, Founder and CEO of Safe Drinking Water for All

Beserra is a environmental entrepreneur who is the CEO and founder of Safe Drinking Water for All. Today she is the only scientist with two Nobel Prizes in the field of science. She is working to democratise access to water.

https://smartwatermagazine.com/news/smart-water-magazine/inspirational-women-water-sector (accessed 05/08/2021)

Albert, Prince Consort and Joseph Bazalgette

Albert, Prince Consort (Victoria's husband) wanted the water problem ("The Big Stink") in London to be solved, as many people were dying from cholera. Bazalgette was the designer and engineer who created the embankment along the Thames which had the new sewage tunnels to take the waste away to the pumping station in East Ham.

Boyan Slat

Slat was the founder of a company to solve the problem of the great garbage patch as he wanted to clean the ocean's water. He designed and created the Great Garbage Cleaner, which now sits in the Great Garbage Patch in the Pacific and cleans the sea by extracting the plastic rubbish.

Archimedes – The principle of water displacement

Archimedes found out some fundamental principles about water called water displacement. If the body is completely submerged, the volume of fluid displaced is equal to the volume of the body. If the body is only partially submerged, the volume of the fluid displaced is equal to the volume of the part of the body that is submerged. (Wikipedia – accessed 05/08/2021)

Further resources

Water Aid

The WaterAid website has lots of projects and resources to use across the curriculum.

www.wateraid.org/uk/get-involved/teaching/ks2-resources

Royal National Lifeboat Institute

There are lots of videos, games, and downloadable sheets for children to learn about water safety.

https://rnli.org/youth-education/education-resources

Maths

Archimedes' Screw – This website explains how Archimedes designed a screw that can move water up rather than down.

www.britannica.com/technology/Archimedes-screw (accessed 05/08/2021)

Water education

This website has lots of teachers' resources and in particularly a good water cycle poster that you can download.

www.usgs.gov/special-topic/water-science-school/science/teachers-resources-water-education?qt-science_center_objects=0#qt-science_center_objects

The Book Corner

The water princess by Susan Verde and Peter Reynolds
Gie Gie lives in a small village African village, and each day she goes to get the water by carrying a pot on her head. She dreams that it will be closer and that it will flow clear. This story is inspired by the life of Gerogie Badiel, a Burkina Faso-born model. Suitable for KS1.

The drop in my drink by Meredith Hooper
This story takes us back thousands of years to where Earth's water began and how life began in oceans and then on the land. It poignantly explores the relationship between water and living things, along with water and erosion. Suitable for KS2.

The river boy by Tim Bowler
An old painter refuses medical support, as he is determined to finish his painting called *River boy*. The story reveals why he wants to do this and is an analogy made to rivers and our life beginning, flowing, and ending. Suitable for KS2.

Water is water by Miranda Paul
This poetic and informative book is about the water cycle and its journey from rain to fog and to snow to mist. The book has beautiful illustrations and is aimed at younger children. Suitable for KS1.

Great rivers of the world by Volker Mehnert
This is a visually rich, well-illustrated atlas of the well-known rivers of the world. Each river has a biography which says where it flows and describes its ecological health. It has facts and questions that will stimulate the wonder of the reader. Suitable for KS2.

The crow and the pitcher – Aesop's Fables
The crow needs to drink the water from the pitcher but can't, as the water is too low. Find out how he manages to get to the water. The moral is that necessity is the mother of all invention. Suitable for KS1/2.

NC subject	Activity	Curriculum connections
English	Water can be . . .	KS1/2 – Comprehension skills develop through pupils' experience of high-quality discussion with the teacher, as well as from reading and discussing a range of stories, poems, and non-fiction.
English	A day in the life of a raindrop	KS2 – Pupils should also learn the conventions of different types of writing, for example a diary written in the first person.
Maths	Water facts	KS1 – Pupils should be taught to interpret and construct simple pictograms, tally charts, block diagrams, and tables. KS2 – Pupils should be taught to solve comparison, sum and difference problems using information presented in a line graph.
Science	Ocean literacy	Spoken language in science – The national curriculum for science reflects the importance of spoken language in pupils' development across the whole curriculum – cognitively, socially, and linguistically.
Geography	The ocean-maker	A high-quality geography education should inspire in pupils a curiosity and fascination about the world and its people that will remain with them for the rest of their lives. Teaching should equip pupils with knowledge about diverse places, people, resources, and natural and human environments, together with a deep understanding of the earth's key physical and human processes.
Geography	The water cycle	Year 4 – Pupils should identify the part played by evaporation and condensation in the water cycle and associate the rate of evaporation with temperature.
History	Canal systems	KS2 – Pupils should learn about a significant turning point in British history, for example, the first railways.
History	Harnessing water for survival	KS2 – Pupils should learn the lives of significant individuals in the past who have contributed to national and international achievements. Some should be used to compare aspects of life in different periods (for example, Elizabeth I, and Queen Victoria).
Music	Creating tunes with water	KS2 – Pupils should learn to improvise and compose music for a range of purposes using the interrelated dimensions of music.
Art and Design	Water from above	Pupils should be taught about a range of artists. KS2 – Pupils should be taught to develop their techniques, including their control and their use of materials, with creativity, experimentation, and an increasing awareness of different kinds of art, craft, and design.
Design and Technology	Making a tippy tap	Evaluate – Pupils can evaluate their design against the criteria. Technical knowledge – Pupils understand and use mechanical systems in their products (such as pulleys, cams, levers, and linkages).
Computing	Green screen fun	Pupils should be taught to use technology purposefully to create, organise, store, manipulate, and retrieve digital content.
Computing	Bug in the water	Pupils should learn how to debug simple programs.

NC subject	Activity	Curriculum connections
Religious education	Water and religion	**NATRE (National Association of Teaching Religious Education)** RE lessons should offer structured and safe space during curriculum time for reflection, discussion, dialogue, and debate; to identify, investigate, and respond to questions posed and responses offered.
PSHE	UNCRC and UNESCO	**PSHE Association Curriculum** KS1 H1 – Pupils should learn about what keeping healthy means; different ways to keep healthy. KS2 H1– Pupils should learn how to make informed decisions about their health.
Citizenship	Guardians of water	PSHE Association Curriculum H1 – Pupils should learn about what keeping healthy means; different ways to keep healthy. H3 – Pupils should learn about choices that support a healthy lifestyle and recognise what might influence these.
Physical education	Water and our health	In either KS1 or KS2, pupils should be taught to swim competently, confidently, and proficiently over a distance of at least 25 metres.

Appendix A: P4C generic worksheets

Developing 4C thinking

We ask big questions
We test our ideas
We give good reasons
We look for evidence
We suggest conclusions

We make connections
We think of new ideas
We explore possibilities
We compare things
We suggest alternatives

justify argue disagree reason
Critical

connect suggest consider imagine
Creative

4C thinking

build on ideas
help others
Collaborative
contribute
share

listen well appreciate give time take turns
Caring

We support and challenge
We talk to each other
We give and take
We are friendly and helpful
We work well together

We let people finish speaking
We listen to others carefully
We imagine how others feel
We don't interrupt
We wait our turn

© Alison Shorer and Katie Quinn (2023), *Philosophy for Children Across the Primary Curriculum*, Routledge.

Identifying philosophical concepts

Connecting? Does this relate to my life experience?

Central? Does this help me understand my world?

Philosophical Concepts

Common? Do we all need to think about this?

Contestable? Can we keep arguing about meaning and value?

Our philosophical concepts

Which are more philosophical?

© Alison Shorer and Katie Quinn (2023), *Philosophy for Children Across the Primary Curriculum*, Routledge.

A new thought – evidence of thinking

Listening to understand, not judge or assess

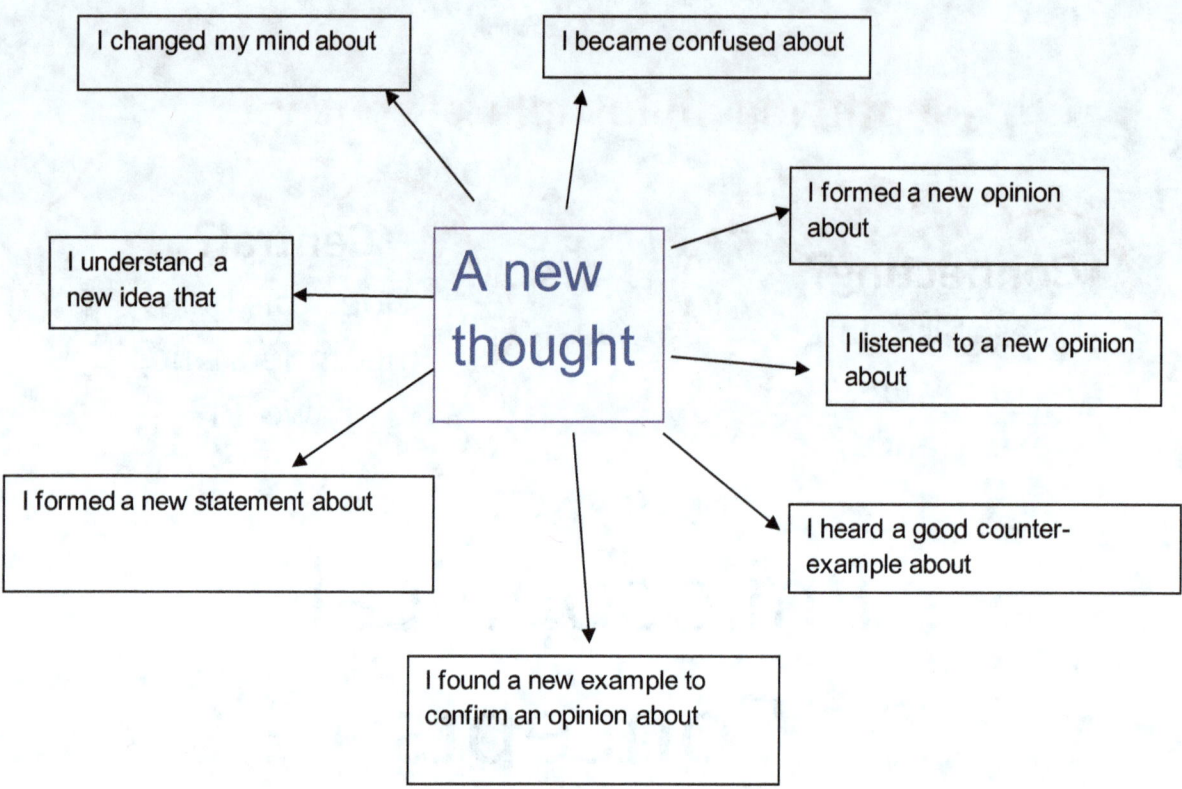

What are you now going to take away and think about?

Designed by Alison Shorer

© Alison Shorer and Katie Quinn (2023), *Philosophy for Children Across the Primary Curriculum*, Routledge.

SPEC Grids

Synonyms	Phrases
Connections	**Examples**

Synonyms	Phrases
Connections	**Examples**

© Alison Shorer and Katie Quinn (2023), *Philosophy for Children Across the Primary Curriculum*, Routledge.

Group, divide activity

© Alison Shorer and Katie Quinn (2023), *Philosophy for Children Across the Primary Curriculum*, Routledge.

Appendix B: Commemoration dates

Commemoration dates you could tie in to each topic

These examples could give any topic a commemoration day to work towards or be used for a whole school focus day. Some extend beyond the areas covered to show further connections which could be made, depending on your chosen focus.

For a focus day for any topic or school issue worthy of philosophical enquiry, please don't forget:

World Philosophy Day on the **Third Thursday in November**

Journeys

27th January	International Day of Commemoration in Memory of the Victims of the Holocaust
21st February	International Mother Language Day
21st March	International Day for the Elimination of Racial Discrimination
12th April	International Day of Human Space Flight
16th May	International Day of Living Together in Peace
21st May	World Day for Cultural Diversity for Dialogue and Development
20th June	World Refugee Day
20–26th June	Refugee Week (UK)
18th July	Nelson Mandela International Day
23rd August	International Day for the Remembrance of the Slave Trade and Its Abolition
21st September	International Day of Peace
October	Black History Month (UK)
24th October	United Nations Day
11th November	Remembrance Day (Commonwealth)
16th November	International Day for Tolerance
10th December	Human Rights Day
18th December	International Migrants Day
25th December	Christmas

Waste

3rd March	World Wildlife Day
21st March	International Day of Forests
22nd April	International Mother Earth Day
22nd May	International Day for Biological Diversity
5th June	World Environment Day
8th June	World Oceans Day
20–26th June	Recycle Now Week (UK)

© Alison Shorer and Katie Quinn (2023), *Philosophy for Children Across the Primary Curriculum*, Routledge.

29th September	International Day of Food Loss and Waste
5th October	World Habitat Day
16th October	World Food Day

Water

22nd March	World Water Day
23rd March	World Meteorological Day
8th June	World Oceans Day
11–17th June	Oxfam Water Week (UK)
17th June	World Day to Combat Desertification and Drought

Resilience

20th March	International Day of Happiness
21st April	World Creativity and Innovation Day
10th October	World Mental Health Day (WHO)
November, 1st Thur.	International Day against Violence and Bullying at School, including Cyberbullying

Heart and lungs

9th and 10th March	No Smoking Day (UK)
6th April	International Day of Sport for Development and Peace
7th April	World Health Day
16–20th May	Walk to School Week (UK)
31st May	World No Tobacco Day
3rd June	World Bicycle Day
6–12th June	World Heart Rhythm Week
14th June	World Blood Donor Day
29th September	World Heart Day
September	Organ Donation Week "Leave Them Certain" campaign (varies)
October	National Cholesterol Month UK

War and peace

21st January	World Hugging Day
27th January	UN Remembrance Day for the Victims of the Holocaust
16th May	International Day for Living Together in Peace
29th May	International of UN Peacekeepers
16th June	World Religion Day
June, Last Thurs.	Armed Forces Day
30th July	International Day of Friendship
19th August	World Humanitarian Day

© Alison Shorer and Katie Quinn (2023), *Philosophy for Children Across the Primary Curriculum*, Routledge.

17th September	Peace One Day
21st September	International Day of Peace (World Peace Day)
6th November	International Day for Preventing the Exploitation of the Environment in War
10th November	World Science Day for Peace and Development
11th November	Remembrance Day (UK)
13th November	World Kindness Day
16th November	International Day of Tolerance
20th December	International Human Solidarity Day

Biodiversity

3rd March	World Wildlife DAY
21st March	International Day of Forests
22nd May	Day for Biological Biodiversity
7th April	World Health Day
22nd April	International Mother Earth Day
5th June	World Environment Day
8th June	World Oceans Day

Time

1st January	New Year's Day
21st Jan - 1st Feb	Chinese New Year (varies each year)
22nd March	Vikram Sawant Hindu New Year (Hindus populations vary)
21st June	Summer Solstice Day (varies each year)
12th September	Enkutatash Ethiopian New Year
30th September	World Maritime Day (last week of Sept)
30th October	Aboriginal Murador New Year
21st December	Winter Solstice Day (varies each year)

Artificial intelligence

8th February	Safer Internet Day
15th February	World Computer Day
5th March	Programming for Primaries Week
17th May	World Telecommunication and Information Society Day
13th September	National Coding Week
13th September	Day of the Programmer
9th October	EU Code Week
30th November	Computer Security Day
2nd December	World Computer Literacy Day

© Alison Shorer and Katie Quinn (2023), *Philosophy for Children Across the Primary Curriculum*, Routledge.

Money

22–28th March	Debt Awareness Week
11th October	National Online Bank Day (US)
12th October	National Savings Day
31st October	World Savings Day
9–12th November	Talk Money Week (varies each year)

© Alison Shorer and Katie Quinn (2023), *Philosophy for Children Across the Primary Curriculum*, Routledge.

Index

air 76
Albert, Prince Consort 267
Aldrin, Buzz 106
Ali, Ala 212
Archimedes 267
art and design 15; and artificial intelligence 25, 35; and biodiversity 39, 49, 59; and heart and lungs 63, 73, 84; and journeys 87, 104, 110; and money 113, 128, 135; and physical education 104; and resilience 137, 152, 162; and time 165, 186; and war and peace 189, 206, 215; and waste 219, 231, 243; and water 247, 262, 270
artificial intelligence 14–15, 16; and art and design 25; books on 33–34; citizenship 31; commemoration dates 279; concept line activity 17; concept-stretching activity 18; curriculum connections 16–18, 35–36; decision corner 18; and design and technology 27; and English 19–20; further resources 33; and history 24; inspirational people in 32; and mathematics 21–22; and music 30; and personal, social, health, and economics (PSHE) 28; and physical education (PE) 29; and religious education (RE) 23; and science 22–23; STEM ambassador 19
Attenborough, David 55

Babbage, Charles 32
bagpipes 74
Banksy 128, 135
Bazalgette, Joseph 267
belonging: concept stretchers 89–91; synonyms, phrases, connections, and examples (SPEC) grid 88–89
Berners-Lee, Timothy 183
Beserra, Anna Luísa 267
Bible 50, 102, 124, 179, 237
binary numeral system 25–26, 35
biodiversity: and art and design 49, 59; books on 57; and citizenship 54, 60; commemoration dates 279; and computing 51, 59; and concept sorting 41; and curriculum connections 41, 44, 45, 58–60; and design and technology 52; and English 43, 58; further resources on 56; and geography 48, 58; and history 59; and inspirational people 55; and mathematics 44, 58; and music 49, 59; and personal, social, health, and economics (PSHE) 53, 60; and physical education (PE) 51, 59; and religious education (RE) 50, 59; and science 45–46, 58; synonyms, phrases, connections, and examples (SPEC) grid 38–39
biographies 143
Bird, Isabella 106
books: on biodiversity 57; on heart and lungs 83; on journeys 108; on money 133; on resilience 161; on time 185; on war and peace 214; on waste 241; on water 269
breathing *see* heart and lungs
British Empire 123, 134
Budde, Ina 239
Burtynsky, Edward 262

canals 258
Chan, Priscilla 131
character analysis 158
children 80, 85, 111; and money 125; and time 178; in war 209
citizenship 15, 31; and artificial intelligence 36; and biodiversity 39, 54, 60; and heart and lungs 63, 80, 85; and journeys 86, 103, 111; and money 113, 125, 135; and resilience 136, 163; and time 165, 178, 187; and war and peace 189, 209, 216; and waste 218, 235, 244; and water 247, 266, 271
clocks 172, 173; *see also* time
codes and coding 25–26, 33, 36, 75, 210
cognitive conflict 5
collages 49, 98
Columbus, Christopher 123
commemoration dates 277–280
computer scientists 22
computing 14, 270; and artificial intelligence 36; and biodiversity 38, 51, 59; and design and technology 110; and heart and lungs 62, 75, 85; and journeys 86, 105; and money 112, 129, 135; and resilience 136, 156, 163; and time 164, 180, 186; and war and peace 188, 209, 215; and waste 219, 233–234, 243; and water 246, 264
concept stretchers 18; on belonging 89–91; on decision pairs 67; on money 115, 116–117; on

resilience 139–143; on time 167–168; on war and peace 191–193, 195; on waste 222–223; on water 250–251
Cox, Brian 183
cryptocurrency 129, 135
curriculum connections 17, 18; and biodiversity 44, 45, 58–60; and heart and lungs 84–85; and journeys 109–111; and resilience 162–163; and time 186–187; and war and peace 215–216

Dali, Salvador 177
Daniels, Ann 106
Darwin, Charles 47
De Vinci, Leonardo 73
decision pairs: for heart and lungs 67; and war and peace 193
design and technology 15; and artificial intelligence 27, 35; and biodiversity 39, 52; and heart and lungs 63, 74, 85; and journeys 87, 99, 110; and money 113, 129, 135; and resilience 137, 151, 163; and time 165, 172–173, 186; and war and peace 189, 210, 215; and waste 219, 231–232, 243; and water 247, 264, 270
DialogueWorks 5, 12
didgeridoo 74
difficult topics 5
dinosaurs 47
divide activity 276
dodgeball 204

Earhart, Amelia 106
Early Years 13
Earth 150, 175
Elizabeth II, Queen 159
emojis 206
English 14, 20; and biodiversity 38, 43, 58; and heart and lungs 63, 68, 84; and journeys 87, 92–93, 109; and money 112, 119, 133; and resilience 136, 143–144, 162; and time 164, 170, 186; and war and peace 188, 196–198, 215; and waste 218, 224–225, 242; and water 246, 252–253, 270
ethics 53
extinction 44, 47

flip books 151

Gandhi, Mahatma 212
Gates, Bill 32
geocaching 27, 35
geography 13, 15; and artificial intelligence 35; and biodiversity 39, 48, 58; and heart and lungs 63, 76, 84; and journeys 87, 98, 109; and money 113, 122, 134; and resilience 136, 150, 162; and time 165, 175, 186; and war and peace 189, 203, 215; and waste 218, 230, 243; and water 247, 256–257, 270
global positioning system (GPS) 27
Great Pacific Garbage Patch 154
group activity 276
Guest, Edgar Albert 144
Guth, Alan 183

Hamilton, Caroline 106
Hamilton, Margaret 32
heart and lungs: and art 73; books on 83; and citizenship 80; commemoration dates 278; and computing 75; and curriculum connections 84–85; and design and technology 74; and English 68; further resources on 82; and geography 76; and history 72; inspirational people 81; and mathematics 69; and music 74; and personal, social, health, and economics (PSHE) 77; quotes on 66; and religious education (RE) 79; and science 70–71; and synonyms, phrases, connections, and examples (SPEC) grid 62–64, 65
heart monitors 75
history 14; and artificial intelligence 35; artificial intelligence and 24; and biodiversity 38, 59; and heart and lungs 62, 72, 84; and journeys 86, 102, 109; and money 112, 123, 134; and resilience 136, 148–149, 162; and time 164, 174, 186; and war and peace 188, 202, 215; and waste 218, 229, 242; and water 246, 258–259, 270
Hopper, Grace 32
Hume, David 81

infinity 166, 179; see also time
inquiry 4
inspirational people: and artificial intelligence 32; and heart and lungs 81; and journeys 106; and resilience 159; and time 183; and war and peace 212; and waste 239; and water 267

Jenner, Edward 81
journeys: and art and design 104; books on 108; and citizenship 103; commemoration dates 277; and computing 105; curriculum connections 109–111; and design and technology 99; and English 92–93; further resources on 107; and geography 98; and history 102; and inspirational people 106; and mathematics 94; and music 100; and personal, social, health, and economics (PSHE) 105; quotes on 91; and religious education (RE) 101; synonyms,

phrases, connections, and examples (SPEC) grid 86–87, 88–89
Kant, Immanuel 174
Kwolek, Stephanie 147
Kyi, Aung San 212

Laird, Elizabeth 125
Learning Pit 155
LEGOs 33, 99
Livingstone, David 106
Longcroft, James 239
lottery 119, 134
Lovelace, Ada 32
Lush Cosmetics 239

Macintosh, Charles 147
Mandela, Nelson 159
mathematics 13, 14; and artificial intelligence 21–22, 35; and biodiversity 39, 44, 58; and heart and lungs 62, 69, 84; and journeys 87, 94, 109; and money 112, 120, 134; and resilience 137, 145–146, 162; and time 164, 171, 186; and war and peace 188, 199, 215; and waste 219, 226–227, 242; and water 246, 254, 270
Mayans 123
meditation 79
mercy killing 208
metacognition 5, 9–13; *see also* Thinking Moves
military science 200–201
Mitchell, Joni 49
money: and art and design 128; books on 133; and citizenship 125; commemoration dates 280; and computing 129; and curriculum connections 134–135; and design and technology 129; and English 119; further resources on 132; and geography 122; and history 123; and inspirational people 131; and mathematics 120; and music 126; and personal, social, health, and economics (PSHE) 127; and physical education (PE) 130; quotes about 118; and religious education (RE) 124; and science 121; synonyms, phrases, connections, and examples (SPEC) grid 112–114
Mother Theresa 212
Murray, Joseph 81
music 14; and artificial intelligence 30, 35; and biodiversity 38, 49, 59; and heart and lungs 62, 74, 84; and journeys 86, 100, 110; and money 112, 126, 134; and resilience 136, 157, 162; and time 164, 176, 186; and war and peace 188, 207, 215; and waste 218, 233, 243; and water 246, 263, 264, 270
Musk, Elon 32

origami 52

pan flute 74
pandemics 236
Park, Bletchley 26
Pascal's Triangle 145
personal, social, health, and economics (PSHE) 28; and artificial intelligence 36; and biodiversity 39, 53, 60; and heart and lungs 63, 77, 85; and journeys 87, 111; and money 113, 127, 135; and resilience 137, 155, 163; and time 165, 182, 187; and war and peace 189, 211, 216; and waste 219, 236, 243; and water 247, 261, 271
personas 6–7
philanthropists 131
philosophizing 13
physical education (PE): and war and peace 204, 216; and waste 219, 238, 243; and water 247, 265, 266, 271
physical education (PE) 15; and art and design 104; and artificial intelligence 29, 36; and biodiversity 39, 51, 59; and heart and lungs 63, 78, 85; and journeys 87, 110; and money 113, 130, 135; and resilience 137, 158, 163; and time 165, 181, 186; and war and peace 189
poetry 170
population sampling 44
populations 48
Post-It Notes 147
Price, Brendon 106
PSHE 15

question chain 143
quotes: about money 118; on artificial intelligence 17; on biodiversity 42; on heart and lungs 66; on journeys 91; on resilience 142; on time 169; on war and peace 194; on waste 221; on water 249
Quran 237

Rai stones 122
refugees 102, 103, 111
religious education (RE) 36; and biodiversity 38, 50, 59; and heart and lungs 62, 79, 85; and journeys 86, 101, 110; and money 112, 124, 135; and resilience 136, 153, 163; and time 164, 179, 186; and war and peace 188, 208, 216; and waste 218, 237, 243; and water 246, 260, 271
resilience: and art and design 152; books on 161; commemoration dates 278; and computing 156; and curriculum connections 162–163; and design and technology 151; and English 143–144; further resources on 160; and geography 150; and history 148–149; and

inspirational people 159; and mathematics 145–146; and music 157; and personal, social, health, and economics (PSHE) 155; and physical education (PE) 158; quotes on 142; and religious education (RE) 153; and science 147; and synonyms, phrases, connections, and examples (SPEC) grid 136–138

Ronaldo, Cristiano 131

Rowling, JK 131

SAPERE 4, 8, 11, 272–273

science 15; and artificial intelligence 35; and biodiversity 38, 45–46, 58; and heart and lungs 62, 70–71, 84; and journeys 86, 95–97, 109; and money 113, 121, 134; and resilience 137, 147, 162; and time 165, 172, 186; and war and peace 189, 200–201, 215; and waste 219, 228, 242; and water 247, 255, 270

Scratch coding 75, 180

seeds 46, 58

semantics 9

sharing 7

skills 10

Slat, Boyan 239, 267

smart cars 105

smoking 71, 72, 84

social conscience 120, 134

spoken language 16, 17

sports 36, 130, 135; see also physical education (PE)

stand-alone sessions 8–9

STEM ambassador 19

subjects 9

success 139–143

sundials 172

Sutcliffe, Roger 11

synonyms, phrases, connections, and examples (SPEC) grids 16–15, 17, 275; of belonging 88–89; of biodiversity 38–39; of heart and lungs 62–65; of journeys 86–87, 88–89; of money 112–114; of resilience 136–138; of waste 218–220; of water 246–248

Taussig, Helen Brooke 81

teachers: and personas 6–7; philosophical 4, 7

themes 5

Thinking Grooves 12–13

Thinking Moves 5, 11–12, 13–14; see also metacognition

Thomas, Donnal 81

Thunberg, Greta 159

time: books on 185; and citizenship 178; commemoration dates 279; and computing 180; and curriculum connections 186–187; and design and technology 172–173; and English 170; and geography 175; and history 174; and inspirational people 183; and mathematics 171; and music 176; and personal, social, health, and economics (PSHE) 182; and physical education (PE) 181; quotes on 169; and religious education (RE) 179; and science 172; synonyms, phrases, connections, and examples (SPEC) grid 164–166

Tinkercad 27

Tower of Babel 23, 36

Toy Story 2 33

trees 49

United Nations 54

Valentine's Day 72

values 7

vaping 69

Wallace and Gromit 33

war and peace: and art and design 206; books on 214; and citizenship 209; commemoration dates 278–279; and computing 209; and curriculum connections 215–216; and design and technology 210; and English 196–198; further resources for 213; and geography 203; and history 202; and inspirational people 212; and mathematics 199; and music 207; and personal, social, health, and economics (PSHE) 211; and physical education (PE) 204; quotes on 194; and religious education (RE) 208; and science 200–201; synonyms, phrases, connections, and examples (SPEC) grid 188–190

waste: and art and design 231; books on 241; and citizenship 235; commemoration dates 277–278; and computing 233–234; concept stretchers 222–223; and curriculum connections 242–244; and design and technology 231–232; and English 224–225; further resources on 240; and geography 230; and history 229; and inspirational people 239; and mathematics 226–227; and music 233; and personal, social, health, and economics (PSHE) 236; and physical education (PE) 238; quotes on 221; and religious education (RE) 237; and science 228; synonyms, phrases, connections, and examples (SPEC) grid 218–220

water: and art and design 262; books on 269; commemoration dates 278; concept stretchers 250–251; curriculum connections 270–271; and English 252–253; further resources on 268; and geography 256–257; and history

258–259; and inspirational people 267; and mathematics 254; and music 263; and personal, social, health, and economics (PSHE) 261; and physical education (PE) 265; quotes on 249; and religious education (RE) 260; and science 255; synonyms, phrases, connections, and examples (SPEC) grid 246–248

WD40 147

Williams, Serena 131
Winfrey, Oprah 131
World War II 159

yoga 204

Zuckerberg, Mark 131

For Product Safety Concerns and Information please contact our EU representative GPSR@taylorandfrancis.com
Taylor & Francis Verlag GmbH, Kaufingerstraße 24, 80331 München, Germany

www.ingramcontent.com/pod-product-compliance
Lightning Source LLC
Chambersburg PA
CBHW080833010526
44112CB00016B/2508